GW00857724

With Best Wishes

from

David

THE SON OF WOMAN

WHO WAS JESUS' FATHER?

by the

Son of Woman

A GODLESS HISTORY
[with italic probabilities]

Bloomington, IN Milton Keynes, UK

AuthorHouse™
1663 Liberty Drive, Suite 200
Bloomington, IN 47403
www.authorhouse.com
Phone: 1-800-839-8640

AuthorHouse™ UK Ltd.
500 Avebury Boulevard
Central Milton Keynes, MK9 2BE
www.authorhouse.co.uk
Phone: 08001974150

First published by AuthorHouse October 2007

ISBN: 978-1-4259-7163-2 (e)
ISBN: 978-1-4259-7162-5 (sc)

Printed in the United States of America
Bloomington, Indiana

This book is printed on acid-free paper.

ACKNOWLEDGEMENTS

I thank Lady Bigz, Radio Presenter on the BEAT FM who helped me to master my computer.

Contents

A LIST OF ILLUSTRATIONS

COVER The HOLY FAMILY reproduced from an oil painting in the possession of the author showing the Madonna and Jesus with Elizabeth and the infant St John the Baptist. Who is the man in the background; the father of Jesus and John? The original is school of Raphael painted in 1518.

ChapterPage

WHO WAS JESUS' FATHER?

BY THE SON OF WOMAN

INTRODUCTION
[With italic probabilities]

"God' is a forbidden word in science"
Sir Fred Hoyle, mathematician, and astronomer.

Genesis says Almighty God made man in His own image. This volume shows that man made an almighty concept - God in man's image.

This book was written because *I believe that the NON-EXISTENCE OF GOD LEAVES A SOCIAL VACUUM* and the fact that respectable people in all ages found the need to *dishonestly* create Him, reveals that OUR NEED for HIS POWER is as great today as it ever was. *However I believe that most people have fallen into a logical error and assumed that if he does not exist he is of no importance. Regardless of God's non-existence* the word 'God' exists and this concept is said universally to be supremely important. *The creation of a replacement God is man's most challenging and rewarding task. It is infinitely nobler,* than blind obedience and faith in somebody else's *rather inadequate* historical God.

If Men and Women are to live happily and peacefully, it is necessary for them to understand some very complicated truths. *They are so complicated that no one man can understand them all, and it is for this reason that no one man can disprove the existence of GOD.* Therefore it will not be surprising if I make errors, and I would be grateful if you would inform me of any.

However if the Pope makes an error when he is infallible he immediately can be discredited as a ridiculous liar. While in his infallible state he has cursed [anathema] any one who does not believe in miracles or disapproves of Christianity. The Pope believes in many pieces of the Holy Cross, which have worked miracles, but these pieces are made of many tree varieties including English oak. Cicero said "Miracles, may be necessary for the piety of ignorant folk; there are no miracles".

The majority of the educated population now have doubts. Scientific theories concerning the creation of the universe and the development of man and his DNA have unsettled the faithful.

The concept of God has affected laws, morality, sex, class, and history. Millions of men have given their lives for it. I greatly value the concept of the need to do good and am concerned that the concept must not be destroyed because scientists are embarrassed by miracles, and journalists interpret their silent embarrassment as anti-god. Parents doubtful of the existence of GOD are too ashamed to pass on a moral message to their children, with the result that bad manners and crime flourish.

If in "WHO WAS JESUS' FATHER?", I show that none of the happenings in history require a God; not even Jesus' ministry or the New Testament; I will have done untold harm. But I hope to publish a book soon that will show that man with the help of computers can perform better than any historical God has ever done. And to show that ideas, like turning the other cheek, which at first sight might look unselfish are in fact, when calculated, the most beneficial forms of behaviour for long term selfish enrichment. If I succeed, there will be no requirement for the Fear of God and I will have done no harm. Unfortunately this second volume has to be a separate book to please librarians as it would have to be sited on a different shelf as it is on a different subject.

*In my future book, probably titled "The **God' Card"** but possibly titled "Cupid's City", I show a non-superstitious, irreligious way of encouraging good manners and honesty for everyone.* Since the majority no longer believe in Hell Fire, this will become very important.

Educated Christians including Anglican Bishops are doubtful of the truth of much of the Bible, and on no authority are they very selective as to what they believe is or isn't true. But due to differences of opinions on details they are shy of talking about it. So other Christians, Jews and Moslems are encouraged to believe in patriotic and terrorist ideas because of ancient texts in which God says kill different types of people. I believe that if we are to have peace and avoid terrorism we must stop educating small children in the belief of miracles and Gods. I believe that through computer records in the future, we can control people so that we do not need to tell them lies about the existence of God. This is why I am sometimes rude about religions because I believe such lies are no longer needed to keep the uneducated in order, and therefore it is my duty to poke fun at the religious.

Why am I, the right person to write such a book? Even if the Pope, the Archbishop of Canterbury, or the Bishop of Durham all knew in their hearts, that there was no God independent of man's invention, *and they must know that God has never spoken to them personally.* They would lose not only their income but also a palace if they said so. As the Quakers say no man that is paid to be good, can ever be trusted to be so, and that is why the Society of Friends have no paid priests.

I have the advantage, over salaried scientists who have to stick to one academic discipline; I can jump the traces from one discipline to another. *I believe my method of writing unproven probabilities or possibilities makes history, more comprehensible, and fleshes out the skeletons of the past. But it is outside the 'yes' or 'no' step-by-step logic of the academic scientists, who are restricted to small concepts, like the splitting of the atom. More complicated concepts like God and morality have so far eluded accurate proof, and therefore discussion. I believe that the most important aspect of science is its ability to change morality. Great scientists like great artists create something new.*

I despise, the Victorians for being unable to talk about sex though they practised it, and present-day politicians who cannot speak of class when their primary motivation is class war and jealousy. I do not respect Mary Whitehouse (the BBC protestor) neither she nor her sons ever attended university. The secret pornographic Museum of AD 1857 of Pompeian paintings and sculptures reveals that the Romans and therefore Jesus' contemporaries would not be offended by my strong sexual remarks.

But I do believe in the war time instruction book Plain Words, recommended by the Civil Service. It carries the story of an officer in the First World War who wrote to the widow of a soldier who urinated on an electric railway line while guarding a station and died of shock. His letter said he had "passed away". So the Bank said he might be in a prison camp and refused to release his money or pay interest on it until after the war; as the unit was behind the lines on the letter date. She wrote to the Officer but by this time the officer and his troop were dead and no authority knew what had happened. The book recommends 4 letter words like "dead". God has failed to publish a chart of good and bad behaviour. So we all rely on grandma's potty training. We dare not go naked or use words like penis, cunt, arse or shit, and the names we are taught to use, are not in the dictionary. So when we grow up we think sex is sin.

So if you are frightened or shocked by the truth. I warn you not to read on. However I have given way to popular demand that were the word f*** is the shortest way of explaining a situation, I will conform to general practice. I understand that many religious people think it is disgusting. *I myself find it extremely pleasurable and think that *** (stars) in the air express my view.*

Innocence is a synonym for ignorance.

ITALICS REPRESENT MY VIEWS

The ordinary type is reserved for generally accepted facts and opinions, which have for the most part been culled from the writings of respected Christian authorities. The *italic*s are for newly created ideas; controversial opinions and my personal prejudices, which I believe, have more probability of being correct than those of the Establishment. *I ask a question, I propose an answer, and if I can see no fault or inconsistency in my reply, I write it in italic,* to warn the reader that he should challenge it.

All the old religions prohibit women wearing clothing between their legs, because disease thrives on stale menstrual blood, for example, Joan of Arc was burnt alive for wearing trousers. It is known that women didn't wear under clothes until the flimsy Parisian Empire styles necessitated them in the nineteenth century. Turkish women's 'trousers' worn under the skirt, are in fact leggings, which go no higher than the thigh. So if I described a man fixing a girls garter, I might add as a categorical fact in italics which at once means it is only my opinion, - *he saw her pubic hair*. This helps to remind those readers who might have supposed that all he would have seen was a triangle of white linen, and at the same time it is short and does not interrupt the pace of the story. I believe a specific statement based on a generalised truth adds essential background colour. I would never describe an historical person as a short ugly man, just because I didn't like him.

The longer portions of *italics* are frequently "unproven probabilities". They are stories, not facts, but I take great care that they infringe no natural scientific law, or historical fact. Since miracles and Gods are not part of natural law, they are deleted from the story.

If history records a miracle I have to show, how someone could have had a motive and the means to cause one to be believed in and recorded. I believe that I have achieved this. *I believe that this proves that History gives no support to paranormal happenings or for the supposition of a God.*

Many Christians defeat atheists in arguments because they challenge them to explain how God occurs so persistently throughout history. The atheist usually explains away one or two instances and then gives up because of the immensity of the task; *I boast that I have achieved that task.*

My probable fictions do not preclude cleverer people than I, writing simpler more probable fictions, but if they are able to do so, they will not be disproving my work, they will be corroborating it. I assure you that the ideas in this book are here because I genuinely believe them and not because of a desire to attract attention to myself or for publicity.

My history of the world may seem inaccurate guesswork. This is because I have left out the 99% of history, which we all agree on. I have concentrated on those parts, which I believe have been wrongly interpreted, and often there is very little evidence to prove either view. But the mere fact that a fiction can be invented to fit the facts means that miracles and Gods are not essential to history.

CHAPTER I
[With italic probabilities]

A GODLESS SCIENTIFIC BEGINNING.

"In the beginning, what was God doing before he made the Universe?" asked the pagans. The Christians replied "Busy creating Hell for the likes of you".

What caused the "big-bang?" Why should we believe scientists who say it occurred 13.7 billion years ago? Because by using the same scientific logic, they made a miraculous smaller bang at Hiroshima. Stephen Hawking who sits in Newton's chair as well as a wheel chair, leads the search for the Holy Grail of physics, a unified theory of the universe. All events in nature can be explained by four basic forces:

1) The strong force, which binds together atomic nuclei.
2) The weak force which causes radioactive decay.
3) Electromagnetism which gives us light and heat.
4) Gravity.

The first two operate only on the subatomic scale; so we are unaware of them; the other two forces affect everything from protons to galaxies.

Even as I write, successful experiments are going on to detect zero-neutrino double-beta decay. The unity of these four forces could be explained if the neutrino has mass. If this unity was the creative force that made the universe, this force could be said to be 'God' or The Creator. I do not deny the possibility of a boring mechanistic God incapable of thought, but I shall continue to call myself an atheist because such a God is so unlike any God believed in by the major religions, who's God, can punish and reward and in some religions have children, [e.g. Jesus (son of God). The unimaginable initial compression where none of the known laws of physics could apply may be hard to understand but it is much simpler than the concept that a God, for which there is no scientific evidence, made himself and then made the universe. Of course in a pre-nuclear age the God theory, despite its mind-boggling complications, appeared to be the simpler concept.

But even in the Bible, God did not make the world out of nothing; he made it out of chaos (pre-existent evil). He was only the chap who put it in order

What was God doing before he created the world? St. Augustine of Hippo in 5th century claimed the world was made "not in time, but simultaneously with time" at the time of the creation. He was correct. Scientists have understood the conditions that existed, one hundred thousandth of a second after the Big Bang. Time and Dimensions started together. However not all contemporary Christians agreed because they sacked Hippo and tortured and killed his priests as heretics, as a result the pejorative word 'vandal' entered the English language. Stephen Hawking believes that a universe with no edge in space, no beginning or end in time, has nothing for a Creator to do.

Each atom through gravity can weigh the whole universe. This poetically could be said to be an ability to "count the hairs on your head". To this extent every atom by its movement speaks to every other atom and if it emits light, it can "speak" to distant stars and this God-like action of communication is on a vast scale. But this God of Light cannot interfere with natural laws, so when I come to parts of history in which God takes an active part, I shall look for reasonable and natural explanations for why people said there was a God at the time. If I fail, I will not regard it as unreasonable if you then believe in God. If I succeed my history is more likely to be correct than conventional Christian beliefs.

But today God and references to his divinity have been expunged from Article 2 of the European constitution concerning liberty and the rights of man, to avoid causing offence. So, if my denial of God's existence causes you offence, you are in the minority. When I write my personal view of history the text will change to *italic*.

'M A R T I A N S' and D . N . A .

When the Pentagon wanted to economise on looking for intelligent life outside earth; Arthur C. Clarke commented that this proves that it is difficult to find intelligent life on earth. The universe is very large. A mere 4.4% is made of atoms, 23% is "cold dark matter" and 73% is "dark energy" which acts as a repulsive force driving us apart. The first stars formed a mere 200 million years after the start of the universe. There are one hundred thousand million galaxies. Our galaxy the Milky Way has a hundred thousand million stars, and the majority of these are three times as old as the earth.

It would appear that life in our tiny solar system, except on Earth, is unlikely, but that in no way reduces the probable number of sites suitable for life in other star systems or other galaxies. Planets in which there are just the right conditions for life to start are extremely rare, but even if only one in a hundred stars has a suitable planet, there are a thousand million planets in our galaxy alone, where life could develop. If life can start on earth, life can start elsewhere and the probability is that it has. *There is, no more logical need for life to have started on the earth than there is for the sun to revolve round the earth.*

Organic molecules such as amino acids have been observed in comets. Experiments have shown that the crash shock of arriving on earth could shake them into peptides, which are more complicated molecules. *Our life may have started with complex D.N.A. chains, which were the garbage of other life forces, which drifted in as flotsam, on inter-stellar dust, or asteroids from other worlds destroyed.*

If, there is intelligent life that can communicate, or even travel across inter-stellar distances, why have they not contacted us? I shall not mean by the word 'Martian' an inhabitant of Mars - there are none but use it for its fictional imagery to represent intelligent life forces from distant galaxies, with the ability to communicate across the starry wastes. *However I believe that most 'Martian' stories are nonsense for they suppose a race that is scientifically clever but historically backward in sociological terms. I believe that the Martians are unlikely to be our very near equals. They are either as far behind us as dinosaurs or so far ahead as to be, more sophisticated than our idea of gods.*

Observe how fast we have developed in the last hundred years. Since some planets were created, millions of years before us, it is absurdly unlikely that the most sophisticated life forces in the universe would be neck and neck with us in development. Unless that 'Life' attempted to contact us, we would not at, our present level of scientific knowledge, expect to have discovered it.

Norman Macrae in. his book titled '2024' wrote, "Civilisation has been allowed to develop. Therefore we can be quite sure that no civilisation hostile to other life is in command of the galaxy. Either there has never been such a killer life form, or any that developed were contained by earlier civilisations with peaceful intentions, or we are in fact alone in the galaxy. All these alternatives lead to a single profound and positive conclusion. Our galaxy is friendly, and it is waiting for us."

Martians *(extra terrestrial life forces)* that could power space ships would be able to manufacture minerals in their own solar systems more cheaply than coming here. We do not have on earth any unique element that cannot be found in the rest of the universe, so it is highly improbable that we should be used as a mine.

We have not yet mined the centre of our own earth where there is sufficient gold to cover the whole surface of the earth knee deep in gold. In the centre of the earth there is sufficient heat for us to cease burning fossil fuels for heating forever and enough space to bury our trash forever. However drilling is difficult because at 8,000 degrees centigrade metal drills would melt unless made of diamonds.

So what could Martians want? *Our only valuable export is likely to be the D.N.A. molecule and that has not substantially changed in ten thousand years, if it was discreetly collected before recorded history, in a Noah's Ark or frozen in test tubes, we would know nothing about it. D.N.A. is very hardy and within their own solar system, they could have bred all the varieties that they require. For instance chopped up cow D.N.A. could be useful in milk making machinery or human D.N.A. could be used for making intelligent loyal slaves. The collection of new slaves from Earth, who had not been properly programmed to accept slavery from birth and who might need complicated transplants to allow them to survive under alien atmospheres, temperatures and gravities; would be far more expensive than breeding them from previously collected stock. New slaves might introduce unsettling ideas about freedom, so even if the Martians required humans as slaves; which is improbable. I would expect this to be a reason for them to hide their existence, in case we should invade with ideas to liberate their slaves.*

It is improbable that Martians can have any use for us, and

our most recent inventions must be as useless to them as a hundred-year-old computer would be to us.

The number of planets having primitive life forces like ourselves, unable to launch a colonial attack, is likely to be as numerous as the grains of sand on a beach, and it would be too boring for them to bother about investigating each one. Besides the time consumption, and effort would be out of all proportion to the gain, needed to investigate, and though the ageing of space travellers slows down when travelling at the speed of light, they could no longer communicate with their contemporaries. No Martian civilisation would send out slow space ships, because by waiting a few hundred years they could send out faster-ones, which would overtake them. So they would probably wait till they could travel safely at the speed of light. But if you travel at the speed of light or faster you cannot see where you are going!

The Martians could not be sure that other Martians would not be hostile so they would not wish to give away their location. Barnard's Star is nearby. It is about six light years away. In a space ship travelling at one hundred thousand miles per hour it would take forty thousand years to reach us. Four times as long as agriculture has been on earth and if their life span was similar to ours, the crew would have to die and reproduce one thousand six hundred times on board their space ship. A message sent to Alfa Centuri would take four and half years, at the speed of light, to get there and eight and half years to get a reply. To Capella it would take forty-five years and the message sender would be dead by the time the message was answered. If only one in a thousand stars had a suitable planet for advanced life, it would be a hundred light years away, or take a thousand years at the tenth of the speed of light and there would be problems steering at that speed.

Since we are still so primitive that we can not understand the language of dolphins, *Martians might be reluctant to broadcast D.I.Y. instructions concerning atomic secrets, which could, as a result of some misunderstanding accidentally blow the world apart, when it took ninety years to reply to our impatient questions.*

We have handed back India and other colonies, and we have freed our slaves. I don't believe couth Martians would want to be our absentee landlords and infect us with viruses; as we infected the New World with smallpox. *They would not want the trouble of administering us and would prefer to let us enjoy self-government. They might think that contact with us, because of our puny knowledge, would put us into a culture shock that might so de-motivate us that we would give up and die.* Like some Eskimos who live on national assistance have taken to drink. *I would be amazed if they tried to contact us and I am sure they have made it an offence for their dropouts to do so. They have not yet heard of glasnost, they might be listening to Hitler's speeches on wireless.* Sir Fred Hoyle says it would take longer than the life of a galaxy, 100,000,000,000 years to colonise the universe.

If there are well socialised Martians (extra terrestrial life forces), it is probable, that they would wish to isolate us as a conservation area, and make sure we were not raided by the natives (uncivilised Martians), just as we stop the natives killing wild life in the Serengeti.

They might desire to conserve us, both for our gene pool, and our independent pool of ideas. Because of the time and distance, it would be quite easy for the Martians to have an effective, Reagan like Star Wars, programme to isolate us. A conservation policy maybe in force now, but long ago, Martians could have come in a space ship and their refuse could be our first life. Or they could have deliberately hurried the process of evolution by leaving the D.N.A. building block that provides fishes with backbones, or maybe they deliberately culled Dinosaurs 63 million years ago to make room for mammals, or maybe they made Homo Sapiens himself.

Early man's obsession with light and the stars could be some mythical memory of a visit. Stonehenge is astronomical. *However, on balance I do not believe in Martian visits, but I do not eliminate them as I do the concept of an all-powerful God. I certainly believe that communication will take place in the distant future and when it does our culture will develop by inconceivable leaps and bounds. Our first contact with inter-stellar intelligent knowledge is likely to be by communicating computers, rather than physically with their biological masters.*

Scientists are mainly agreed on how the solar system developed from the big bang and there seem to be few loose ends. But how did life start? The primordial soup had suitable constituents and chance, over millions of years, developed it with the aid of radiation. Eric Smith of Santa Fe institute says "Life is an elaboration of something very simple, it looks easy and inevitable." Metabolism came first; it could have led to the development of RNA. Some types of molecular chains out-competed other molecular chains for the planets resources, and gradually led to the kind of molecules that life depends upon, long before the first living thing oozed forth.

The earth has been bombarded by millions of asteroids; these contain carbon and nitrogen in the right proportions to have had life. Hans Pflug thinks asteroids are fossil living matter because they have non-earthly amino acids. Sir Fred. Hoyle suggests in "The Intelligent Universe" that life could travel deep frozen on comets. Organisms as complex as humans, could not survive the journey through space. But some bacteria have the ability to survive the years of freezing on the journey and short periods of boiling, such as the inner layer of an asteroid would suffer on entering the earth's atmosphere. Other bacteria are able to reconstitute even after bombardment by radiation. Some even live in the heart of an atomic reactor. Hoyle finds it hard to believe that they would have acquired this immunity if they had developed only on earth where this ability would have no Darwinian advantage. He also believes interstellar dust contains living microcosms as dust can enter the earth's atmosphere slowly without burning up.

The self-generation of very simple life, out of complicated molecules, is a simpler supposition than the self-generation of a God who was immediately so sophisticated that he could create life.

However Professor Hoyle thinks the odds on producing by random the 200,000 proteins in our cells are 1 to 50,000,000,000 ,000,000,000, and at one re-arrangement per second, each would require 1,350 billion years or 300 times the age of the earth. If science does eventually show that life developed on earth rather too early to be probable, this does not prove the existence of God but rather suggests the interference of Martians. How then did life become so quickly sophisticated? The process would be speeded up if we were the remains of gigantic colonies of symbiotic genes. Mitochondria are symbiotic bacteria; lichens are a fungus plus algae. D.N.A. could be a well-behaved virus that does not travel normally through air but only in sperm and genes. Hoyle says "diseases are foiled evolutionary leaps" and viruses could produce genetic changes and by being infectious could easily arrange for their sexual partner to have suffered the same change.

Mitochondria live within every human cell and have separate spirals of DNA, which reproduce quite separately at different times. *This suggests to me that they were once quite separate living organisms that took shelter in animal cells.* Mitochondria enable us to use Oxygen and consume the waste products from our cells. It would seem that bacteria could pass their D.N.A. not only to their children, but pass short lengths of their D.N.A. to neighbouring cells. 10% of our dry body weight consists of free-living bacteria, for example cows have some, which help them eat grass.*The following fiction sets out the possibility that we might be made from the reconstituted parts of Martians on a dying planet.*

Once upon a time there was a Martian inhabited planet that was suffering from some terminal disaster. They could see no way of getting a live breeding pair safely on to another healthy planet. Even if they could achieve that, they felt unable to send out a full Noah's Ark. This might have been for many reasons. 1) Because the gravity was very strong and they had never invented viable space ships. 2) Because they had used up all their fossil fuels early on to keep themselves warm on a cooling planet. 3) Because they feared an immoral minority, their C.N.D. movement had prohibited nuclear development. 4) Because an atomic war had not left them enough time to plan a fleet of space ships.

These Martians were reluctant to see a thousand million years of their D.N.A. development destroyed. So, though they could not arrange to send out their complete spiral of molecules they arranged for a massive number of space resistant chains of D.N.A. packaged with viruses designed to help link the chains together in sensible ways. They believed that with the help of Darwinian selection, it would only take a couple of billion years for sophisticated animals to reconstitute themselves on arrival in favourable environments. When, by chance or deliberately the planet blew itself apart, it launched random comets, asteroids and dust into interstellar space and they hoped some of these would land on receptive planets such as the Earth.

We think of D.N.A. as blue prints for hardware but they could also contain software i.e. books of instructions written in D.N.A. code, just in case there were intelligent beings who on arrival, could speed up the process of reforming the D.N.A. Unfortunately the present day Earthlings can only partially read the D.N.A. molecule, though they did notice that some very primitive creatures did have absurdly long D.N.A. chains. These software D.N.A. chains could have been designed by the Martians to be read two ways, like a Bible and as unconscious thought patterns like the way birds remember to build nests.

I agree that this is rather like sending loose jigsaw puzzles and hoping the box will re-combine, simply by being shaken by chance. But if there are a lot of boxes and the picture is variously damaged by random radiation in transit, there is a chance over millions of years of it being reformed rather more quickly than forming itself de-novo. My thesis does not depend on your acceptance of these ideas but it simply gives more time for natural selection to have had its way.

Professor Dawkin's Memes (Ideas)

The creation of the planets took billions of years, the development of genes [the D.N.A. molecule] took thousands of years, but the development of ideas [memes] used to take hundreds of years to spread throughout the world, but as a result of T.V. it now only takes minutes.

Memes are replicating ideas that spread by imitation, with longevity, fecundity and copying fidelity like genes. It is a word much used by Professor Dawkins in "The Selfish Gene" a book I strongly recommend. Memes are achieving evolution at a rate several orders of magnitude faster than genetic change and seem to be speeding up. "Examples of memes are tunes, ideas, catch-phrases, clothes fashions, and ways of making pots or of building arches."

The following is another extract from the Selfish Gene: - "When you plant a fertile meme in my mind you literally parasitize my brain, turning it into a vehicle for the meme's propagation in just the way that a virus may parasitize the genetic mechanism of a host cell. And this isn't just a way of talking - the meme for, say, 'belief in life after death' is actually realised physically, millions of times over, as a structure in the nervous systems of individual men the world over.... Consider the idea of God. We do not know how it arose in the meme pool. Probably it originated many times by independent 'mutation'. In any case, it is very old indeed. It replicates itself by the spoken and written word, aided by great music and great art. Why does it have such a high survival value? It provides a superficially plausible answer to deep and troubling questions about existence. It suggests that injustices in this world may be rectified in the next. These are some of the reasons why the idea of God is copied so readily by successive generations of individual brains. God exists, if only in the form of a meme with high survival value, or infective power, in the environment provided by human culture." God is an extremely cheap and effective way of making ignorant believers do what you want them to do because of the fear of Hell and being unable to escape an all seeing God, and is therefore popular with rulers.

I hope this book will put some memes in a meme pool because they can make culture evolve a million times faster than genes. I regard them as so much more important than producing genes; I have had a vasectomy. We alone can rebel against the tyranny of the selfish replicators, genes or memes because we have the ability to be altruistic.

GHOSTS, AND MAGIC

The Christian Church is so embarrassed by their phrase "Holy Ghost" for God that children tell me that I have got it wrong; the phrase is "Holy Spirit".(*Whisky?*) I personally do not believe in ghosts, but some genuine people are convinced. *I cannot explain their belief.* The following ghost stories show that some were tricks. Some Roman Catholics attached candles to the backs of crabs in a village graveyard, to convince Protestants that there were ghosts. And my father, who was the Resident of Government House Ishapur, India; a 16th century Dutch edifice had a Major General staying the night. At a well-lubricated dinner, father told the General the story of the house Ghost, saying however he had never seen her, my father went to relieve himself, and met a white nurse returning from night duty who was also staying in the house whom the General had never been introduced to. My father quickly threw a mosquito net over her and told her to act the part of the ghost. As he showed the general around the house she emerged from a fireplace and was so convincing, that the Major General fled to his bedroom and locked the door and thereafter believed in ghosts.

In Jamaica a family vault was opened after a decade and the skeletons with un-stolen rings on their fingers, appeared to have got out of their coffins, some of which were on the floor, and some standing upright, when they had originally been neatly placed on shelves. The skeletons appeared to have been dancing; one was suspended by his hand, which was stuck in a coffin on the top shelf. The locks had not been tampered with. The whole district was convinced the devil himself was involved. However a visiting hydrologist, a few years later discovered that 10 years before, there had been a freak rise in the water table. This could have floated the coffins on and off the shelves, as it rose and fell over a period of a few weeks, but of course at the time of the opening every thing was bone dry.

Water is the cause of most ghost stories; messages miraculously appear on the wall, these are, but old writings, which appear through distemper, which has been made transparent through dampness. The sound of a person going up, or downstairs, is often heard. This is due to moisture movement in the bottom step, which causes a slow motion pressure release all the way up the stairs. Often, the occupants going to bed left the living room door open so the rising warm air dried the stairs.

When I was a student, I had my bedside light and an electric fire operated by the same switch. Ten minutes after switching off the light someone took three paces across the darkened room, and once knocked some papers to the floor. I eventually discovered that the fire dried one side of a heavy mahogany chest-of-drawers. After the fire was switched off this timber sucked in moisture and the side minutely with a creek adjusted its angle which half a second later caused the other side to adjust with a creek, a cheap cupboard leaning against it, then adjusted with a third creak.

Telepathy may, or may not happen, but the messages never seem to be reliable and they are frequently so blurred, that they are virtually useless. I myself almost believe in it because of a statistical oddity. When driving my car, if I observe a girl on the sidewalk with her back to me that excites my lust, there is a fifty per cent chance she will turn and look at me, while the unexciting ones virtually never turn round. I agree that girls that affect me may be wearing something sexy and therefore maybe looking for male approval, and they may hear a difference in the note of my car engine, which has ceased to accelerate. But if the metabolism of my body is severely affected they nearly always turn.

Surveys show that one third of the population have been aware of an abstract presence or power, a sixth only once, 2% feel a presence every day. *God cannot believe in equality if he has forgotten to contact two thirds of the people.* Those that felt the spiritual side of religion was important, were three times as likely to have had such an experience. Churchgoers had twice as many experiences as non-church goers, but not in church. Experiences usually occur at times of emotional overloading; suggesting the conscious valve was relaxed. 50% were triggered by distress, and 70% of the recipients were alone, only 7% occurred during religious services and these were usually amongst adherents of minority ecstatic religions. These experiences were usually interpreted, as the presence of God or a massive remembrance of a dead person at a time of trouble; such that they seemed to be present. Often they lasted only a few seconds so their recipients were unable to check them out.

"The main purpose of the central nervous system is to exclude the majority of impulses coming into it." says Jonathan Miller. I believe that because most experiences have the same lack of meaningful logic as dreams; it is much more likely to be the unconscious, coming through at a time of stress, like a dream but when one is awake. It could be an atrophied sixth sense, but if this is the case, it is so atrophied that unless we can build up the signal, and we do not know how to, we cannot use it as a tool because it is so inaccurate. Very, very few people feel they can switch on or off such experiences.

Magic is so discredited by science, you may be surprised that I deal with it at all but astrology takes up more space in our daily papers than Christianity. Sympathetic magic is a pantomime, mimicking a natural happening and thus hopefully causing it to happen. Some examples are: -

The belief, that driving nails into a model of a person, containing some hairs from their head or nail clippings would actually harm them.

The cannibal belief, that by eating an enemy chief, his knowledge, cleverness and strength will transferred to the eater.

The belief, that by producing wet sperm and releasing one's own tensions; one would remind the sky to rain.

Infectious concepts like; I will be weakened if I touch a woman when I am on the warpath, because women are weaker than men.

The Chinese burn paper houses, clothes and bedding for the dead, so that they will have real ones transported to them, in the smoke.

Arabs in 1900 still believed that a knot in a handkerchief would stop, a bridegroom consummating. In 1718 in Bordeaux a person was burned alive and in 1702 in Ashiutilly, Scotland a person was put to death because they had tied knots.

The idea of transferring troubles or sins onto scapegoats is magic.

A man carrying a heavy load of firewood can transfer it onto the back of a donkey. Language permits a man to transfer a load of troubles onto another, thus primitive man believed it must be possible, because nearly all thought is language, and something that can be said, must be able to be done. Upon this basis the early Greeks practised Pharmakos. A riddance ceremony whereby annually two people were loaded with the town's abstract ills and diseases, they were driven around the town having their testicles beaten with wands. [Incidentally the word testicles was invented by a Pope and means 'little witnesses'] Once outside the town they were frequently killed not as an offering to a God but simply to stop them re-entering the town. *Adam and Eve could have been Pharmakos victims.* The decision to kill Socrates could have been influenced because he was born on the annual day of Pharmakos.

Jesus believed in Magic he cast out the devils from a man and made them enter some geese, *a real God would not have needed to harm the geese, but it made it a much better piece of showmanship.* For instance the Israelites would not eat blood because they believed that the soul of the animal was in its blood. They had to protect themselves against the vengeance of the souls or ghosts of the animals they had killed.

Surely we should look for advice from modern educated writers and not accept Bronze Age ideas concerning God.

Magic unlike science never learnt from failure, failure was simply explained away. Cannibals found that when they ate big men they did not become bigger, as the logic of sympathetic magic decreed would happen. Rather than disbelieve in magic, they argued the essence of the man must be in something they didn't eat, namely his soul; the soul must reside in his last breath, which escaped.

Agriculturists planted the dead in graves so that they might grow miraculously like seed, or journey down to the under world where both the good and bad went. The northern herdsmen burnt their dead, so that the Fire God would send their souls up to heaven in the form of smoke. Both agreed that if the priest or witch doctor did not perform the correct rites, the soul would hang around on earth and upset the natural order of things. This had the advantage that it made the priests rich, and gave them explanations for the inexplicable, and the chance to frighten people with supernatural happenings.

The Greek peasantry embarrassed the Athenian nobility when honouring Zagreus, later called Zeus, by eating raw meat, direct from the carcass of a bull, on their hands and knees. I believe this custom arose, because they believed that through sympathetic magic one obtained the strength of Zagreus, who on account of his big penis had been nicknamed 'bull'. It was essential to eat the whole carcass at one sitting to prevent the bull's essence, or soul from escaping. This was followed by an ancient incantation of words which prohibited any one from placing meat on leaves or covering up their food; this was designed to prohibit gluttons taking an unfair quantity of meat and hiding it for another day and so allowing the essence to escape. These misunderstood table manners, thousands of years later when fire, plates, cooking pots and metal knives had been invented, had the effect of prohibiting the use of plates or putting the meat in a cooking pot. The early Christians [Clement] scorned the Olympian gods on account of this. *But I think the last laugh is on* the Christians who drink the blood of their God in St. Peter's in Rome.

Dr M. A. Murray in 1921 thought the witchcraft in Western Europe was the leftover of Teutonic religion, and though this viewpoint is now challenged, because witches were so ignorant that they did not know what they believed.

I shall never the less talk about witchcraft and astrology in seventeenth century England because we know so much more about it than ancient magic and there are some parallels. Convicted witches were often very old lonely widows, with physical deformities, who were desperately poor and relied on village charity. *When the fairly poor turned them from their door, their undeserved plight made them hateful and angry and their only hope was to frighten the children into giving them some food. When by chance their curses actually happened they were judged guilty.* Witchcraft seemed the only explanation when misfortune struck the deserving, because God was meant to be good. Misfortune could be far worse than it is today, because there was no fire or theft insurance, National Health or Social Security. Epidemics, fire, and earthquakes were regarded as 'acts of God'.

When Divine Providence was exposed, as a worthless idea, the clergy invented the pangs of conscience. *I have never had any, only embarrassment at my accidental stupidities.*

Doctors and midwives, as late as the 18th century, believed that deformed children resulted from indecent sexual relations, rationalising that the state of mind of the f***ing couple, could influence the embryo. Fig leaf philosophers taught that ill health and monstrous births punished incest and adultery. Victorian clergy preached that the punishment for fornication was venereal disease and cattle plague was retribution for ill treatment of farm labourers. In Africa today witchcraft is produced as an explanation for impotence, barrenness, and failure in examinations.

We still use planetary astrological words such as - 'jovial', 'mercurial', and 'saturnine'. Astrologers in the seventeenth century were consulted because they could read and write, and there was no other citizen's advice bureau. Both witches and astrologers were excellent agony aunts. Like psychiatrists they gave confidence to their clients and helped them to make up their own minds. The pretence that stars could influence behaviour, relieved clients of a sense of failure and guilt. Sometimes they responsibly advised patients to consult a doctor if they felt the disease could be cured by medical or surgical treatment. Because they were illegal one could trust them with illegal secrets. A man on the run could ask them where best to hide. They were purveyors of cheap legal advice. They were private detectives because they kept informants and frequently learnt their client's secrets by secretly overhearing their conversation in the waiting room. Their advice was frequently as obscure as the oracle of Delos or one of Christ's parables, so if it was wrong, it could be put down to misinterpretation.

Capricious Fortune, Fate or Chance were classical ideas, but after John Wesley's death, the Methodist Conference resolved the question of who had spiritual authority to administer communion by casting lots, believing God would influence the lots. *In modern times, seeing life in terms of the lucky break remains the philosophy of the unsuccessful.*

The Roman Catholics believe; Holy wine, bread, water and relics can do miracles; if presiding priests say the right incantations over them. By consecration [*magic*] places can be made Holy. Exorcism is a form of white magic. By denying the Roman Catholic claims to manipulate God's grace for earthly purposes through magic and the intercession of Saints; the Protestant clergy lost power to the astrologers and witches, who could still claim they were able to cure the sick and find lost property.

Magic must always be false, because were it true it would be called science. Magic is logical like science, it puts its faith in order, but mistaken notions form its basis. Magic preceded both religion and the law. Blessings and curses are magical ideas; in religion they became the vow or the prayer; in law, they became the judge's sentence.

Excessive excellence instead of being praised, as it would be today would be called black art by the jealous, and therefore excellence was not a characteristic anyone wanted to achieve. *In this way a belief in magic was a brake on progress, and induced wicked egalitarianism. But magic made men behave themselves, because they were taught that misfortunes and illnesses were punishments for moral lapses. Now that we think they arise from natural causes, the bad can be bad with no fear except of the police. Men no longer keep quiet through shame when they suffer God's punishments, rather they boast of their bad luck, to get our sympathy.*

Religions pose abstract powers that are hard to disprove and are created by men like Moses and perpetuated by hereditary cliques so they can order the masses about with ritual, pretending the orders came from God. "Everyone must obey the state authorities, because no authority exists without God's permission, and the existing authorities have been put there by God". (Romans 13.1). Bertrand Russell says "What we 'ought' to desire is merely what someone else wishes us to desire. Usually it is what authorities wish us to desire – parents, schoolmasters, policemen and judges".

Sir Walter Raleigh wrote, "The art of magic is the art of worshipping God". Magicians believe that man can make God do as he is told, by ritual, just as scientists believe that man can make Nature do as it is told, through formulae.

APES, ICE AND FIRE.

The first apes were 35 million years ago, 15 million years ago they divided into hominids from which man evolved and pongids from which modern apes are descended. A fictional ape at London Zoo asked, "Am I my keeper's brother?" We are probably descended from an African Eve 200,000 years ago. Darwin's Survival of the Fittest has been corroborated by finding that gorillas' and chimps' D.N.A. is 98% the same as our own, and at least one white human baby has been born with a two inch tail. Female chimpanzees are matriarchal and promiscuous; typically they have 13 male lovers and know nothing of the incest taboo. They can use sticks as levers, make sponges of crumpled leaves and throw stones.

When the forest receded, due to climatic changes, and women stood up to look over the high grass, using two legs, instead of four, the pelvic bones in order to adjust the balance narrowed the hole through which the baby was born. This was a distinct Darwinian disadvantage; many women and babies must have died. When a foal is born it can run with the herd shortly after birth. Desmond Morris advances this idea or meme in another worthwhile book called the Naked Ape. In order to get through the pelvic hole, babies' heads were under-developed in such a way that the short learning period that all animals have was substantially extended. This slower development called neoteny, enabled man to learn communication through hand signs and speech. Man has many Darwinian disadvantages over more primitive animals. Women may have had to stand up in order to free their hands for the carrying of babies. Chimps do not need to be carried they can hang onto their mothers body hair with their hands and feet. Women had to solve the problem by developing clothes with pouches in their folds. In turn clothes and furs encouraged fleas [humans have more varieties that can live on them than any other species]. Hairlessness made the treatment of skin diseases easier, and in turn made clothes more desirable, which in turn enabled men to extend their range into the cold North. Mankind's hairlessness, taught us how to use fire to guard against the cold and ice.

Man's hairlessness may be due to men and women, or their ape ancestors, living on an island to escape dangerous animals while asleep. Head-hair does not get wet when standing up in water or even swimming. But body hair is difficult to dry without towels and fire; the sun is unreliable, so hairy people died of cold induced diseases on their return from fishing or hunting on the mainland before reliable boats were invented.

There has been a pattern to the **Ice Ages,** they usually last 100,000 years with warmer windows of 10,000 years. During an Ice Age, the sea level drops by 360 feet and there is three times as much ice. This enables man and animals to bridge, not only the English Channel, but also the Bering Straits. As recently as 30,000 to 10,000 years ago Australasia was only a short sea journey across the Wallace Line. 35,000 to 25,000 years ago the grassland steppes stretched from Hungary to Mongolia while Europe was covered in ice. *Ice covered mountains must have separated tribes living in valleys from other human breeding stock and this could explain separate languages.*

The ice advanced to its maximum 18,000 years ago. The "Climatic Optimum" or "Thermal Maximum" (the warmest period in the ice ages) occurred 6,000 years ago. In AD 1200 - 1800 there was a mini cooling period, and the Thames used to freeze, but the return of the ice age was delayed by global warming as a result of pollution. From 1880 onwards it has been nearly as warm as the "Climatic Optimum".

Traces of human fires 20,000 years old have been found in Africa. **Fire** enabled men to drive animals to their death, by creating forest fires; it also enabled men to sharpen sticks to provide spears and make palings to constrict wild animals. It provided him with light, so he could nap flints in the long dark cold evenings, a job requiring great skill. It enabled him to shape wood i.e. hollow tree trunks to make canoes. Wheat seeds could be made into bread, by cooking, and raw meat made tender. But like all good things he over used his power over fire, both intentionally and accidentally. He burnt the forests and the dry grass and accidentally changed the climate and created deserts. Cave paintings show that in 3000 BC pastoralists were able to obtain grazing all over the Sahara. He was so successful at killing animals that Man's numbers increased and the number of edible animals and plants decreased sharply.

The invention of fire, was man's first great achievement. It was so important that fire became a great God. Naturally the skill to make fire miraculously from two pieces of oak made the igniter as important as the hunt captain. He became 'King of the Wood', Druid, Witch doctor, High Priest, Magician. At Christmas time we commemorate him by burning the oak 'Yule' log. He was so important that Christ's birthday was changed from its real date to Yuletide.

Sir James Frazer's Golden Bough is the mistletoe which goes golden as it dries which is the soul/life of the oak tree because it lives on, when the tree sheds its leaves. Even today we touch wood in memory of the oak trees magic. Since souls could leave one body and enter another, the soul of the oak tree could enter the high priest. The Norse hero Balder was killed by mistletoe.

The Present Tense Creates Immortality And The Human Soul.

Because the shape of the skull affects the voice box Dr. Laitman thinks the first speech possible was 300,000 to 400,000 years ago. Modern man's brain size did not develop until 125,000 years ago and these Neanderthals, buried their dead, looked after their sick toothless brothers, and were big strong men with heavy skeletons, who used their front teeth while working on hides. They only had an expectation of life of 29½ years, and had short thighs like Eskimos and lived in a cold climate. But we are probably not descended from them, as they died out 30,000 years ago. Modern man with tools and language has probably been in Africa for half a million years, and for fifty thousand he has buried his dead. As hunter-gatherers, man wandered and populated Europe and Asia. The cave paintings of France and Spain are 35,000-10,000 years old. More people live in Tokyo today than lived in the whole world at the start of the agricultural revolution.

Man is not as strong as a lion or as fleet as a horse but language has helped man to co-ordinate a team and has given him a major advantage over his prey when hunting. It helps him to lie and deceive, and mislead his prey or adversary. *It was for purposes like this that language was invented.*

It is hard to philosophise without using words and much of twentieth century philosophy is about semantics, proving that those Greek and eighteenth century philosophers made errors because ordinary language was inadequate or had led earlier philosophers into errors. Bertrand Russell for instance in the 20th century asked; "Is the King of France bald?" Some answered 'Yes there is no King, so he has no hair', some answered 'No, there is no King, so he has no head to be bald'. Bertrand Russell regarded his answer, which is "Nonsense", as a great philosophical discovery. It was a third category, not true or false. *I believe that Gods are not true or false but nonsense. I believe that just as sophisticated language confused many philosophers, the absence of future and past tenses in the early languages of primitive man, confused him and caused him to invent gods. The first words that man invented must have been nouns or verbs. Nouns are the spirit of whatever they describe, as soon as a mountain or a tree has a name, it has a personality, and it can be linked with any verb just as a man can be. All verbs must have started with the present tense only, and therefore dead ancestors when spoken of must have appeared as much in the present as their surviving children. This produced a logical problem. Language said dead ancestors existed, but they didn't exist like ones children, so they must exist like ghosts or spirits.* Spirits of alcohol evaporate *and live* in the air.

Humans invented personalities for inanimate objects like trees, stars, and the weather; this was poetic not scientific but it helped to make the dead survive as ghosts or immortal souls. *Other people's misleading has led us to God.*

One could say, "The tree moves", to say the tree is moved by the *wind is as inconceivable; as the idea of the earth revolving around the sun.* Empedocles of Sicily was the first man to find air. He noted that the inside of a pot put upside down on water was not wet. *If one believes that the tree moves itself, it has a spirit (a personality) like an animal or a man. So it is not surprising hundreds of nouns became spirits, and because men boast, they grew to be powerful spirits, and a powerful spirit is a God.* Powerful dead ancestral chiefs, whom one turned to for memories of their advice, became powerful Gods, together with powerful nouns like individual volcanoes or the sun. "It" (i.e. the inanimate category) had not been discovered. All nouns were "thou". All unique nouns and ancestors could become Gods and that is why some say there are more Gods than people in India today. These Gods did not have the power of Allah. These Gods were often immoral tricksters like the pre-Christian Germans and Africans believed in.

The soul of man is but the breath of life and the last breath belonged to, and floated up to, God. A spirit is disembodied but it could move about and be powerful. Others thought the soul was in the blood and that it went down into the underworld, if it lingered it was a 'shade', a weak ghost. When language acquired a past tense, the soul could die, but if it did, there could be no rewards and punishments in Heaven and Hell, *so the literate aristocracy perpetuated the fraudulent belief in rewards and punishments so that they could make the illiterates and semi-illiterates obey them.* Modern science shows us that consciousness [the soul] is an internal construction in the brain to represent the external world; it is part inherited and part added to as a result of learning. It enhances social understanding, sympathy, and communication. It helps; model building, pattern-recognition, and prediction. But it is not wholly personal because linguistic skill and the resources of its cultural group, limit it.

I include this table because many people seem unfamiliar with large figures. 100 is shown as 10^2. The number of stars in our galaxy is 100 billion = 10^{11}. An erg is a Joule 10^7.

The Roman Empire used	10^{24} ergs of energy.
We now use 100,000 times more	10^{29} " " "
A 10 megaton hydrogen bomb	10^{23} " " "
Krakatoa	10^{25} " " "
Sun Flares	10^{31} " " "
The Sun	10^{40} " " "
A supernova	10^{49} " " "
Explosion of an entire galaxy	10^{58} " " "
Quasar	10^{61} " " "
Big Bang	10^{80} " " "
No. of atoms in known universe.	10^{80} " "

The universe is finite to science. Ignorant people believe in an infinite God because large numbers baffle them.

C H A P T E R   I I
WOMEN
or the HISTORICAL BATTLE of the SEXES

The HUNTER GATHERER'S DIVISION OF LABOUR.

In a typical hunting group, of fifty, there would be no individual private property save a few hand tools or skins, no fixed abode save the grave, no marriage or sexual taboos such as incest. Being illiterate, the laws would be what the leader said they should be *and as a result he would have priority use of all the women for his sexual delight.* This would genetically improve the race better than our present system; in as much as the best men would tend to be selected as leaders and have priority access to women. He would look upon all children as his sons; though scientifically speaking they would probably be the sons of previous leaders. There would be no proper Gods, just a few ghosts, or spirits of ancestors.

Women could not be taken hunting because mothers usually fed their babies every few hours with breast milk, for four years. The trapping of animals depends on deceit; a baby's cry would give the mother's position away. This meant that women had to be the gatherers of seeds and berries, firewood and water. The men grew taller and stronger in order to hunt better. To this day men score more in tests of spatial ability, while the female gatherers can see better in a dim light and have sharper hearing. Hunter-gatherers deserted the old dried up lands and chased the vast herds that roamed the areas where the ice had been, all over Asia and Europe. The men might have to journey long distances to find animals, and then follow the wounded animal further still. The women had to make themselves attractive to encourage the men to carry the heavy carcasses back to the fires they kept alight. It was their job while the men slept, to prepare and cook the meal.

This ancient Trade Union division of labour was to lead to the ownership of land by women.

Soon women found that wild wheat was getting harder to find, gathering was getting very difficult. *One day a woman tethered*

*a horse and made it walk on bare stone to trample the wheat grain.
The horse dropped some manure on it. Upset the woman shovelled it
to one side by a fence post where nobody would tread on it with their
bare feet. Next year there seemed to be a lot of wheat amongst the
weeds on that very spot. The following year she used fire to clear a
small field where she could sow and grow wheat.* With the reduction
of trees the land became drier, grass fires spread out of control more
easily. The number of wild fruits and wild animals reduced still
more, but with bread, the population grew. Competition became
fiercer and the quantity of naturally occurring foods decreased i.e.
too many fruits were eaten for them to reseed themselves, too many
cows or horses were eaten, so the size of the herd reduced.

In the ancient world, when agriculture was starting there were
more Goddesses than Gods. *They believed that Creation and fertility
was much the same thing,* so a Goddess created the world, during
the period when man thought that women produced children through
parthenogenesis. The word is from the same root as Parthenon,
the Greek Goddess' temple, and means birth without a man, virgin
birth.

PROSTITUTE GODDESSES

Trees, mountains and animals all failed to perform miracles
or maintain as interesting personalities as the new Goddesses did in
their theatrical brothels. Every tribe that spoke a different language
had a different Goddess to strengthen their tribal identity but though
their names differed they all had a great deal in common.

In an ordinary farming family, the woman would be
responsible for planting, working the fields, cooking; and looking
after the fire, the food stores, and medicinal herbs. She was also a
sexual partner and trainer of children between whom she would settle
disputes. She would wear the family jewellery as decoration and as
a result became the family's bank.

Today in a sample survey of 515 horticultural societies,
women in 41% of the cases are in charge of cultivation rather than
men. However I cannot cite historic evidence for the domination of
men by women, because I am writing of the era, before there was
writing and trade, and before the population explosion brought on

by peaceful horticulture. My case is based on myth and religion. However ca 2,350 BC Urukagina's edict "Women of former times each married two men, but women of today have been made to give up this crime." This suggests a change.

In Catal Huyuk Turkey, probably the most ancient city in the world; with a population of approx. 7,000 persons between 6,250 – 5,720 B C there are many female figurines, with prominent vulvas, navels and breasts. Marija Gimbutas reports that there are 30,000 miniature-Mother-Goddess-sculptures from 3,000 sites in S.E. Europe, dating from the Neolithic period.

Before there was trade or sufficient wealth to make it worth while to be a thief, there was only one way to become richer than your neighbours, prostitution, the sale of the 'Jewel' which you can sell many times but always keep. The female leader or Goddess did the same, only on a grander scale. She might not actually cook but she would be responsible for maintaining the village fire, by which sacrifices to herself or her grandmother would be made, in practice it was the village festival barbecue. The 'Goddess' was also responsible for the village granary in case of famine. She became the good 'witch' or medicine woman, because being rich; she could maintain a large supply of herbs.

"Prostitution is the oldest profession" is a well-known saying. *i.e. it came before the church, army, the law, medicine etc. I say the church was founded on the brothel. I do not like the negative vibrations of the word prostitute so I shall substitute the word Goddess.* A goddess according to the *puritanical* Oxford Dictionary is "a woman one adores".

Ancient goddesses were well fed, well dressed and they were more able to maintain their beauty and cleanliness better than the agricultural workers. Because they did no work, their hands were, not callused. Just as the mother was head of the household, so they were mother to their village or small town.

Sex for fun must have been the most interesting activity for an ancient civilisation that had a steady food supply and which was in no danger of attack because of the protection of a desert or the sea. Ancient man must have been willing to bring his surplus to his Goddess, just as modern man pays a day's wage to attend a Madonna Concert. He would take it to her as the mother of his tribe as insurance in case he died or his crops failed, then she would feed his family from the tribal granary.

The Indian Goddesses have different names to represent different moods, such as anger. They usually have three aspects somewhat like the Christian Trinity; they are three in one, but all female. The Greeks had a similar trio: - Parthenia, the virgin, represented the creation of life and rebirth. Demeter the corn or barley mother represented fertility and summer. And her daughter Persephone was the bringer of destruction and death, and the hope of resurrection. She returned annually from Hades, which was not a Christian Hell; but a home for the dead, both good and bad. The Greek goddesses existed for thousands of years before the Greek Gods.

The Goddess Astarte made every woman, both high and low born, serve as a prostitute, and she had to give at least one fee to her church. No shame attached to this behaviour. Constantine stopped it in the 2nd century AD at Byblos, Paphos and Cyprus.

The original Goddess must have been a beautiful young girl who because she enjoyed dancing, singing and sexual embracing was besieged by men with gifts, and society's admiration and adulation. Thousands of years later jealous puritans would sneeringly describe her as a nightclub prostitute. As she grew richer and older, she would run a brothel, which gave greater safety in numbers. The job like all jobs in the ancient world would be passed on by hereditary to her daughters. Soon it would be the largest house in the village. Later it became a palace incorporating a hotel with a stage overlooking the square. In middle age, she developed into a universal mother who looked after the corn stored for the years of famine and preserved her appearance with fine textiles and jewels and acted as judge administering justice through her brother. She described herself as the priestess in charge of her hostess daughter, but in fact was ruler of the village. If she had a large congregation, she would have had helpers, just as singers have backing vocalists on stage today. When she was dead, her successor would declare her to be an immortal goddess, to explain how she could continue to speak in the present tense, and she could be credited with all the unpopular pronouncements. Finally a statue would be erected to her memory, and the palace called a temple.

Her domination, of the strong men through sex, could be supplemented with a little fear, and magic to keep the children and simpletons in order and even poison in extreme circumstances could be used to reduce others with a little diarrhoea.

Men are not like lions that can ejaculate 80 times per day or rams that can impregnate fifty ewes. It is true that when a man ejaculates, he produces 250 million sperm, but in the normal sex act he cannot divide this number, even amongst two women. The number of women, he can satisfy per day, is limited to a tenth of the number of men that a woman can satisfy. *A desirable and experienced woman can cause dozens of men to ejaculate into her and thus enslave them sexually. In an agricultural area, a woman could mate once a year with every man, even allowing time off for pregnancy. Women are more capable at orgies than men. Any resultant children could join the temple staff, which in any case looked after other people's unwanted orphans.*

Gonorrhoea led to infertility; Syphilis had not been imported from the New World, and AIDS was unknown; so promiscuity did not necessarily result in death. A woman f***ing with one hundred men has scarcely any more children than one that is monogamous. In order to give herself protection from violent physical abuse and to give those watching sexual excitement, she would f*** in public or in the room that we call the Holy of Holies were any cry for help for assistance could be heard. She could administer chastisement because her congregation was shy in public and feeling sexually submissive. There was nothing wrong with sex for fun, until man invented the genealogical tree as a defence of private male property and privately owned kingdoms. She would initiate the male teenagers in her sex school, by imprinting her smell and image on them early, the girls she could initiate with her tongue. She practised the oldest profession. She used her sexual powers to make men slaves and belonged to no man, she was the great goddess and all men belonged to her. Her tribe was taught to worship her from birth as a mother, at puberty as a lover and she wore the tribal wealth as gold bangles. She had the authority to appoint the chief bouncer, executioner, judge, general, king or call him what you will. His job could be inherited within a family, but only through a woman.

Goddesses supported the arts. They invented the first

sophisticated language. Sanskrit is not the first language, but it is old and not over modernised, it has a hundred words for our one word 'love'. They commissioned sculptors, painters, and architects. Goddesses used scent, incense, frankincense, myrrh, oils, and unguents, because they knew that smells penetrate straight to the unconscious and are very important in sexual recognition and pair bonding. Priestesses would dance and sing. Singing was even more important than it is today, because there were few musical instruments. They had pipes and percussion and maybe some strings.

When money was in its infancy, long long before the Lydians invented coins; transactions must have been very difficult to do. *The ordinary family farmer must have found it virtually impossible to buy a sword from a passing salesman. The salesman had no shop, he sat outside the temple, and he lodged at the temple and shared a bed with the Goddess if he was lucky. The goddess was the only person who was rich enough to have excess goods in sufficient quantity to trade with. She was quite likely the owner of the village shop.*

Textiles were very important, as they could be carried great distances by men or beasts, and be used as gifts to the goddess or for barter. Her House/Brothel/Temple would be carpeted and curtained, with fine materials, and she would not only dress up in exotic costumes, but have a wardrobe, so that the villagers could dress up too. This was equivalent to the twentieth century's custom of hiring clothes from Moss Bros' for weddings and festivals.

She would be in charge of the grain stores and the alcohol jars that she could ration out at festival time. She would be the doctor, chemist, and witch keeping a store of all the medicinal herbs and hallucinatory drugs like soma. No single household could keep them all, for occasional use. She would store the perfumes and unguents, being the biggest user, and maybe the rare art works or tribal insignia. She would be in charge of the treasury, protector of the gold and silver and a big user of jewellery for musicals and pageantry especially at festival time. Thus she would be bank manager, and with inside financial information and the sexual confidences of her lovers and patients she could foresee the future. This power could be augmented with magical tricks. Travellers needing accommodation would come to her door because her temple or home would be the largest. She would be the news source and be possessed not only of carnal knowledge but tribal, historical and scientific knowledge. Most of her scientific knowledge would be 'magical', which is a synonym for incorrect scientific knowledge.

Just as an ordinary mother settles disputes between her children, so a Goddess would act as Judge. She would be peace loving and so would have no army. Full-scale war would destroy her, but she might employ a few bouncers to punish thieves, for the new private property needed protecting. But in the early days the world population was small and there was lots of new land revealed by the receding ice. Who would want to walk a hundred miles and kill a pretty woman? If they enslaved her through capture, and raped her, she would win in the long run because she could poison their food. Weapons were simple, there was no iron, and it was hard to kill anyone with them. So there was peace and prosperity a golden age of LOVE.

Goddesses lasted as a concept for at least as long a period as the concept of God the Father has done. The prostitutes' temples were taken over by men with the coming of metal and swords. After Alexander the Great conquered the area, the temple at Jerusalem was dedicated to Olympian Zeus, following the practice of the local inhabitants. 2 Maccabes 5,6 3 in the Bible records. "The Gentiles filled the temple with licentious revelry: they took their pleasure with prostitutes and had intercourse with women in the sacred precinct".

WOMEN OWNED LAND;
MEN OWNED ANIMALS.

The Agricultural Revolution was the solution to the damage done by fire, in slash and burn societies, it is only the crop, not the land that belongs to the grower. But in places where the land was watered by ditches from the river, a really great step forward was taken *by the women; they invented* private ownership of land in order to grow their wheat. However Jonathan Sauer says the first cereals were unsuitable for baking and they were grown to make beer. The idea soon spread to every conceivable type of crop. They built houses near a water supply. With fire, distant men had melted copper and bronze and one could barter corn and hides for knives and spearheads. Civilisation was about to begin.

Hunter-gatherers only owned personal portable possessions. Private property is the basis of the Agricultural Revolution, which increased the food supply 1,000 fold. When the wild animals decreased in number, men domesticated and bred herds. With red hot brands they marked the animals with their ownership. Private ownership encouraged men to capture, conserve, protect and breed animals, rather than wastefully kill them for just one part, say a horn. Men set about killing lions and tigers to protect their herds with the result that there are no wild lions left in England. As we do today; the animals were milked, or bled, their wool shorn, and their eggs taken. The invention of bread and systematic planting however meant people no longer depended on the bloody butchery of animals.

Sedentary villages established themselves on river islands and on oases where wild animals and wild men could not steal the corn. The desert was a silver lining, because its inhospitableness provided protection from attack, and insufficient grazing, for animals that would have supported a nomadic class or tribe of powerful or rich men who might have taken the power from the agricultural women earlier. It was in agricultural villages that sophisticated language and primitive writing was born. The calendar was discovered to help with planting cycles. In Ur they built with mud bricks set in bitumen mortar in 4000 BC. Trade with measured weights of metal took place.

The bread eating villages quickly grew with a safe supply of food. Their populations were so great, that they were safe from the attack from any one group of hunters. Runaway starving herdsmen kept turning up and stealing food. Laws were made to make stealing a punishable crime, so they begged for work. Because there was no money, *the women had landless male workers dependent on food handouts. This was probably the start of slavery.*

Popular opinion had decided that ownership of land was a winning idea, well worth defending, even when the owners were defenceless children. The starving new arrivals could not of course set up their own farms, because it takes nearly a year to grow a crop, and the best land was already taken, any new land might require a lot of work. It might require draining, or a ditch to supply it with water, or clearing of tree roots or stones. Planting valuable crops like olives or date palms took more than a generation to pay off. In those days unlike today it took a human lifetime for olive trees to fruit and dates take 20 years. Therefore women had to feel certain that society was stable and that *their daughters* would inherit the land without any trouble.

I cannot stress too highly the importance of land ownership. When the community owned it, it quickly lost its productivity and grew weeds. Recently this has been proved by the collapse of Communism. As a result of this agricultural revolution, the concept of perpetually owned private family property was born. The certain inheritance of this property was the primary creative force in the creation of: -

1) Marriage, [together with the concepts of virginity and adultery, to preserve inheritance]
2) Laws administered by a single King descended of God to protect it.
3) Slavery of non-landowners.

But this is later, in the mean while the *women owned the land* because the collection of seeds and berries and everything to do with plants was women's work, while men dealt with animals, which grazed on common land because they had no fences.

The Naxi; who are some of the most remote people in the world live in Chinese Tibet. They practise azhu which means that the woman takes a partner or friend for sex but both he and she continue to live with their respective families. The women own the land.

MATRILINEAL INHERITANCE & DESCENT.

With matrilineal inheritance, paternity is unimportant, and restrictions on female sexuality are ridiculous, so what is now called prostitution caused no problems.

The Agricultural Revolution gave women power, because horticulture (seeds and vegetables) were women's work. This traditional [trade union] division of labour had been in operation for 15 million years according to a zoologist and with the coming of agriculture it was strengthened, so for four thousand years women had the advantage over men. It took a bitter and terrible fight to change it, but that is later. *All gardens and fields belonged to them.*

This is still so in the Darien, men do not own land. *This meant that the women were the landowners, and land is capital and that gave them a distinct advantage over the landless men who did not realise this to begin with. Men were only too happy to avoid boring work in the fields and enjoy the excitement of the hunt, which is why women became richer than men. Animals need more land than wheat, per calorific value of food output. As the population grew the animals declined in numbers and the wheat increased. Men had not yet learnt that it was honourable to be a thief, a tax collector, or an enslaver of women.*

All societies have to have power structures, and power can only be wielded through love, reward, and fear, there are no other ways. Reward is popular today but difficult to organise without trade, and there was virtually none at this time, certainly no money. When love wanes it seldom turns to hate, but as soon as fear is relaxed it nearly always turns to destructive anger. Women are loved by children for their breasts and by men for their c***s, they are more loved than men who on the other hand are feared for their strength. There were a great variety of societies, far more varied than today and it is very hard to be pedantically accurate when the hard facts are potsherds and grave goods. But I have tried to distil from other more specialised writers the essence of matriarchal importance. I present it here as being a society common throughout all early agricultural societies, especially those in the Middle East where civilisation was born.

The Stone Age female figure carvings such as the one at Willendorf are said to be 'Venus figurines' or Mother Goddesses. *I feel Venus and Goddesses are later inventions. I believe they are more like individual dolls used for sympathetic magic, like the wax images, which witches stick pins into, but for the purpose of making individual women pregnant, because male impregnation was not understood.*

"Mater semper certa est". [It is always certain who the mother is.] Before marriage was invented and the necessity for a woman to be faithful, it was hard for a child to know whom his father was. Matrilineal descent means inheriting through the mother. Men can't give birth to children; there is no natural method of them knowing which children have their genes. If men owned a piece of land they would leave it to their sister or their sister's child. In the hereditary chain, women were twice as important as men.

The Hittite patrilineal society flourished in Anatolia 1700-1190 BC they abolished the matrilineal kinship of the ancient Hatti governance in the third millennium BC. The Hatti royal house practised brother-sister marriages, like in Egypt. The male ruler married his sister who as *tawananna* was a priestess with considerable economic and political power, such as the right to collect taxes from cities. Her male child became king, not because his father was king. When incest became illegal, inheritance still passed through the *tawananna*

The earliest historian, Heroditus 490-420 BC, because he came from a Greek society which had for generations been practising marriage and patrilineal right, cannot believe contemporary Lycian genealogical records which showed that the status of children was defined solely in accordance with the maternal line. The king's sister chose the heir to the Lycian kingdom from her children, not her brother's. Menelaus only becomes king of Sparta when he marries Helen. Strabo says that the Ethiopian kings do not leave their sceptre to their children but to their sister's children. In Ethiopia and the Balearic islands a woman sleeps with all who bring her presents and the woman who sleeps with the most, is judged the most beautiful.

The Venerable Bede records that the Picts choose their Queen through the female line, rather than the male. The women leave their estates to their daughters not their sons. Fathers were like fallen leaves from the mother tree.

In 1914 the Trobriand Islanders of New Guinea had a well-established tradition of matrilineal descent and their laws revealed that the child had no substance from the father, only the mother and they had no idea that the man is father to the child despite having marriages.

Early man must have found it very difficult to discover the basic principle that men had anything to do with the production of children without counting the days and months of pregnancy. Since the tribal system of counting might consist of 1-10 followed by the word 'many' as in some languages today, it would be impossible for the child to count or create a calendar. In promiscuous societies especially those that had orgies at festivals it must have been impossible. Women who, had been f***ed by four or five men or even by one they could not recognise in the dark on a festival dedicated to a God, recorded the child, as a child of the festival's God. This statement on occasion might be doubly true, because it was thought that if the priest wore the mask of the god, the soul of the god entered him, and if he then f***ed the girl wearing the mask, it was truly the god's child. One must remember no shame attached to such behaviour, fathers never helped with the support of their children, it was the duty of the girl's brother and he liked extra children, as modern men like pensions.

Most mammals mate only when the female is in oestrous: a brief period around the time of ovulation during which the female advertises sexual receptivity by distinctive visual and scent signals. Most primate males are known to murder infants that they did not sire. Human females do not show obvious external signals, this makes it much more difficult for the human male to work out when conception has taken place, and which infants are his. This means that men fed all women they copulated with regardless of parental success. In Palaeolithic times it was natural for a woman to be pregnant. There was no particular reason, for any one to speculate on how it occurred. However it was commonplace in Europe, India and China to keep the population down by infanticide, even in recent times Polynesian tribes have killed two thirds of their children.

A nomad had no possessions to leave his children. Hunting group loyalty was all that mattered; having a group fractionalised into genetic families would have only weakened it by rivalries. But mothers must have known who their children were and emotionally bonded strongly through their milk. Most mothers, as today must have been rulers of their immediate families.

Society was very free; virginity, monogamous marriage, divorce, and other restrictions had not been invented, as they were not required. The idea, which is current today, that a woman's cunt is private property and can belong to some one other than the woman herself, had not been developed, (i.e. a husband who can use it exclusively or a father who can sell it for bride price).

Children lived with their mother, the mother lived with or near her mother and therefore with or near her brother or mother's brother. There were just as many men about as there are in a family today. Modern writers call it 'avuncilocal'. The mother might be head of the family, but her current f***er would never be head, if the head was a man, it would be her brother. Matrilineal societies are on the decline today because the incest taboo puts a big strain on brothers and sisters being so friendly. Muslim children cannot marry anyone who has had the same breast milk, ie not only brother or sister but adopted children. However they believe intercourse is insufficient to produce children and a prayer to Allah is essential. This reveals that the Muslim Mullahs are as ignorant as their ignorant peasantry, since Australian Aborigines who have never heard of Allah are able to have children.

J.J.Bachofen 1861 AD a Swiss judge and classical scholar with a great command of ancient languages, is the great exponent of mother right, preceding other forms of government; despite disapproving of it. An example of his high flown prose is "The opposition between egg and snake, between the primordial feminine-matter and the masculine kinetic principle, is expressed in two terms which play a prominent part in the religions of the ancients: these are the terms sanctum [*the untouchable*] and sacrum [*the consecrated*].....The sanctum stands under the protection of the chthonian [*underworld*] powers, the sacrum is dedicated to higher gods". *Sadly, I believe his belief in Matriarchy [rule by women] has been dismissed because he is such heavy reading!* I added the translations in brackets. But Christians at that time and Bachofen was a Christian, thought that Adam & Eve were the first people in 4000 BC. Bachofen's idea, that mother right [matriarchy] was dominant 4000 to 2000 BC is suspect in the West today because we are now aware that there were humans before Adam & Eve. Likewise Karl Marx and Engels, as scholars, believed that matriarchy was dominant in the early agricultural historical period, but because their Communist ideas failed; their other ideas are no longer respected.

I believe that when early agriculture was being discovered [I call it the horticultural period], I believe women had more power than at any other time in history, this expressed itself, or was due to, society being matrilocal and matrilineal. I believe warlike matriarchy was unusual, though much more frequent than now as is instanced by the Amazons and Bodica, together with the Goddesses of war Minerva [Roman], Morrigan [Celtic]. Matrilocal societies [where the girl continues to live in her mother's house] tend to be more peaceful than patrilocal societies, because when villages fight one another; it frequently means brothers have to fight each other, rather than brothers in law.

Archaeologists are agreed that households were generally matrilocal at the beginning of the horticultural period because the houses were twice the size they were later as a result of monogamy's reduction in family size.

Incest taboos by encouraging exogamy have helped to destroy female family power. Women by being forced to live in a different location to the one they were born in loose their friends,

I disagree with modern historians who think that surveys world-wide of 20th century matrilineal societies, which shows that power is substantially in the hands of men, is proof that ancient societies were not matriarchal. Because the societies they describe are by no means innocent of other modern customs, such as marriage, incest taboos and in one case the natives have Spanish horses! Incest taboos put a great strain on brothers and sisters living together. Furthermore the research is too prudish to discuss the power of the prostitute, thinking that to be something too shameful to mention. For example the Etruscan Queen Tanaquil was the mother of Kings from 616-510 BC as temple prostitute she presided over 5 days of orgy and then sacrificed on a pyre the lusty youth who had acted the role of God. This sort of thing does not happen today.

The Romans did not have matrilineal descent, except for slaves and this social divide brought it into disrepute. Codex Iustianianus 3.32.7. "It is the law that the slave girl takes her status from the mother and is unaffected by the position of the father". If a noble woman marries *[f***s with?]* a slave the children are noble, if a noble man marries a foreign born woman the children are dishonourable.

INHERITANCE & OWNERSHIP

The agricultural revolution could not work without private ownership of property. Private property could not work with out law and order, and a clear pattern of inheritance rights. The difference between the rich and the poor arises easily when a farmer becomes twice as rich by inheriting a second farm with a house. In this way in a few generations some men and women can have free time for more civilised pursuits, and are rich enough to employ craftsmen, which leads to the development of urbanisation. Free men or women working for themselves, work harder than slaves, or communal co-operatives. Aristotle argues that what belongs to the greatest number of owners is used the most carelessly. The children will not work hard improving the land, under their parent's direction, unless they know for certain that in due course and time, they will inherit the land. Since men die, it was necessary to make memories exceed a generation, this was achieved by the invention of clear lines of inheritance, blessed by custom, and supported by the new invention of writing.

New professions were required, judges, scribes and surveyors. New laws and punishments were made; theft of land was made a capital crime. It is hard to catch a nomad who steals a jewel but it is easy to catch a land thief, the law came to be respected, everyone could see it was working.

In places safe from wild men and animals, like oases and river islands, civilisation was born. Peoples without the concept of private property, -virtually the whole world, outside the Fertile Crescent, remained hopelessly backward.

No one family of farmers was strong enough to repel a gang of nomad raiders, so a general or King had to be appointed with the right to raise a national service army for defence, by beating a drum. This army became useful in the form of corvée labour to construct large drainage works.

Before society had schools, or methods of testing ability, or incorruptible voting systems, the important thing to avoid was quarrelling and fighting, when succession took place. Every time a king was killed, civil war broke out. Civil war is the vilest of wars. The difference between a clever and an ordinary advised person, is not critical when a judge is administering four or five basic laws, even today we leave judgements to juries, which are unselected for their ability.

Kings and Queens defended the farmer's hereditary inheritance of land to encourage the farmers to defend their own inheritance. Before writing was a general accomplishment, it was essential to have an easily understood and rigid system of inheritance; there can be very little error if you stick to inheritance through the mother. *Chaos and civil war are often the result of inheritance through men. Confusion can arise when the King dies; a woman who has not spoken to the king while he reigned says he f***ed me one dark night more than twenty years ago and my son is older and better fitted to rule than his generally known young children*

The protection of private property in general, as opposed to the protection of a particular piece, is essential if the whole community is not to starve. More peoples have given their lives defending this great truth, than to any other cause in the history of the world. It is fashionable to sneer at these martyrs who fought to establish our affluent life style, by saying that they were only fighting for their personal land, or that they were merely tribal patriots. This is substantially true but was not the designer of the system whereby land is privately owned, clever to use these selfish motives for the general good.

All private property must have originally been obtained by theft from the communal store of property. But the original value of the land is a very slight element in its present day value, underground ancient agricultural drains, fencing, propinquity to roads and buildings have created the bulk of the value. This can be seen by the difference in price between Western farmland and virgin jungle in Brazil. The agricultural revolution has so softened us, that Western European prisoners of war preferred Japanese slave camps to the choice of becoming hunter-gatherers in the jungle.

However God did a sex change when the new scientific discovery blazed into the human consciousness that it is men unaided by women that have children. The creator must be a man. [See my paragraph on "women are bags" later in this chapter.] The majority of the early books of the Bible *record the male take over,* with long lists of men 'begating' men.

Because men tend to rule through fear, rather than weak womanly love, most Gods were terrorists, or jealous bullies. Zeus hurled thunderbolts, and teased lame blacksmiths. Allah had a nasty whip and threatened Hell Fire. *They often arose out of memorials to dead chiefs who at best were fair judges, who dealt out punishments including death, and at worst were greedy patriotic mass murdering conquerors. I agree the following sentences and may be many others in this book may be over simplified and exaggerated but I write them to show the overall trend. Rule through female love with sexual overtones gave way to rule through male induced fear through violence, in the more civilised countries ameliorated by ritual and pageantry. The 'Mafia' pimps took over the prostitutes and called themselves priests, kings, or Gods. They boasted that their gods were both more cruel and powerful than their enemies' gods; this helped to frighten their enemies and make their own men more obedient. The Gods were constantly at war, every time one was defeated there was one less, eventually there was only one God in the West, but in gentler India the Gods married and had large families.*

NOMADS HAD MALE SKY GODS.

Nomads can get lost at sea, in the forest or the desert. When locating their position, the stars are very helpful. In the North among the herdsmen the most important gods were male sky gods. The names of the days of the week record some of them Saturn(day), Sun(day) and Moon(day). There was even an unimportant God that created the world, that had been invented to give some sort of explanation as to how the world started, and the obvious thing to do was to give him a name and draw him as an old man with a beard. Without our present knowledge, it must have been easier to think a Spirit created the world than imagine how the world could create itself. As knowledge and reasoning gained ground this spirit gained status, and eventually became Chief God but this is much later.

I believe Gods are invented by humans and therefore they reflect the political arrangements at the time of their creation or are simply dead people who have become gods to preserve their memory. This view is supported by the fact that there was no kingly type God before mankind was organised enough to have kings.

As the population increased, there became a shortage of animals to hunt, so men captured them and branded them, and herded them. The domestication of animals is the other half of the agricultural revolution, and the two halves were constantly antagonistic. The division between Cain, the agrarian farmer, and Abel the herdsman, is the greatest division that there has ever been in society. The domestication of animals taught men their role in procreation and the practice of forced mating of animals naturally led to rape and domination of women. Nearly all-nomadic societies honour thieves as kings; it is so easy to be successful at it. When there was drought, the nomads drove their animals to the village well or riverbank, and ate the cultivated wheat, they could not understand private ownership. As a result villages only grew in naturally protected places. There were no villages in the middle of the jungle where attackers could not be seen until it was too late. The illiterate nomads were quite uncivilised compared with the villagers, but they learnt how to ride bare back on wild 4' 0" high horses and how to attack and run away quickly.

The history of civilisation is the history of defence against nomads. The heaviest engineering feat in the world is the Great Wall of China, which was designed to keep the cattle of the thieving nomads from being driven through it. Rome fell when the Hun's cattle were driven over the frozen Danube. Hadrian built a wall to keep out the ancestors of the Scottish Lairds who were cattle rustlers, and the English built a fence, remembered by the phrase "beyond the pale" to keep out the landless Irish. However the Nomads seldom stole the land because they didn't know how to farm. They loved to visit the goddesses with gifts of hides and meat but sometimes they quarrelled about excess charges, or were plain greedy and they destroyed the village crops, killed the inhabitants and smashed the temple, all so that they could steal the prostitute's gold and silver.

Eventually this became such a regular occurrence that the villagers bought off one local tribe who promised to defend them from attack by other tribes. If this tribe had to give up hunting and nomadism to live near the village, they soon got bored of hanging about doing nothing, except looking after sheep and goats, and so they stole other nomad's cattle, which caused endless wars. About this time developments in brewing made alcohol much more easily available, - wine was invented - and under its influence these men were brave enough to bully the women, and call them scolds and witches, because they were frightened of *the women's new invention of writing.*

After a few generations the protectors grew more powerful than the protected, and they seized the power of judge and king and created another ethnic class of rulers who believed in male inheritance, women were no good to them, they were less efficient bullies. If the King needed help and there was no more powerful King, he could only call upon the moral force of custom and that was not strong enough to protect him. *So he called on the Magicians and they invented a warlike God who could punish and kill people beyond his reach. As long as people believed in him there was no need for him to exist, and he was very useful even during peacetime. The King said to the farmers 'give me some of your crops and I will see you don't get attacked'. 'Why do you need so much' said the farmers? "Ah, well" said the King "I have to pay protection to God." So a system of taxes/voluntary sacrifices arose to pay for the killers (Mafia like part time soldiers) who were needed to defend private property. Thus was born taxation, the second profession, (soldiers), and a male God.* God frequently threatened to destroy cities in the Bible by way of punishment. It is obvious that boastful nomads *[the Jews]* required an *imaginary* God the equal of real historical Gods like Amenopsis II who made a habit of destroying cities.

If religion because of its need for orthodoxy requires the destruction of cities, and Deuteronomy 15 written in 400 BC, says all the inhabitants must be killed. *I say why not kill religion rather than people?*

However men were regaining power to equal or exceed women for more peaceful reasons at the same time. Since large animals were the responsibility of men the new inventions of the plough and cart gave them importance. With the invention of metal and the sword they became more frightening. Women had less time to rule. The making of clothes became much more complicated and time consuming with spinning, weaving and sewing, using up the remains of their time which was mostly in the fields

I do not believe that marriage was made in heaven. I believe the pimps that ran the brothel who called themselves priests, (the third profession), invented it. Men flourished on the sacrifices that they demanded for God and were too pompous in the stage productions to be funny men; they brought with them jealous gods who were terrorists with thunderbolts. Some of their gods demanded all firstborn male babies as human sacrifices. *This reduced the number of men in the subject race, after all only women who worked in the fields were useful. Some priests thought it best if pimps (priests) were celibate so they would not be soft with their lucrative prostitutes.*

Roman Catholics preserve this celibate tradition. *However in time, the complications of their retributive tortures, which they called justice, caused them to learn from the local people how to read and write.*

WOMEN ARE JUST A LOT OF OLD BAGS.

Illiterate nomadic herdsmen were domesticating cattle and they made a scientific discovery.

A tribe for safety moved on to an island with 10 cows; they took no bulls because they were difficult to control and never produced milk. However these cows soon ceased producing calves and milk. A scientific discovery was made. Cows on their own can not make calves. It is the bull's semen that makes calves. Mother earth does not grow wheat; it is the seed that makes wheat. Therefore women have nothing to do with the production of children; they are not fertility goddesses they are just bloody bags for marvellous men to put their seed into.

Apollo says in Aeschylus' play Eumenides lines 657-661 "The mother contributes nothing to the substance of the foetus, her womb is merely a receptacle for semen". English soldiers returning from the 1940 North African campaign called women a 'bag', this is a translation of 'bint' and a dozen or more other Arabic words which when translated all mean 'bag'. Vagina is Latin for sheath or scabbard.

Learned doctors long before Christ said they saw with the naked eye Homunculi, minute fully formed babies in men's sperm, *no doubt the same men who saw the man in the moon.* Leibniz thought that the sperm contained pre-formed human babies complete with their allocation of original sin in their souls, packed like Russian dolls one inside the other; the sperm contained another like it and so on ad infinitum, in fact the whole future human race. It was obvious that women just kept men's seed warm, like a bird keeps its eggs warm. Women never even touched the male seed; it went into a bag, which we now call the afterbirth. Aristotle 384-322 BC said only men could ejaculate a conception fluid.

But do not be surprised by their ignorance. Even in this century our two foremost sex experts, Kinsey and Masters, both said that it was a widespread and erroneous concept that women could shoot sex liquid in a trajectory because they assumed like Freud that the clitoris was an atrophied, stunted penis; which it is not. But it now appears that women can, in just the way Hippocrates 460-367 BC said they could deep within their bodies. Regnier de Graaf agreed in 1672, but neither he nor L. Severly in 1985 is famous in the twenty first century.

The belief in Homunculi believed in by Jesus' educated contemporaries was not disproved until 1827 AD when Von Baer saw a woman's egg in his microscope. In 1854 the fusion of egg and sperm was observed. Since then women are being reinstated, the married women's property act was 1882 AD.

The new science of genealogy was born; it is no accident that so much of the Bible is given over to male genealogical trees. The amazing thing is that Eve and Sarah get mentioned at all. Matrilineal descent gave way to patrilineal; marriage was invented but that was not enough for the ruling classes. In order to make sure which children are yours, it became popular to put your women in purdah, in harems and covered with the veil, and be protected by eunuchs. Despite the very large number of eunuchs, you had to be very rich and very keen to have them, because two out of every three slaves you had castrated died from the operation. It was not a punishment, you chose your best slaves, it really is a very horrible thing to do, but virginity, and faithfulness was more important than life. The punishment for a woman's adultery was death; the punishment for a man's adultery was a congratulatory laugh. *Who can believe that God invented marriage, and this double standard?*

I know it is thousands of years later, but during the middle ages, the Germans, *being a backward people,* went through a similar stage of development, they tortured to death hundreds of thousands of innocent women as witches. They said they were ugly old women who danced naked around a cooking pot. *I don't believe that rheumaticky old women dance, I guess they were young, and the Christians were jealous and the ceremonies were much more like a Club Mediterranee barbecue or chorus line in a nightclub.*

I quote from a Guide Book to Sicily. The heading is "CHTHONIC DIVINITIES" (*which implies earth mothers which live in the underworld*). "Before there were gods, there was only the Goddess. She was essentially, motherhood: the source of life most apparent to primitive people since – as it seemed – woman bore children of herself, parthenogenetically.---- a belief of great antiquity, holding that the wind impregnated women."

Persephone was the Greek equivalent of the destructive woman into whose womb men wished to climb into, to die, so that they might be resurrected. The Indian Hindu goddess Kali is one of the goddesses that arose to fight this male domination; she was the prototype for the western witch. She is a very sexy goddess, who is depicted with a necklace of skulls, dancing on a copulating couple. From some of her Muslim male devotees we have obtained the word 'thug', and Calcutta is named after her.

Captain Cook describes the Tahitians as "People who have not even the idea of indecency, and who gratify every appetite and passion before witnesses, with no more impropriety than when we satisfy hunger at a social board with our family and friends." "They seemed to be brave, open, and candid without suspicion of treachery, cruelty or revenge; so that we placed the same confidence in them as our best friends."

So certain were they of the new scientific truth that males made babies, that 'couvade' spread throughout the world. It was practised in every continent, and even in the 20th century in Brazil and by the Basques in Spain. Because the Christians have deceitfully prohibited sexual education you may not have heard about couvade.

Couvade is the custom of the father going to bed at the birth of his child and simulating the symptoms of labour and childbirth while the mother returns to work as soon as possible after the birth and waits on the father the same day. You may think it sounds so idiotic and ridiculous that you can not believe that anybody ever believed it. So before you jeer too loudly check that you are not a believer in the corollary.

The deity had a sex change, Goddesses were disgraced they were not fertile; they were old bags. Only a male God could be fertile, only a male God could create. This is the corollary; the manliness of God depends on the theory that women are old bags. And a woman is not allowed to become Pope.

It is sad that nearly all we know about the old matriarchal societies is from the abuse the later male societies hurled at them.

They come out in a poor light because they were fighting for their life and had to do some nasty things just to survive. The men took away their sexual freedom, they stoned them to death for adultery, they took away their civic rights, they stole their land and denied them land ownership, they refused to educate them, and they relegated them to being the personal property of men with no higher status than slaves. Is it any wonder that they replied, with poison and magical spells? It was really the men who behaved abominably.

St. John the Divine in Revelations, *reveals his personal God is not Christ, but the green eyed God of Jealousy when he describes the last remnants of the peace loving matriarchal establishment* as the Great Whore of Babylon that drank the blood of Saints and Martyrs.

MARRIAGE

"Marriage ain't a word it's a sentence."

The typical fairy tale, tells of a handsome hero who left his friendly father's kingdom to wander across seas and mountains to a strange kingdom where the king is running a competition for his beautiful daughter. The man that can kill the dragon, run the fastest race or solve a riddle can marry her. The hero wins, the king resigns, and foreign people who have never seen him before, accept him as their king. These stories always seem very odd to children, why did he not stay behind and inherit his own kingdom? *Because of course the inheritance only passes through women. The king resigns because he has no personal rights to the throne. The people accept a stranger because the marriage must be exogenous to avoid incest. The marriage is the crowning; it is the formal appointment to office.* Incidentally the first Olympics may have been a bridal race for a princess.

Some people think that because God is the third party in a marriage and that God decreed marriage, it must be very ancient. *I believe it was invented to make clear the rights of males to inherit agricultural land. The lower classes always imitate the aristocracy so marriage became a popular idea.* Professor Dawson lecturer in Chinese and fellow of Wadham College writes that as late as 104-87 BC. Confucians "introducing the concept of marriage to ignorant natives so that they could practice filial piety, to people who were unfamiliar with the whole idea, so that for the first time, man began to know who their fathers were."

Male inheritance forced man to invent recorded marriage contracts, complete with virginity and compulsory faithfulness for women, polygyny and later monogamy. Monogamy has the advantage that there is no imbalance between the sexes and by allowing slaves to marry, kept them more docile. The rich could always have extra concubines [women with wifely duties whose children do not inherit]. *The marriages had to be standard, because writing wills and administering justice was still very difficult.* In order to clarify inheritance, the eldest son of the first wife (loved or unloved) preceded subsequent sons who might be born earlier to second wives. A very important part of marriage is its public demonstration. The King of France always had to f*** his bride while a hundred courtiers looked on. This accounts for the amusing consummation ceremony when the King of Spain sent his representative the Duke of Alba to marry by proxy his fourteen-year-old French bride and watched by the court; he had to put his foot under the bedclothes until it touched naked flesh.

Slavery was an important influence in the invention of marriage. If in battle you captured a male slave he frequently ran away back to his tribe, however if you raped a girl she sometimes liked it and stayed because of the love that she had for her children. This caused women to frequently change villages, and led to men owning the land.

Slave masters were paid, not the slave when he entered your service. Likewise one did not give your bride money in a civilised way, like one gives to a prostitute; one gave seven years labour, or cattle to her father, you did not ask her, you asked her father. Having got her, she was like a slave; Moses' law allowed you to beat her. She was murdered by lapidation [death by stoning], if another man raped her. Hebrew law allowed a man to divorce his wife at will but never allowed a woman the right to seek divorce. A man, who raped other people's women, was looked up to, and he was expected to rape his own slaves. The rich prohibited their wives from going out of the house; often locking them up with eunuch prison guards, and hiding them in the heat, under stifling black garments, on the rare occasions they were allowed out. *Men carried penis images, with which they could threaten to dilate women, blunt lumps of iron, steel had not been invented, and they called them swords.* In the name of morality they stole the prostitute's fee, they hired their own slaves out for f***ing and they terrorised women with their male gods that demanded child sacrifice.

The Encyclopaedia Britannica says, "Warfare was the earliest source of slaves in the Ancient Near East. Originally, captives seem to have been slaughtered; later women and then men were spared to serve their captors."

From a biological point of view, the human capacity to pair bond develops much more slowly than it does in birds or dogs which have 20 to 60 days. If it were not so we would all become fixated on our first love. *Often part of the first pair bond, becomes an essential, in subsequent pair bonds, i.e. the partner has to have blond hair or a dark skin. Mal-imprinting can produce a craving for fetish objects like black stockings, velvet, or rubber because it was present at the first important ejaculation. Despite all this marriage is still popular in the 20th century. Most societies were so keen on marriage that they married their goddesses to old or new gods; especially Creator Gods that had been invented to explain 'The Beginning' but which previously had taken very little part in day to day life. It also gave the gods a chance to have children and this meant that your neighbours' gods could be your god's, brother, or sister. So that you did not have to fight them to prove your god was superior.*

'In Christianity, neither God nor Christ married, *so can there be marriage in heaven?* Christians are quite *"kinky"* about sex; they hate it. Roman Catholic priests are celibate, so are monks and nuns. They can't bear nakedness and think of sex just for procreation, not enjoyment. This causal argument came not from Christ but from Aristotle. It was spirit against flesh. Judaism is the same, but definitely allows sex within marriage. I can just understand the logic of nuns keeping themselves for God.

Photo Permission BM

Recently acquired by the BRITISH MUSEUM

Ishtar was the Goddess of Love and Prostitution.

ISHTAR

She delighted in bodily love. Other goddesses regarded her as the senior Goddess. She was the opener of wombs, forgiver of sins, and her title was "she who begets all". She was around at the time of Gilgamesh [known nowadays as Noah of the Ark}. She ruled Uruk at the time of Abraham. She was worshipped in Babylon and Assyria. She became identified with many other Goddesses; Astarte, Aphrodite [She always had Venus as her star]. Palestinian worshippers called her Astoreth or Asterah, amd more of them at the time of Jesus worshipped her than ever worshipped the male God of Abraham and Moses. The Sumerian Inanna was also identified with her, the belief that Jesus rose from the dead was possibly copied from her arising.

Hammurabi who erected a needle of stone with hundreds of laws written on it, a thousand years before Moses; called her the Lady of Battles, and had her represented as standing on a lion.

Most pre-literate societies permit pre-marital relations. 70% if you allow for the male double standard whereby it is approved but kept secret. What is normal behaviour in one society may be a deviation in another. The Encyclopaedia Britannica 16-600 says: - "Virtually any sexual act even child-adult relations or necrophilia" *(corpse f***er)* "has somewhere at sometime been acceptable behaviour". In Nepal I have personally seen the beautifully dressed child sex goddess who is the reincarnation of an historical young child who died while being fucked by the king who loved her. Some shamans (ecstatic communicators with the godhead) were transvestite or homosexual.

Eskimos lend their wives to keep guests warm. American sub-arctic people preferred to marry cross cousins i.e. his mother's brother's daughter but not parallel cousins. Missionaries soon put a stop to this incest. Many tribes insist with punishments such as death, for disobedience, that all marriages must be exogamous (outside the tribe or group), others the opposite - endogamous (within the tribe). The Lacedaemonians allowed their wives to be fecundated by the handsomest men among citizens and foreigners. The Librians judge children at seven years old, on their appearance, as to who is their father, because they are a promiscuous society.

The feudal *droit du signeur,* the right of the first night, which belongs to the master who has granted his serf the right to marry, institutionalised an already well-established practice. Central Europeans, until this century, had a nice custom for the landlord. The bride had to sleep with the landlord on her first night of marriage to an employee. It gave the bride a chance to see the inside of a great house and feel the kiss of clean linen before she returned to her straw beside the pigs. Jewish girls in Russia still shave their heads to look unattractive on their bridal night, although the communists have done away with landlords. *Religious custom is often perpetuated long after the need for it has gone.*

Marriage was invented to solve the problem expressed by Telemachus in the Odessy "My mother says I am his son, I myself do not know; for no one of himself knows his father". Menander expresses the same problem "A mother loves her child more than a father does, for she knows it is her own, while he but thinks it is". Pater est quem nuptiae demonstrant [the father is he whom the marriage designates as such]

FOUR ANCIENT CIVILISATIONS & INCEST

THE MIDDLE EAST

Humans were living on the Iranian plateau in 100,000 B.C. Mesopotamia means "the land between the two rivers", the Tigris and the Euphrates which run into the Persian Gulf and is now part of Iraq. This was the cradle of civilisation. By 10,000 years ago wheat was grown, animals were domesticated, and the calendar invented. The world's oldest excavated settlement 7,500 BC is in Catal Huyuk in Turkey, where Goddess figures have been found. The Sumerian creation story starts with the Goddess Nammu [the sea] who creates Ki [the female earth] and An [the male heaven] their son Enlil [the air] separates them, and incestuously with his mother makes vegetable and animal life.

The Sumerians used seals to legalise documents from 5,000 BC; the wheel from 4,000 B.C. and they developed wedge shaped Syllabic writing from 3,200 B.C. to 2,800 BC. .Many stories were written in cuneiform script on clay tablets in Sumeria, a thousand years before they appeared in the Bible. Cain and Abel are called Enten and Emesh, they quarrel without murder. Emesh the farmer proving to be the greater. The king Zisudra escaped the flood like Noah.

Inanna Queen of Heaven went to the underworld before Ishtar and Persephonne. She even killed a dragon like Perseus and St.George. The king to be crowned had to marry Inanna who was represented by her priestess. A thousand years later they had developed astronomy, mathematics [multiplication tables and quadratic equations] and time reckoning. Women at this time had a wide variety of jobs including the world's first stenographers. Naditu priestesses traded and exported money, land, slaves and grain. Sometime between 2,350-2,150 BC Sargon united the north and south, and Urukagina put an end to polyandry (Having many husbands).

It is hard to date the male takeover. *I believe that the sacking of Uruk by Semites; - the city of Gilgamesh - was the beginning of the end of the feminine civilisation of love, and the triumph of the male rule by fear.* Abraham a Semite left Ur (Urtuk); about 2,000 BC. Male inheritance for the aristocracy of Semite rulers became de rigueur; but 2,000 years later Roman slaves inherited through their mother showing that the change moved through the social classes slowly. As a general rule amongst the Gods, the sons became in time more powerful than their mothers and fathers.

Civilisation progressed because the Sumerians had to invent for their Amorite speaking illiterate conquerors a new written language that was able to throw out the fossilised defects of Sumerian. The new language was Indo-European and spawned Zend [Old Persian], Sanskrit, Greek and Latin. Metallurgy improved with the need for weapons, money was measured by weight. Knowledge of geometry was the equal of the Renaissance but not of the Greeks. The 360-degree circle, the 60 minutes, and the 60 seconds, were invented. They thought that there were 360 days in a year. Astronomy was studied; later generations linking it with magic turned it into astrology, which has since spread worldwide.

Elam in SW Iran with its capital at Susa came temporally under the 3rd dynasty of Ur. Sovereignty was hereditary through women; the new ruler was always the son of the sister of some member of an older sovereign's family.

Sacred prostitution was highly respected in Sumerian and Babylonian times, and their earnings produced the income for the temples. There were many expert and professional types. Some worked from the Temple others in the streets and taverns. Herodotus describes a national service for women. He says every woman in the name of Mylitta must sit in the temple of Ishtar and offer to lie at least once with any man that throws her money, ugly women may have to hang around for four years, but tall handsome women soon get home again.

THE CODE OF HAMMURABI
OF BABYLONIA c.1752-1686 B.C.

This is the Lex Talonis famous for the quote **"an eye for an eye and a tooth for a tooth"**. It sets forth a standard of law, which was not equalled until Victorian England abolished slavery. It was streets ahead of Roman law, which classified women as imbeciles, and the Laws of Moses, which came hundreds of years later *and was a mishmash based upon it.*

Known laws were an advance on the Vendetta whereby a family member had to punish someone in the guilty person's family more seriously than the original crime. This is reasonable, if a thief steals one sheep he will frequently get away with it so if he is to fear any form of punishment, he must loose say 5 sheep. But having lost 5 sheep he is morally bound by the rules of the vendetta to steal 25 sheep. That is why an eye for an eye and a tooth for a tooth is very generous.

The 282 laws on the Stella deal with the following themes:- Libel: corrupt administration of justice: theft, receiving stolen goods, robbery, looting, and burglary: murder, manslaughter, and bodily injury: abduction: judicature of tax leases: Liability for negligent damage to fields and crop damage caused by grazing cattle: Illegal felling of palm trees: Legal problems of trade enterprises, in particular the relationship between the merchant and his employee travelling over land, and embezzlement of merchandise: trust moneys: the proportion of interest to loan money: the legal position of the female publican: slavery and ransom, slavery for debt, runaway slaves, the sale and vindication of slaves, and disclaimer of slave status: the rent of persons, animals and ships and their respective tariffs, offences of hired labourers and the vicious bull. Adoption, the wet nurses' contract and the legal position of the children of the concubine, and the wife who could keep her children. The legal position and inheritance of certain priestesses. Women could trade on their own account independent of their husbands and could be Judges, elders, witnesses and scribes. Marriage was monogamous. If a wife decided to return to her father or was divorced by her husband she took her bride price [dowry] including any real estate with her. A woman could divorce her husband on the grounds of cruelty or adultery. A husband could divorce his wife at will.

Hammurabi marriage rules on the whole were reasonable, for example wives could own slaves, but both parties were punished by death; if mother and son incest took place, however only banishment if father/daughter incest took place.

The codes of Hammurabi c1752BC exact the death penalty for

certain kinds of theft; housebreaking; connivance in slave escapes; faulty building construction which resulted in fatal accidents; black magic; kidnapping; brigandage; rape; incest; for causing certain kinds of abortion; and for adultery committed by wives. Masters could substitute family or slaves to suffer punishment for crimes that he has committed. Wives, concubines and children could be given as debt pledges and if not redeemed would become the slaves of the creditor but only for 3 years, previously it had been for life. Hammurabi's rules were practised not just preached in the towns of the Near East cultural area which includes the Egyptians, Hebrews, Moabites, Phoenicians, Ugaritans, Arabians, Aramaeans, Sumerians, Babylonians, Assyrians, Hittites and Iranians. The concept of an eye for an eye, a tooth for a tooth was widely accepted as unchallenged truth. One must pay the correct price; one must never escalate the injustice done one. It made trade possible. It stopped the blood feud getting out of hand. The statue on the dome of the Old Bailey in London is of a woman *[matriarchal dominance]* with a sword for punishment and scales of justice representing the idea of tit for tat or balance, *which I believe to be very important.*

But as more and more savage nomads conquered the agricultural villages, slavery for women and men became more established. For example Middle Assyrian Law 55 says that if a man rapes a girl he must be bound to her in an indissoluble marriage and his totally innocent wife must become a prostitute. The father could expose unwanted infants on hillsides but mothers must not induce an abortion because their child did not belong to the mother.

Slavery became well established, and slaves were sinful if they committed suicide, because it was stealing from their owner. Today the law prohibits euthanasia, because we are God's slaves.

E G Y P T

In 10,000 B.C. the Nile broke through the cataracts and huge swamps and lakes in central Africa dried up. There are thousands of paintings showing animals at Tassilli 5,000 B.C. in the centre of the Sahara desert, and at Fayum. Man's agricultural fires hastened the coming of the desert in many areas.

The Nile's endless supply of water and rich silt, which it

brought down each year, made an ideal site for the growth of an agricultural civilisation. Despite the protection of the desert you could still be attacked by your neighbours up or down stream but in 3,100 BC the Kingdom of Upper Egypt combined with Lower Egypt, which was symbolised by the snake in the Pharaoh's diadem. This military conquest by an ethnically similar race meant that men got their foot in the door of power and most Pharaohs were male but inheritance through the female was important.

Akhenaton married first his mother, then his maternal cousin Nefertiti by whom he had three daughters, one of whom he married as his fifth and last marriage. Both his sons married their half sisters. The queen Haatshepsut ruled in her own right and used all the royal names of a king except Mighty Bull. Tutankhamen married aged 9 his slightly older half sister in the 13th century BC and was possibly murdered after he became Pharaoh but before he was 20 years old.

The Ptolemies a Greek ruling house revived incestuous-ness, 10 or 11 out of 15 marriages were full brother and sister. Arsinoe II became a goddess on her death. Cleopatra VII who gave Caesar a son is probably the most famous queen born of this incestuous line.

The ordinary people through out historical times were not incestuous, there was no formal religious marriage service, but monogamy with an occasional extra concubine prevailed. However property was held conjugally two thirds to the man and one third to the woman.

Herodotus 484-430 BC said "It was the Egyptians who first made it a matter of religious observance not to have intercourse with women in temples." *This implies that it had been normal throughout the rest of the world.* However his sentence "the people also in most of their manners and customs exactly reverse the common practice of mankind" reflects the known high legal status of women in Egypt. Herodotus was a Greek, and the Greeks were male dominated. In Egypt women owned property, took part in public life, and mixed freely with men. As dancing courtesans, they could earn money.

The greatest Egyptian goddess, Isis incestuously married her brother Osiris. They abolished cannibalism, taught the making of wine and bread, founded the legal system and religious worship. Life after death was the central religious theme. This is exemplified by the Pyramids.

Slavery was not fundamental to New Kingdom agriculture; everyone including priests could be compelled to do corve'e work, (for example building canals) though you could pay some one else to do it for you. But it did mean that many men were separated from their wives, which suggests that marriage was not all-powerful.

The wealth and power of the Pharaoh *came from his or her ability to see the future.* They took Nilo-meter readings as to the height of the Nile and these were relayed back so that the exact time of the flood could be forecast. Lunar calendars preceded ones based on the sun. The observation that the Sirius Star is brightest and rises with the sun when the Nile floods; *may be led them* to measure the length of the year as 365 and a quarter days. Their traditional calendar omits the quarter day. Flood warning was important because any person or animal left on the land was likely to be drowned. After the silt had been deposited, it was hard to recognise the boundaries of one's land without the help of a surveyor; this helped to produce a class of scribes.

It is fashionable today to praise societies, which practice equality, yet I believe that the difference between the Pharaoh and the fellahin (peasant) must have been the most extreme in history, and yet it was successful and stable.

The Atlantic Ocean is named after Plato's Atlantis, and because Egyptian mummies have cocaine and nicotine in their remains some scholars think Atlantis is submerged under Lake Titicaca. *I think this is nonsense, but I see no reason to be surprised that the seafaring Canary Islanders who built in the centre of Tenerife changes of level that look exactly like the changes of level on the pyramids in South America may not have been blown by the prevailing winds and currents to South America or Mexico.* Thor Heyadal supports this view. The Canary Islands could not have had prosperous colonies in West Africa, because it was colonised by the Mosquito and the Sahara was a desert

Primitive mobile hunters, who were driven by Asians across the Bering Strait, populated the Americas, it is unlikely that such primitive peoples would know about or have a use for calendars. *However seafarers would know about calendars and star positions, and it could explain South American sculptures with Negro features and others, which are bearded.* The bearded Spaniards when they arrived thousands of years later were expected as a result of ancient traditions and were accepted as rulers.

Plato speaks of Atlantis as a continent sized piece of land. Before there were roads, the sea and rivers were the highways. *Cocaine and Nicotine come from America. But the trade was probably infrequent, as the return journey must have been full of peril, if a couple of returning fleets sank with out trace, this loss of life would leave very few who would know the route. Therefore a couple of search parties returning to America could have only found sea and therefore assumed that the land had been covered by the sea in the same way that the Thira volcano had virtually disappeared*

M I N O A N   C R E T E

In the Old Testament, Crete was called Capthor and was thought to be the original home of the Philistines. Man first arrived on the island of Crete five to six thousand years BC. In 2,000 BC palaces began to be built, not temples, because the palaces doubled as temples. They developed efficient sanitation, fine clothes, high fashion, wall paintings, furniture and priestesses who carried snakes. They ploughed their fields and grew grapes and olives and imported bronze from Cyprus.

Cattle cannot swim. So they must have developed boats large enough to import cattle and bulls. *Soon they became the greatest trading nation on earth. There was no trading competition, for no other nation had developed such large boats or honest traders; they ruled the Eastern Mediterranean through respect not force.*

They invented an alphabetic script, which the Greeks later adopted. Our capital A is descended from their writing; it is an upside down drawing of the head of a bull. Michael Ventris' translations reveal that Crete was a centre for mother right. Herodotus, a Greek said to be the first Historian in the world, says the Lycians who practised matrilineal descent came from Crete. They take their names from their mother not their father. If a noble woman marries a slave the child is noble. If a man marries a foreign born woman the children are dishonourable. The women leave their estates to their daughters not their sons. They use coins for money. Women from time immemorial have ruled them. The fertility of the earth and women are combined in myths. Water is like sperm it fertilises the earth. Fathers were like fallen leaves from the mother tree. They were as unimportant as women in Roman times who had no hereditary part in the family tree.

Plato's (b. 428 BC) assumes that God is a '**she**'. "The universal nature which receives all bodies must be always called the same; for while receiving all things **she** never.....". His account of Atlantis 399 BC was of a lofty civilisation whose people were "famous throughout all Europe and Asia both for their bodily beauty and for the perfection of their moral excellence". He heard the news as a small boy, in after dinner conversation, from Solon who had heard it in Egypt. If Plato's 9,000 years is 1,000 years plus 8000 months the date is close to 1628. Magnus Pike and Patrick Moore say that around 1500 BC, Thira swamped the shores of Crete putting an abrupt end to Minoan civilisation and giving rise to the Atlantis legend.

Mavor believes it was Atlantis. Bristlecone pines in California suggest 1627 BC, so modern science says in 1628 BC the volcano Santorini, which was an island in the caldera of the island of Thira near Crete exploded and sank below the sea. Three times as great as Krakatoa, it must have been one of the most destructive natural catastrophes in the history of mankind on Earth. Thirty-five Cubic kilometres of solids were expelled. The Mediterranean was blacked out for several days the sea waves were up to 300 feet high; buildings 100 miles away were demolished. I believe volcanism, and its sulphuric acid was enough to destabilise the Mediterranean peaceful trading culture.

Crete was probably a colony of the nearby island of Thira 70 miles to the north which had a very advanced *civilisation* before it was blown up by the volcano. *If it was 'an act of God' that destabilised this peace-loving civilisation it proves that there is no altruistic God that rewards the good on earth. They may have worshipped the Earth and its tremors, and it could with its magma and lava, be the origin of Hell and the Devil.*

Peace never returned to the ports and fishing villages the Minoans traded with. The Greek states of the Mycenaean world warred and vied with one another. Mycenaean graves 1450-900 BC with their emphasis on weapons, military scenes and armour are a complete contrast with the sophisticated craftsmanship and design of the civilian objects in Minoan (Cretan) graves before the volcano erupted.

However, Minoan ideas survived, an Etruscan calendar of offerings is the same as a Cretan Phaistos disc from a thousand years earlier, and their word 'apa' for 'father' is thousands of years later, the word for 'father' in Hungary.

The Mycenaeans are Homer's Achaeans of the Trojan War period. Helen's name is pre-Hellenic and goes back to a pre-Greek period. She was a patron goddess of sailors and daughter of Zeus *rather than the monogamous wife of Menelaus. Being very ancient, she reinforces my view that women were once more important than men.*

Cretan culture was based on advances in dairy production. The bull presented quite a problem, before the invention of reliable ropes, chains and barbed wire. It was difficult to bring a lot of wild bulls over on boats, and difficult to control them when they arrived, they had a nasty habit of breaking loose and trampling on corn or worse still goring humans. So they decided to only have a few bulls and keep them underground in stone buildings.

These stone houses developed into a tunnel with passages in and out so they could pass a stream of cows past one bull, and get the cows out; with out letting the bull out, this was called a labyrinth. In this way they could have big bulls that would genetically improve the herd and the bull owner grew rich on trading bull semen, and so was able to build a palace *on top of his monopoly.*

In Knossos, Crete, the palace has 1,500 rooms, no fortifications but drains and showers.

Modern townsmen dare not walk in fields with cows. But to take 100 cows 50 miles across ancient Crete before there were stonewall lined roads to meet a bull could have been a problem. Hammurabi's law column reveals that stray cattle are a serious problem particularly bulls, before ropes that never frayed were invented. Milkmaids are happy to milk cows but I have never heard of them milking bulls of semen! If ownership of bulls was restricted to the few; it must have made it extremely profitable, it could have been an aristocratic monopoly.

Desc: Goddess holding serpents, c. 1500 BC from Palace of Knossos,Crete
Credit: [The Art Archive / Heraklion Museum / Dagli Orti]
Ref: AA367491

This fresco at the Palace of Knossos in Crete

In the illustration it looks as if the bull has been stretched out by his back legs and has put his front legs forward to avoid over balancing with the power of his thrust. The back legs in the picture are damaged and restored in an area where a rope could have restricted the bull's charge. The toreador on the right is a girl, her boot tops could be a rope. *If the bull's rear legs were tied he would be unable to charge beyond a chalk line where one could wait safely to grab his horns and if the passage was narrow and you finally landed behind his tail he could not turn round quickly to gore you.* Even if I am wrong; a rope could have been used while practising with a bull bred and trained like a circus animal. When the bull came to the end of its tether, balance would cause it to throw its head up.

The Theseus myth locates the bull in the roofless part of the Labyrinth under the Palace Square at Knossos, where all the spectators would see would be somersaulting boys and girls. They were not like Spanish Matadors who kill. "They took the bull by its horns" and jumped it, just like athletes on leather horses in gyms. Instead of a springboard they used the bull's neck muscles to give them extra levitation and they competed like modern ice skaters or Russian Olympic girls to do the greatest number of somersaults or gyrations in the air.

Visiting foreigners hoping to marry the princess (Goddess) in whose genealogical power was the appointment of the Minos (King); *did not enjoy the* selection process and gave the sport a bad name. It is possible that the bull remained in his subterranean roofless passage under the main square and all that the protected spectators saw were the aerial gyrations of the athletes and music drowned the noise of any accidents. *Could the secret to the exit from the Labyrinth, be the terrifying experience of being thrown out by the bull's horns into the public square?*

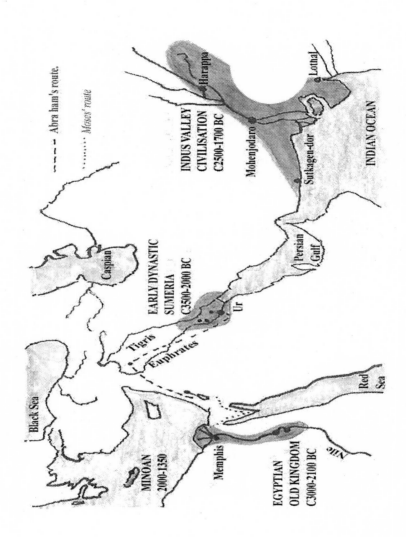

MAP OF FOUR CIVILISATIONS

The INDUS VALLEY CIVILISATION MOHENJODARO:

In 1900 BC the population of the Indus valley exceeded that of Egypt, Mesopotamia and Crete combined. Mohenjodaro with a population of 80,000 was the largest city in the world. Both Harappa and Mohenjo-daro were laid out on gridiron plans with drainage, and had granaries larger than any other in pre-classical times.

Each time the cities were flooded they were rebuilt. For hundreds of years standards rose at each rebuild. Then something happened to cause the towns or cities to be rebuilt to lower and lower standards each time, until they appeared to be squatters uninterested in rebuilding.

Conventional historians say the Indus was overrun by Aryans whose books, tell of great conquests. Unfortunately carbon dating shows the Aryans came 200 years after the towns were deserted, and they were pastoralists who wouldn't have wanted to squat in towns. There is therefore a serious mystery, which cannot be explained by archaeologists. An obvious explanation for this mysterious decline; would be that the inhabitants caught a virus which progressively made them more and more mentally defective, but there is no such virus today.

How did mankind learn that incest is wrong, if there is no God? It would be impossible without long term genealogical records to detect the effects of incest especially before marriage was invented. Even today the effects are guess work. Morton S Adams MD & James V Neel MD PHD say in 'Children of Incest' – "although there is an abundance of anecdotal material, objectively assembled series do not seem to exist".

Since Gods are made in the image of men and it was usual for ancient Gods like Zeus to marry their sisters. There must have been before writing was invented an organised stable society that insisted on incest as a moral solution to avoid quarrels concerning land inheritance and divorce. After several generations the people would be unable to rebuild their cities, and when incest was identified as the problem, the disastrous news and horror would travel world wide and never die. Only one illiterate sailor need arrive in America and Australia.

Could incest be the solution to the mysterious demise of the Indus Civilisation?

In the National Gallery in Trafalgar Square there are many paintings of Europa flirting with bulls. Zeus had to pretend to be a bull to seduce her. *She must have been an important Queen to have Europe, a continent, named after her. We scarcely have a named woman in later history with the exception of Cleopatra.* Her son Minos became King and is sculpted with a bull's head. *This must be nonsense. A sculptor who was asked to make a portrait of a dead king he had never seen, whose name was Bull; might well sculpt a man with a bull's head, to commemorate his monopoly ownership of the best bulls.*

The roughly contemporary Greeks at Troy made a hollow horse into which men climbed. But bestiality is so shocking for Christians that the making a decoy wooden cow, *which was covered in a hairy cow's skin,* into which Pasiphae the wife of Minos climbed, is frequently suppressed. The bull then f***ed the sculpted cow. Later generations thought the Minotaur sculpture of a bull headed man (the Minotaur) was a child of Pasiphae.

However I do not think human and bull DNA can mix. Europa's daughter in law Pasiphae *could have been head milkmaid, and rather than be f***ed herself while crouching in her hollow cow she could with her hands have milked the spurting bull's semen into a bowl. This could be taken 20 miles in small jars strapped between women's breasts to keep it warm, to where the cows were grazing.* It was much too dangerous to allow bulls loose in the countryside.

Daedalus was the sculptor of the cow he was also the first man in the world to fly successfully. He glided off a cliff top on a rising thermal. His son Icarus is said to have flown so high that the sun melted the wax fixings of the feathers. I think h*is flying machine disintegrated because he flapped his wings too strongly, which explains why he rose higher than his father*

MOHENJODARO

The Indus valley civilisation flourished from 2,600 BC and disintegrated in 1,900 BC and disappeared by 1700 BC At it's peak the population exceeded that of Egypt, Mesopotamia and Crete combined.

Mohenjodaro with a population of 80,000 was bigger than any other city in the world. They were traders and many of their seals have been found in Mesopotamia 2,000 miles away. They had a language and a script with over 40 letters, but no one has deciphered it, and both are unused today.

They probably invented the wheel for ox-carts. They had kilns for bricks and for pots made on a wheel, but they had no iron. Their tools were made of chert a kind of Quartz. The towns at Harrappa and Mohenjodaro were laid out on gridiron plans with drainage, and had the largest pre-classical granaries.

As a result of plate tectonics, the Indian sub-continent was driving itself under, and raising the Himalayas by a few inches and by balance it raised by a few inches the Indus valley that was the other side of the fulcrum. This caused the river to flood an ever wider and wider plain and meant that the settlers had to repeatedly rebuild, raising the height of their mud mounds. Each time they rebuilt the size of the buildings and the standard of the craftsmanship increased, until two thirds of the way through the period when the standards deteriorated at each rebuild, together with the quality of the pottery until they were nothing more than uncivilised squatters camping amongst the ruins. The flooding does not seem to have increased in frequency or seriousness although it was approx. every 40 years through out the whole period and today of course the area supports an even greater population.

This mysterious desertion of civilised towns in what is now Pakistan may be a clue to another historical mystery, why the Gypsies left *India.* 'Gypsy' is a corruption of the word Egyptian a country through which they passed. *Their colour schemes alone show that they come from Rajasthan.* The stamping foot in Flamenco dancing is pure Gypsy. The percussive steps in classical Indian dance also communicate the beat to the musicians, who also follow the erotic undulations of the dancer's body round the hips in Egyptian 'belly' dancing. In all three dances the performer contributes to the rhythm rather than following the beat which tends to happen in the West, and the women are proud, sensual and challenging, and show no subservience to men.

Mike Edwards assistant editor of Geographic Magazine writes in June 2000 "No one can say with certainty why the sub continent's long civilisation came to an end". Sir Mortimer Wheeler in the 1940s and 1950s suggests on the basis, of 30 unburied skeletons found at Mohenjodaro, that there was a massacre, but he has no other evidence, for a conquest. As a result conventional historians say the marvellous Aryans whose books tell of great conquests crossed the Himalayas and overran the Indus Valley.

I think they are all wrong. Carbon dating shows the Aryans came in 1500 BC, 200 years after the towns were deserted, and they were pastoralists who wouldn't have wanted to squat in towns. The Aryan conquerors had horses but no word for elephant and no idea about farming rice, which the Harrappans had farmed extensively. The cities were empty. There were a few local, inferior, uneducated, dark skinned, country people, called the Dasa, who did not practice urban incest. The upper classes like both Buddha and his father married their first cousins. The Aryan conquests of the Ganges valley were made 500 years later.

It must be the most horrible disaster in the history of mankind. Destruction by volcanoes or a rise in the sea level may be awful but the minority that survived would still carry on their civilisation and language. Nothing survived no laws, no customs, no hereditary line, and no land ownership. There is therefore a serious mystery, which cannot be explained by archaeologists. Things have not been helped by the British engineers who used the Harrapan ruins as a primary source of hardcore for the building of railways. But there is still enough left, if Pakistan was rich enough to excavate.

A possible explanation for this mysterious decline would be that the inhabitants caught a virus that progressively made them more and more mentally defective, but there is no such virus today. Their sanitation shows they were the cleanest people of antiquity, so disease is not indicated.

I will therefore try to solve the riddle, using insufficient evidence. First I will steep myself in the knowledge of the time, resisting any knowledge which came later, and then I will plan a utopia, which will ameliorate all the topical problems I can observe at Ur. I would simplify legal problems to produce an easily governed law-abiding contented peasantry. As an idealist desiring equality, I would stake out the property into equal lots. The use of gridirons suggests a desire for equality, and there are no palaces, which suggest altruistic socialism.

I would observe that private property was the most important verity to maintain, and that inheritance must be clear and perpetual, and absolutely fair between the sexes. Nearly all the problems in the law courts, at that time, arose because of promiscuity, complicated money transactions and written contracts. *I would fail to think of the idea of wasting five years of the life of every child by sending him to school, to learn to read and write. I would simply observe that most people could not read and that writing was a boring task. Likewise I would fail to invent a plentiful coinage and only notice that "money seemed to be the root of all evil", because the majority had difficulty checking the scales and counting. I would think of writing and money as a bodge up method of sorting out difficult problems, which should not be there in the first place. I would find the selling of daughters into slavery for a bride price horrific and sorting out divorces a nightmare. I would regard the transfer of parcels of land, as a recipe for disaster because seashell counters could be inflated over night by the arrival of a new supply, and precious metals were in such short supply, there was physically insufficient to go round. I would think that a system that depended on putting all women into veils and locking them up was crazy. I would abolish all slavery, because I believed in equality, though I would keep the corvée system for men. I would restrict the movement of people to avoid the spread of disease, in particular physical contacts like marriage between strangers. I would conceive of the family as an indivisible unit that owned a well-watered plot of land, which was large enough to supply all conceivable needs. The dream of self-sufficient farming, inherited by its genetic owners should reduce the number of contracts and so the number of quarrels. Have you spotted what it is that will make them all go mad?*

There is one more clue. Who hid before 1,000BC hoards of gold and copper in the Ganges area which the local people did not know how to use, and who buried the unbelievably valuable treasure found on Herod's estate on the Red Sea? *Was it from the Indus valley civilisation?* If you cannot guess what the disaster was that overtook the most civilised society on earth, it is because the fig leaf philosophers have put a tea cosy on it. Astronomers seeking the origin of the universe found it by observing background noise. Let's listen to the social hum unimpeded by the tea cosy and see if we can hear an echo of the social error which destroyed the largest and most civilised of ancient societies. Let us go to a New York prison and listen. "You MOTHER F***ER" are likely to be the first words you hear, addressed to the prisoner in the next-door cell. What can he mean? Does he really suppose that the prisoner, who has been locked up for four years, has recently been pumping his mother with sperm?

No I don't think so. I think he is trying to attract attention by saying the most horrific thing that he can think of saying. But surely 'murderer' is worse and God also prohibits that. I am afraid 'murderer' is a damp squib, it is nothing like as shocking as 'mother f***er'. Is this just because there is a sexual overtone? Surely 'mother rapist', or 'corpse f***er' is worse, i.e. someone who loves necrophilia and maybe likes murdering them first so that the body is still warm. Logically these are worse, unless he is on a grapevine from which we are detached. A mother and son in a loving relationship in bed together, is that worse than murder?

It could be incest, something so awful that even the pornographic magazines that illustrate buggery, dare not talk about it. A psychiatrist I spoke to, thought it just as frequently practised. I asked him about the percentage of mental and deformed children that would result from brother /sister and mother /son f***ing. His voice dropped and he said he knew the results were very bad. Yes, I said but what percentage. So I asked him to look it up, after six months he had failed to find out. "Since you know it's very high," I said "they must have taught you it at Medical College". "Oh no, they never mentioned it". He had learnt it on the grapevine.

Myrrha by a ruse with the help of her nurse slept with her father the King of Cyprus. An ancient instance, showing that it is not always the grown up that instigates child abuse. The King had modern views about incest, and patriarchy and when he found out; he was so furious he tried to kill her. So she turned herself into a myrtle tree and produced myrrh and bore a son called Adonis, whose name means Lord and who was a handsome God who took over the job of being annually resurrected. Jesus was given myrrh at his birth and also was resurrected.

INCEST

The Bible says that God told us to execute incestuous people. In my attempt to show that God is not necessary in history, popular knowledge of the incest taboo is my most difficult conundrum. So why does everyone on every continent know that incest is frightful? If there is no God, and there is no legend concerning a Martian that told them. The only conclusion must be that a scientific study revealed that children born of incestuous mating produce deformed children. However there is no such recorded study. Smoking was only discovered to be unhealthy after hundreds of years when the majority of Westerners practised it and statistical analysis was in every day use. Even though it is fairly obvious that the lungs are filled with smoke, it took a long time for it to be associated with cancer of the lungs.

I cannot imagine how the vast variety of different ailments suffered by a small minority could be identified with incest, unless the majority practised it over successive generations.

I am certain that people who are stupid enough to practise couvade, or believe that women are bags, and who do not know the names of their great grandmothers would be quite unable to fix the wide variety of defects occurring, on to any common cause, unless it was blatantly obvious.

If a family had a common defect it might have been because they ate different food, or had a virus in their granary, it was not till the nineteenth century in England that a comparatively obvious cause for cholera was discovered.

We now know about haemophilia in the European Royal families but then they have well known genetic trees and live thousands of miles apart, which make it comparatively easy to detect.

For example the Tobriand Islanders this century believed that the mother alone conceived the child, they did not know the significance of the male sperm. However marriage was general, and there were severe incest rules between brother and sister and incest between father and daughter was taboo. But in their mythology the origin of love magic is based on a brother and sister.

Levi-Strauss agrees with me that incest prohibitions are not generated through legislation, observation of mental or physical defects or Freudian principles. Freud thought, the incest prohibition was invented by a hunting group whose young men murdered their leader for monopolising all the women and then felt guilty about it and so decided to marry outside the group and respect their dead father as a God. Freud today is discredited, he refused to believe his women patients when they told him they had been sexually interfered with by their fathers, he thought women were naturally dishonest and they were but lecherous imaginings.

Encyclopaedia Britannica 16 599F says, "All [societies] have incest prohibitions. These are not based on genetic knowledge." In 10 480 B "There is no innate aversion to intercourse with sister or daughter, though some evidence from Kibbutzim and elsewhere may suggest that common rearing may diminish sexual attraction".

The universality of the incest taboo preceded the taboo on cannibalism. *I do not think respect is powerful enough to make practising cannibals observe the incest taboo.* The Hua tribe in New Guinea still believe that a MAN can become pregnant by eating possum! How do they know incest is wrong?

Today there is still no conclusive evidence that all incestuous marriages are so dangerous that laws should prohibit them. 2% of ordinary marriages produce genetic defects. Morton S Adams M.D. & James V. Neel M.D. P.H.D. say in 'Children of Incest'- "although there is an abundance of anecdotal material, objectively assembled series do not seem to exist".

I agree that a small number of children born of incestuous parents do have birth defects, but because it is illegal a disproportionate number of parents were 'odd' in the first place; i.e. a mentally deficient father rapes his 13 year old daughter, or a genetically crippled son f***s his 50 year old mum, which puts both parents in categories which are more likely to produce congenital defects than incest on its own.

Even then the chances of a deformed child are highly unlikely. Since it is thought, that in pre-classical times 50% of normal children died before puberty, the number of abnormal children would be greatly reduced in the next generation. It is only in the following generation that the trouble really occurs, modern theory, not observation, implies that the incidence of defects increase geometrically with each generation that repeats the incest.

When brothers and sisters f*** repeatedly for seven generations, by my theoretical mathematical projection, they would produce more than 80% of surviving adults with noticeable horrific defects. By sheer guess work I suggest that 2% of the first generation of children would have unnatural defects, and this would be doubled when a defective child had a sexual union with a brother or sister, so 4%. However each generation the odds might double, so if those children had children 4% + 4% = 8%. If their children in order to conform to the law and wished to avoid being stoned to death or sent to hell by their God copulated with their brothers and sisters. Next generation it would be 16%. Still I think unnoticeable. But the 5th^h time round it would be 32% still not obvious. But the by the 6th^h generation it would stop doubling and rise to 50% and the increase to 66% and then 75% when it might become noticeable

At this point a woman might have had 3 deformed children by her husband, and then have an affair with a non-family member, immediately there would be no problems and since she would have thought of herself as a bag. She would realise the deformed children for which she was being criticised, were not her fault. She might have another deformed one by her husband and then realise by having a child by an old deformed generous man who had given his sister lots of deformed children with a different deformity; she might guess that incest was a disaster.

The only reasonable explanation for the universal knowledge that incest is wrong; must be that before history was recorded, there was a society that practised it for many generations, it is only after several incestuous births that physical and mental deformities would become obvious. This is why I think there must have been a society that stipulated that non-incestuous relations were illegal over a period of several hundred years and then dissolved in the most ghastly and horrible physical and mental mess sending it's citizens out to find un-contaminated people. The horror would be so intense that the news would travel worldwide and never die.

Even if incest was legally compulsory, long chains of incest over several generations would always be punctuated by secret love affairs, and the absence of mixed brothers and daughters in one generation, would break the sequence. The sequence would also be broken when the opposite sexed parent had died young.

There are only eight genetic families on Tristan da Cunha, yet the doctor is not worried by the prospect of genetic defects.

The Peruvian rulers were incestuous.

Cleopatra VII came of a long line of brothers marrying sisters, and she is famous for her beauty and her brains. Rarely incest actually improves the stock, it is also theoretically a way of changing the species, *and we may be descendants of incestuous apes.*

We know that patriarchal inheritance superseded matriarchal inheritance before the birth of writing, and therefore written wills. It must have been obvious that the only simple and direct way for land ownership to be transferred on death was for the existing family living in the house to own it. I believe that there must have been an organised civilised society whose female ruling aristocracy insisted with puritan like strictness that everyone was incestuous in order to preserve family ownership of land.

The result after many generations must have been a predominantly mental population, not just subnormal and stupid as in Rampton Hospital, but highly intelligent and criminal as in Broadmoor Hospital, together with the majority suffering defects that made them look like the victims of thalidomide. The sewers must have got blocked up, but the people had been trained to shit in them, the results must have been worse than doing it in the fields. Cholera, smallpox, the Black Death, yellow fever and other plagues must have descended on them decimating their numbers. A scene worse than Belsen, a medieval painting of hell, or a leper colony combined. I will not go on to describe the full horrors lest they keep you awake at night.

When the penny dropped that this was caused by incest, the people rebelled against their incest insisting rulers. There was no Lenin to take the reins of power. They were suddenly a rudderless society, permanently in civil war, with no ruler, no respected aristocracy, no accepted customs, no religion, no inheritance rights, no laws, no order, and as a result theft and. terrorism was the norm.

If a philosopher had diagnosed incest, the idea would have taken a thousand years to travel as many miles and we would know his name. If on the other hand the discovery was made by a people unable to write in foreign languages, the message would travel in a tea cosy and I would be obfuscated by the wool over my eyes and only hear the prisoners raised voice and the psychiatrist's lowered one.

Leprosy is scarcely infectious at all, and only in the very early stages before the ancients usually diagnosed it. There is no reason why lepers like Aids victims should not live amongst society. However for thousands of years they were segregated especially when parts of their bodies started dropping off, which happens when they are at their least infectious state.

Why? *I believe that the infectiousness of some diseases is discernible, - a sailor arrives ill, soon the whole town is down with the disease, starting with his landlady. When the Indus valley society disintegrated, the remainder of the inhabitants not only were the products of incest, which explains their slow decline. When fleeing they arrived amongst normal people, with their sorry tale, they were not welcomed because of the fear of the plague. They were treated as lepers. I imagine the population of the Indus valley even reduced to one third would exceed the population of hunter-gatherers in the whole of the rest of India.*

Their predicament was so dramatic, that the news in garbled form blew to the ends of the earth as religious knowledge. One illiterate sailor, is all that is needed to spread the idea that incest is bad, arriving in a wrecked boat, in America so that the Hopi Indians can know, or in Australia to tell the aborigines. He does not need to make the return journey. If criminals in New York know it four thousand years later, every sailor must have known it, and it would have been to his advantage to tell it, especially if he was ugly and the island on which he had arrived was small and suffering from too much inbreeding, he could explain his children would be wholesome.

Thor Heyedal with his balsa raft Kontiki and papyrus boats Ra I and Ra II shows that such journeys are possible. The Hawaians knew about Noah [Nu'u] before the Christian missionaries arrived.

The worldwide prejudice against incest is very garbled. Although there is general knowledge that incest is unspeakably horrific the different shapes the theory takes is nearly as varied as man's ideas of God. For instance Medieval Christians prohibited sexual relations between children and their godparents and the marriage of godparents that looks to me like a literal translation from another language that has lost the raison d'être of the prohibition. Likewise the classical Chinese cannot marry a cousin with the same surname, but can marry one with another surname i.e. his mother's brother's daughter or son.

The Tallensi of Ghana also traditionally practise incest rules based on language. The Grandfather calls his son's wives 'mother' so he cannot have sex with them or with his distant cousins because they are called sisters. But he can copulate with his real sisters because they are not called sisters.

Australian aborigines who look physically very like the dancing girl from Mohenjodaro will not speak to strangers until they are assured that they are not consanguineous. The sea journey from the Indus to Australia is only twice the sea journey to Ur where they traded regularly. To trace genetic defects to incest is very hard but made easier to demonstrate if all the inhabitants were descended from one boatload.

Herodotus the first historian did not write till a thousand years later, and he could not read proto-Dravidian any more than we can today. Westerners did not reach India until 3,000 years later to research forgotten Indian history.

At the birth of patriarchy, long before Herodotus was born, his god Zeus married his elder sister, Hera; other gods that married sisters are numerous Isis & Osiris, Janus & Camisa. The Sumerian God En-ki has to marry his own daughter and his grand daughter to create sweet water and to make the soil fruitful. Fryja the goddess of sexual love in Scandinavia had her brother Freyr as her sexual lover. Frigg married her father, Odin. Quetzalcoatl slept with his mother. Hathor was Hourus' mother and wife. Enki the Sumerian God f***ed his own daughters; so his jealous wife planed to kill him, then changed her mind and rejuvenated him by putting him in her womb.

The Fon of Dahomey regard Mawu-Liza as the creator God. Mawu [the moon] is female; Liza [the Sun] is male.

They are twins in permanent sexual union and they run the

world through Da a serpent. It is only natural for man to imitate his God, *or more correctly for his gods to imitate the emerging customs of the times. This implies that incest was once approved.*

In 136 BC there is evidence of legalised brother sister marriage. Greek immigrants in Roman Egypt took detailed and meticulously accurate household census returns every 14 years between AD 20 and AD258. Despite the fact that only 40% of all families had a son and daughter of marriageable age, 15% to 21% of all marriages were between brothers and sisters. This means that at least a third of all brothers and sisters married by preference with in the family rather than marry out side the family. These full brother sister marriages were not occasional pre-marital sex between siblings, abnormal but condoned, but lawful, publicly celebrated marriages with wedding invitations, contracts, dowries, children and divorces.

Nowhere today is incest practised legally, but attitudes as to normality can vary. *In 1960 in urban Japan more than half 11 to 15 year olds slept in the same bed as at least one of their parents.* Is Wordsworth *f***ing* his sister, or a modern man doing it with a condom, really deserving of the death sentence?

Cannibals by eating people can get a lethal disease that has only recently been discovered. Why did God tell cannibals not to f*** their sisters, but allow them to think that they could make themselves cleverer by eating a clever man? *I can only think that the message reached them with such super charged emotional force that it was greater than the mere fear of being eaten. If man discovered for himself that incest is wrong, and modern scientists cannot point to any orderly body of facts to prove it, surely there must have been such a society as I postulate. I cannot prove that this horror happened in the Indus valley but it occurred somewhere or there is a need for a messenger or a God. The Church has failed to use this piece of evidence as proof of a supernatural power to prove the existence of God, but it is the only historical scientific evidence that I have difficulty explaining away.*

If incest is universally distasteful to people who have not been taught to disapprove it, I am surprised Moses would want to execute them, when he made no prohibition on child abuse. As a general rule, religious prohibitions are only put on the customs of neighbouring religious practices that are likely to steal adherents from that religion.

Why can the Jews and Mohammedans not eat pork when the trichinosis larvae can be eliminated? Or do all taboos, even incest, have a longevity that is not justified, because of the tea cosy of the fig leaf philosophers refusing to talk about sex?

I believe that nearly all religious laws are public health laws and are as silly as the Medical officer's insistence on air bricks and ventilated lobbies to WC's, to suck away miasma or stop cholera jumping out of the WC, but before these rules were abolished in the 1980's, millions of people had to be unnecessarily cold and some even died of hypothermia.

My Nanny said "Never eat in public." I envied the other kids their water ices. "Why." I said, she did not know. Being rebellious as a grown up I have always made a point of eating on the 'hoof'. In Morocco I learnt why, I saw some starving children watching me, their digestive juices giving them agony. There is much wisdom in ancient rules if only one knew why they were made.

I have sunk myself in imagination into the Indus valley culture for days at a time over years and I have not found a single pointer that says my theories are untrue. But there are pointers each of which would take a hundred pages to explain and then wouldn't amount to much. For instance, if Indians are kindly people who don't want to kill animals why are they so horrid to the untouchables? If the shadow of one falls on you, you must not join your community until nightfall and you must wash yourself because you have been contaminated. (i.e. Go away and check that you haven't got a rash or spots.) The untouchables are the original population discovered by the conquering later arriving Aryans, *that is to say the dispersed inhabitants of the Indus Valley. The defects of incest would have taken many generations to disappear, so surely this is a senseless remembrance of a health rule. Just as my Nanny's remark was a remembrance of hunger in England. I, who am too sceptical to believe in God, am certain that I am right about incest in the Indus valley, but my general philosophy is not proved wrong if it is disproved, as the Pope's would be if he were disproved on a non-essential matter, because I do not claim infallibility.*

A society that demands that its members be incestuous, and prohibits sex and marriage outside the home, may seem strange, but it would be very stable, every one would know who was married to whom because they would be married without the need for a ceremony at birth. Surely it is less strange than one that stones to death for adultery and makes women wear a veil. Such a society would sound fanciful if the Moslems had not preserved it. Likewise; a society; in which, the fathers exchanged their daughters for cows, or contracts of slavery for seven years; would seem much more repellent. Indians don't eat much meat today; even in those days there may have been a shortage of animals for the bride price. Remember the matriarchal system was half way towards incest already, in so much as a man thought of his sister's children as his heirs; it was the logical next step to make his heirs his genetic heirs. In matrilineal societies the child's uncle, (mother's brother) took the role of father.

For the whole family to sleep in one bed seems economical, making brother and sister and inter- generational love convenient. It cements the family more firmly together. Besides, one's offspring are more genetically your own.

In the hunter-gatherer days, a group of 50 remained integrally together. Efficient farms only required grandparents, parents and children. It was not obvious that the reduction in numbers made a genetic problem. The family could remain on the same plot for hundreds of years, despite increasing family size, for five reasons, - because the original allocation of land would be many sizes larger than necessary, because they could throw out the animals rather than their daughters and live on cereals which require much less land per useful calorie, because their farming methods would improve, because plague, flooding, and war would decrease the family occasionally, and because finally the increasing number of natural abortions due to incest, would restrain the increase in numbers.

Wheat, which was the staple diet in the Indus valley, is unaffected by inbreeding; maize is affected *but I think they did not know about maise.* Incest amongst the lower animals does not produce as many biological imperfections as it does amongst humans.

I do not think the English can be smug. Archaeologists confirm that houses in Britain were twice the size of monogamous Gaulish ones. This seems to confirm Caesar's account of their different marriage practices. "Wives are shared between groups of ten or twelve men, especially between fathers and sons but the offspring of these unions are counted as the children of the man with whom a particular woman first co-habited." De Bello Gallico v.14.

The early Greeks tell the story of a primitive Arabian patriarch who had fifteen sons and one daughter. All the brothers carried staffs because swords were not available, and they drove these into mother earth outside her door opening to show what they were doing to her inside her tent. The girl got tired and sore, - as it was more or less non-stop, so she manufactured some look-alike staves and stuck them in the ground, one at a time, to get some rest. However one brother met another brother whose staff he had just seen preventing him entering, carrying his staff! They were both furious and went off to punish her for adultery with a stranger.

Although the story says they are all her brothers, we should take this with a pinch of salt. In English law 1980 style all children born to a married couple are said to be the sons of the women's husband even if the D.N.A. says they are the sons of the woman's lover. Many primitive tongues do not use the word brother even with this degree of scientific accuracy. The communists use it to mean others in a group, *in this case it probably means within an age group.* But the use of this word does show that there can be no incest taboo or monogamous marriage, yet there is adultery because the patriarch owns his group and therefore none of his women must mate with strangers. Strabo [20 BC] says the punishment for this sort of adultery was death. *Hunting group loyalty was all that mattered; having a group fractionalised into genetic families through marriage would only have weakened it by rivalries.*

Strabo reports, that amongst the Arabs, rule over the clan is by primogeniture, all blood kin hold property in common, they share their women, it is first come, first served, and they cohabit with their mothers.

It is folk law to assume without scientific evidence that incestuous relations automatically produce monsters as punishment against God's law. Not everyone believes in the transubstantiation of wine and bread into the blood and flesh of Christ, another popular superstition.

Though today incest may tend to produce genetic defects, when in a hundred years research is done by D.N.A. testing the minority of close relations that are not compatible could be identified and warned not to have children. But I believe the majority of fathers and daughters; mothers and sons; and brothers and sisters could mate with impunity. It is high time all aspects of incest are freely discussed on T.V. Before we harden our incest laws we should evaluate statistical studies as to the probability of genetic disorders not just accept the laws of Moses.

The breeders of horses, cows, dogs and rice would never have had their successes if animal incest had been banned.

CHAPTER IV
THE OLD TESTAMENT
BIBLE WRITING

The oldest preserved copy of the Old Testament was a tenth century AD one in Leningrad before the finding of the Dead Sea Scrolls. The Scrolls are about the time of Christ and where they quote the Bible the text is incredibly similar.

As mentioned before it is probable that with the exception of one copy of the book of the law, Deuteronomy found in the ruins of the temple, all the Jewish literature was destroyed by the Babylonian enslavement. It may have been reconstructed during this exile from memory and or on their return. Moses' law had binding force on the Jews by the fifth century BC, the prophets by the 3rd cent BC, and the psalms and other books achieved their status in the 1st century. BC

Hebrew was written in consonants only, without vowels until the Christian era. For example 'mn' could be translated as 'amen' (that's certain), 'amon' (master builder) or 'amun' (baby). I do not know enough Hebrew to categorically say that one could not say in ancient Hebrew; 'God is brave', or 'God is strong', or 'God is warlike'. But abstract phrases would typically be rendered much more physically like instructions to a sculptor "God with a sword in his hand," or "She was naked" to mean 'sexy'. It wasn't until c.1200 AD that the Bible acquired chapters and c.1550 AD with printing that it was divided into verses. The early Bibles had a continuous flow of letters there was no space between the words, no accents, or breathing marks and hyphens were rare. For example:-GODISNOWHERE can be read as God is now here, or God is no where. And in French SANGREAL can mean the Holy Blood or the Holy Grail depending on which side of the G the break should appear.

Would a real God be content with such slovenly expression when he could easily make a video tape today which would clear up all the scholars' difficulties and sell at a profit, after all the Bible is still the best selling book. *God is an appalling communicator; he still hasn't got a www page! He really is incompetent, it's all very well saying that because I am a sinner, I am not worth telephoning, but there must be one good person on the web.*

"The fundamentalist student might pause to wonder at a God who goes to great trouble to provide predators with beautiful (genetic) adaptations to catch prey, while with the other hand giving prey beautiful adaptations to thwart them. Perhaps he enjoys spectator sports." Dawkins.

A D A M   &   E V E

Archbishop Uscher 1581-1656 of Armagh, Ireland, literally dated the arrival of Adam and Eve as 4004 B.C. *The Bible is a first class historical record,* but one must remember that the early parts were written thousands of years, after the events had occurred, and therefore the information had to be passed on by word of mouth. 'Chinese or Chain Whispers' show how difficult this is. Before the first records were written the story must have been verbally passed on for 25 generations, and during this time the Jews travelled more than a thousand miles and considerably changed their language.

The Bible consists of a number of different stories; the first chapter of Genesis tells how God created mankind [the word that does not mean man; but both men and women]

My comprehension of the story is: - Adam *& Eve the first recorded people in the Hebrew family tree were the first gentlefolk, and were probably brother and sister. Adam's penis communicated (spoke) to Eve and they ate of the seed (apple) of the tree of (carnal) knowledge. Their father kicked them out of his delightful cultivated privately owned estate at Eden for the sin that is too shameful to mention (incest). [All dead ancestors became Gods when they died. Their ancestral father whose name had been forgotten is referred to as God.] Everyone's earliest father's name must be forgotten, so to be respectful in the days when there were many gods, he was called 'god'. Just as actresses today call any one whose name they don't remember 'darling'. Surely if someone is their great, great, great great grandfather, an illiterate person at a loss for their correct greater title would find it so much simpler to say they were a God.*

At this time there must have been lots of Gods; Exodus 34 11-16 "for thou shalt worship no other God, for the Lord is a Jealous God". In Genesis one God created the world in seven days. *Surely the God that planted trees in the Garden of Eden is a different God and occurs in quite a separate text.* For a couple of generations; timber is of no real use for buildings and olives trees did not bear fruit as quickly as they can be made to do, today. *But if this God is just the human father of Adam, it makes sense. It makes him a good father who practices long-term selfishness for his children who he is expecting will inherit his land.*

The book of Genesis appears to be the result of the merging of two separate stories. In 1753 Astruc divided the book of Genesis into two, one in which God was called 'Elohim', and one in which God was called Jehovah; this explained why there were two contradictory accounts of the creation, Sarah's age, the number of animals in the Ark, etc.

Some archaeologists think Eden is the fresh water spring at Dilmun, Bahrain; which is mentioned in the story of Gilgamesh 2,000 BC.

If this story was copied from the more ancient Sumerian, the creator's name was Lilith, a matriarch. Rabbis up to the 7th century AD in Talmudic myth said that Lilith was Adam's first wife who abandoned her partner after he denied her equality, and as a demon vowed vengeance on the successor Eve by murdering children and pregnant women. *Lilith helps to substantiate my theory that women were more important than men in the early days of the agricultural revolution.* However that made Eve's position as first woman untenable, so some said Lilith was his second wife, but that meant that one of his wives must be his daughter! Lilith a Sumerian was later called Inanna who gathered men from the street to bring them to the temple for sex. Lilith refused to be sexually submissive to Adam. *It was just too embarrassing,* so now they do not believe in her.

In Hebrew the words Adam and Eve mean Mr Man and Mrs Life. When the Bible stories were assembled in chronological order; a *teacher of professional bards, might easily have asked, "Who is the first ancestor on the list?" The child when repeating it might forget the importance of 'the list' and simply describe Adam as the 'first man', and go on to teach that phrase by rote. I am sure that the phrase originally did not intend to suggest that he was the only man; otherwise* the narrator would not go on to say that Cain said

"Everyone that findeth me shall slay me....and the Lord set a mark on Cain lest any kill him".   Enoch, Cain's son built a city.   Who produced the people to fill it?

Cain and Abel took wives. *Who were these women, Eve herself, or her daughters?* By the time the story was written, God had prohibited incest, surely, this embarrassment would have caused them to rewrite? *I don't think they were embarrassed because they understood the words 'man' and 'woman' as an eighteenth century woman would understand the words 'gentleman' and 'lady'. Adam and Eve were the first gentlefolk; their sons married barbarian women from the surrounding countryside. A snob today could say, "Nobody sends their sons to State schools". The hearer would understand that he meant 'nobody' who was 'anybody'. Tracing your ancestry back to Adam and Eve is a very snobbish thing to do.*

For example I am a snob, and I trace my ancestry back to God who Luke says begat Adam. Because a Pope said the Merovignians were descended of Noah and King David and through marriages I can trace my family tree back to Charlemagne whose family twice married Merovignian Princesses. The DNA may not go back because some of the women may have preferred the stable boy to their husbands!

In the 4th century AD, using a literal translation, St. Augustine of Hippo (in North Africa) created the concept of "original sin" as a Roman Catholic belief, and made women out to be worse than men. *This gave the story a new false meaning, which is absurd.* The reason why Eve acts and Adam is passive is because at that time, societies that cultivated land tended *to have matriarchal societies and inheritance through women: (i.e. Adam was a second class citizen).* However the writer of Genesis and *the misogynist* St. Augustine wrote at a time when women were 5th class citizens as they are today in India. *They were seriously misled by prudish 'fig leaf' poetry* that produced a thousand-year problem for women, *which is why I use precise words like 'f***'.*

If Cain's "mark" were related to the LAW OF MENU, which separates a man from his relations, this would make his son's task of populating a city still more difficult.

For violating the paternal bed,
Let the mark of the female part be impressed on
THE FOREHEAD WITH A HOT IRON.
For drinking spirits a vintner's flag:
For stealing sacred gold, a dogs foot.
For murdering a priest, the figure of a headless corpse.
With none to eat with them
With none to sacrifice with them
With none to be allied to marriage to them
Abject, and excluded from all social duties
Let them WANDER THE EARTH;
Branded with indelible marks,
They shall be deserted by their paternal and maternal relations
Treated by none with affection;
Received by none with respect
Such is the law of MENU".

Early history is always taught to young children, because it is at the beginning, as a result of 'fig leaf' philosophy, it is devoid of sex. If we turn to the end of the Adam and Eve story we realise that it was written *by a prude for children*, because they end up wearing 'fig leaves' over their sex organs. Entering into the spirit of this poetical tale *we at once realise that the miraculous talking 'snake' means 'penis'.* Mankind has always given his sexual parts funny names. 'Naked' and 'Crafty' are the same word in Hebrew, therefore the snake could originally have been 'naked' not 'cunning'. A snake, which is limp, can stand up like a cobra and the hood expands. A penis becomes erect; the knob at the top becomes prominent. Many languages even as far away as the Daribi in Melanesia use the word snake for penis.

Adam is said to be the Son of God, *Jesus is therefore his second son, and it is odd that the second son is immortal whereas the elder one died.*

When I drew out my family tree, nobody told me how to do it, but I quickly found it was necessary to have horizontal lines to relate brothers and sisters, otherwise one got into a hopeless muddle. I think a skeleton of connecting lines is essential; a 'tree' would have to be upside down, rather a senseless name if you start at the top with Adam.

> *A real skeleton of an ancestor or a drawing of one in the sand helps to give structure to the relationships. Thus the skull would represent God. To the top rib one would fix the clay seals that would represent his children, i.e. it would be Adam's 'rib', his name would be first as he was the eldest. The second rib would, show Gods grand children, i.e. Cain & Abel. The third rib His great grand children etc. I maintain that Eve was shown on or of Adam's rib. And in prehistoric times a technical argument developed between those who said this means that Eve is Adam's sister and those who said the ancient genealogists may have considered it OK to put daughters in law on the same rib or line. This, in c.1500 BC still a thousand years before it was written down, was an incredibly important question. Incest was now one of the worst crimes in God's law.*

> *The sages were very keen not to be descended from a criminal ancestor and since they couldn't be a hundred per cent sure, they diplomatically decided to record the technical problem and leave posterity to decide. Therefore they decided the wording of the bardic rote should be* "Eve was of Adam's rib". As dozens of generations passed and they went to Babylon as slaves, language changed. *The phrase became meaningless. Young wags asked are they Siamese twins? Ha,ha,ha. The sages sat down again, at a loss to understand the phrase, which made them, look ridiculous. They evoked that universal panacea God and said,* "The LORD GOD caused a deep sleep to fall upon Adam and he slept; and he took one of his ribs, and closed up the flesh thereof". Other phrases in the story have a faintly incestuous feel relating to a genealogical skeleton [bone]. "And Adam said of Eve, this is, bone of my bone, and flesh of my flesh". Later when they mate God says "Wife: and they shall be one flesh", *the word bone is omitted because penises do not have any.*

> *Since I have shown people, even if they weren't gentry, were living before Adam, the idea that he was thrown out for having normal sex must be nonsense. Incest could be the whole raison d'être of the story. Adam & Eve could have been thrown out for committing it. Because Methuselah etc. couldn't have lived 900 years; Adam was born c.2000 BC, which fits in with my time scale on incest.*

Today the Black Sea is 3 times the size of England. The Black Sea was a lake, half its present size due to it being 500 feet lower than the Mediterranean. In 5,550 BC due to earth quakes, salt water flowed 200 times as fast as present day Niagara Falls, from the Mediterranean and the water level rose by 15 to 30cms a day, flooding 60,000 sq. miles says Walter Pitman. Archaeologists are searching the seabed for ancient signs of habitation; they think Noah may have lived here. *I think it quite likely that the Ark fled to the shoreline famous for the Golden Fleece.* If Noah was this early; a great many generations must have got lost in the telling of the story. *The Sumerians who wrote about Noah could have journeyed down the Euphrates*

INCESTUOUS ABRAHAM

The Bible is essentially a historical record from start to finish. The Bible story of Abraham was written more than a thousand years after he was dead, when the Jews were settled once more in Canaan. *Before Abraham, in what I allege is the matriarchal period, counting systems were being invented. It is possible that time was measured in terms of menstrual flow;* or lunar months. For instance Methuselah lived 969 years. *(969 months is 80 years 9 months or less if you work on 28 days) However, this may be an over simplification, because their ages would still have to be counted from a puberty ceremony* [Bar-mitzvah, aged 13 years], *for them not to have had offspring as children. Since I am suggesting that the counting be based on menstrual flows, which start at puberty, this is not too surprising.* This makes Methuselah die in his nineties, I expect at that time a remarkably long life. The Jewish religious calendar is still tied to 12 lunar months of 354 days so that approx. every 3 years they have to add a month to keep in step with the sun's 365¼-day year.

But by the time we come to Abraham, c1800 – 1550 BC a less exaggerated system was in operation and by halving their age one can reduce them to a natural span. *This probably arose because the text said something like 7½ hands i.e. 37½ fingers (years) but because at the time of writing everyone was on the decimal system, it was translated to mean 7½ pairs of hands i.e. 75 fingers (years) which was the age that Abraham was, when he married Sarah who was 10 (20) years younger, i.e. 27 years old. Incidentally the Masai of East Africa in their language have two years for every one of ours because they differentiate their dry season from their wet season.*

I shall write my interpretation of their age then put the Bible age in brackets. It is true that the text says that Abraham was very old and Sarah was barren I think this means he was 37 not (75). I believe it relates to the fact that Isaac was conceived when he was 55½ (111) years old, which is why we find his son Isaac marrying a 2nd cousin who is his own age rather than a 1st cousin which upsets the horizontal ribs on the genealogical table. I believe the stress on how old he was relates to this jump on the family tree. For Sarah to have children at (91) years old would be absurd, whereas 45½ years is enough for her to think that missing a period of menstrual flow is the menopause rather than the start of a baby. She would hardly have had a great king propose to her in her seventies whereas many Jewish women of 35 today could attract a middle-aged king.

Sarah probably lived in a black goatskin tent, so low that she would have been unable to stand up in it, like the Bedouin today. The word Hebrew [Hapiru] is not a tribe but means, a gang of itinerant labourers who hire themselves out for work, and sometimes gang together to attack towns, naturally people of this sort have left no archaeological evidence.

The Bible is in a considerable muddle as to the identity of the king, who gave Sarah rich gifts and wanted to marry her.

THE INCESTUOUS HOUSE OF ABRAHAM
Not earlier than 2,207 BC or later than 1207 BC [1800 BC usual]

TERAH (lived near Ur of the Chaledese, and had two wives)

HARAN

LOT

f**ed his two daughters

NAHOR m MILCAH

LABAN the Syrian

JACOB m. 1st LEAH and m. 2nd RACHEL

JOSEPH Egyptian scribe

ISAAC m REBECCA

Many brothers + DINAH of foreskin fame.

Abraham's 'rib'

HAGAR concubine ABRAHAM m SARAH
Egyptian maid   his
                     half
moved   sister
to
Canaan

ISMAEL

MALAHATH m 2nd ESAU

marries first

ELON the Hittite

BEERI m BASHEMOUTH a Hittite

JUDITH

So the idea that, she was a suitable wife for a God Pharaoh who usually married his sister because there was a shortage of Goddesses with impeccable genealogical trees, sounds miraculous to me; even if they could have crossed the Sinai desert twice with a flock of sheep. Their second choice, Abimelech is more likely, who is a persistent claimant, because they also tell the story again in relation to Sarah's daughter in-law. If both stories of the Pharaoh and Abimelech are true it makes Sarah appear like a prostitute. I don't think she was classy enough to be a Goddess / prostitute. A Pharaoh would give his father-in-law a river or canal bank not a few wells. The rich gifts, "sheep, oxen he-asses, men-servants, maid-servants, she-asses, and camels." *sound much more like fantastically memorable gifts from a Canaan King Abimelech than the sort of thing the Pharaoh would give his wife. By the time the story was written all trace of Abimelech and his descendants would have disappeared, most probably genocidally murdered by the Jews. I believe that Abimelech's name was left out in one version, and he was only remembered by the phrase 'very great king' which could have been the cliché name for the Pharaoh during the reign of Solomon.*

Solomon could have identified him as the Pharaoh, to provide a precedent, so that he could marry the Pharaoh's daughter. Solomon married seven hundred wives one of whom was a daughter of the Pharaoh and had three hundred concubines.

So my version of this story is: - c.2000 BC Sarah who lived on the fringes of Ur-uk near the future city of Ur of the Chaldes on the Euphrates river; the most civilised place on earth, got fed up with being excluded from society as a day labourer. She left Ur-uk with her father and uncle Haran and left them behind at an area called Haran. She married Abraham, her half brother (they had a father in common) which is in accord with my theory that incestuous behaviour was compulsory in the Indus valley c2,300 - 1,750 BC and probably fashionable in land-owning societies such as Ur-uk and being upwardly mobile, they set off from Haran to find new land in Canaan taking with them 17 (34) year old Lot the son of Haran.

They walked with their flocks up the Euphrates to the headwaters and then down into Canaan, which wasn't quite as dry as it is now. *Sarah probably went out in front as a scout, in the same way as the nomadic Kurds in Turkey do today when travelling with flocks [transhumance].   They send the prettiest unmarried girl, way out in front; to spy out danger; on the basis that no one would want to kill a pretty girl.*

A civilised king, Abimelech whose territory they were passing through, heard she was Abraham's sister, so he offered to marry her. *Abraham was just a tricky liar,* deliberately saying Sarah was his sister and not mentioning that she was also his wife, but since she was barren *he didn't much-mind parting with her.   Does this mean that God likes to talk to liars?* But Sarah loved her tribe *and did not want to leave it, even to become Queen of a town she could not speak the language of,* so she told Abimelech the truth that she was married to Abraham incestuously and purloined the wedding gifts. Abraham's *dirty rough swarm of goatherds* frightened Abimelech, so he gave the Hebrews gifts and the use of wells for their flocks and let them settle down on the outskirts of his village.

Sarah had learnt the latest techniques of genealogy and was determined to found a dynasty. Unfortunately she was barren so she encouraged her Egyptian servant Hagar to have a child by Abraham. *When Sarah's menstrual flow stopped she thought it was the menopause but it turned out to be Isaac, a son,* so being horribly jealous she evicted Hagar and her son Ishmael and they both would have died of thirst in the scrub if they had not chanced on a well. Because Mohammedans say they are descended from Ishmael they think that the Jews need punishing, *a viewpoint as foolish* as the Christian view that women are second-class citizens because of what Eve did.

Sarah having left all the other urban gods behind; only had her cooking fire which travelled in the Ark and was regarded as a God. This God became a Nationalist. To me Nationalism is the vilest crime known to man. Most people regard Nationalism as good. On Nurse Cavill's statue in Trafalgar Square they hoped to write her famous quote "Patriotism is not enough, we must love our enemies." But the followers of the Old Testament have altered it to read FOR KING & COUNTRY. PATRIOTISM IS NOT ENOUGH. *The Jews belief that they are the chosen people is ridiculous. It got them into trouble with another nationalist Hitler.*

Joseph Heller said, "Where the ark was, there was God. Where the Ark is today, God knows".

Historians say Monotheism was first believed in 15th-14th cent BC so it is likely that Sarah and Abraham c.1800 BC are the first recorded monotheists. Paul Johnson in the history of the Jews says "Abraham .... paid tribute to local deities, known generically as 'El'. El was a standing stone, a penis. Elohim as in the Bible is especially respectful it is the royal plural. The Bible describes God in this period as the most powerful God, a God who can act in other God's territories. It is not until Isaiah that he becomes the only worldwide God. There were of course masses of Gods and Goddesses in Ur but because they all had statues and temples, Sarah could not bring them with her, so she only had the *God of her cooking fire* which she never let go out. *I believe it was this chance that introduced monotheism.* Similar portable altars containing Holy Fire were frequently carried in 550 BC in Iran, more than a thousand years after Abraham. *I believe that is why the great Zoroaster's Ahura Masdah, is described as God of fire and light.. Monotheism reduced the quarrelling*

Africans today make tribal scars on their faces in lieu of a tribal identity card. Sarah introduced circumcision as her tribal identification. In a ceremony using a knife made of flint or possibly silver, (have you ever tried cutting meat with a fruit knife) she circumcised her husband aged *49* (99) and all their men including Ishmael aged *6½* (13). Ishmael's descendants were so keen on the idea that they extended the custom to teenage girls who had their clitorises cut off in lieu, and sometimes the labia as well, accompanied by drums outside the tent so that their screams should not be heard. *This helped to keep women faithful, by reducing their pleasure in f***ing.* Praise the Lord!

Sarah's nephew Lot didn't want to overburden the Abimelech lands with his flocks and he wanted to be independent of Sarah, so he went to live outside one of the most civilised towns in Canaan called Sodom were they enjoyed sex for fun, reading, writing and trading. Sodom was raided and the total population was being taken away as slaves. Abraham with 318 good fighting men raided the slave lines and freed them all, for this service he declined payment. Soon after, volcanic action destroyed Sodom and everyone except Lot and his two daughters were killed. Lot's wife died as she escaped. Lot being a shepherd had a second home out of town in a cave on a mountaintop that protected him from the fall-out. The action is in the name of his two daughters, who are now head of the family, because their mother is dead. Being very loyal they got their father to f*** them both, so that even if he died of the after effects, as his wife had done, the family seed would go on. *The word 'drunken', to make us think that Lot did not know what he was doing, I take to be a prudish comment added later to record a ceremonial Bacchic style rite with libations of alcohol. Could it be that the Bible writer said that God had saved them because they were incestuous i.e. didn't have sex outside the family, unlike the other Sodomites?*

Sarah being a woman, I believe, was more important than Abraham: but when the story was written, men were dominant so nobody mentions it, but Sarah is one of the last women to have a very active role in the Bible. *The battle for power, which Abraham won, is exemplified in their lives. Abraham frightened Sarah into* submission by offering her only son Isaac as a burnt offering to her God.

Viewed from the Kedron River or from the road the pinnacle called the Twin cedars of Olivet before it was approached by a bridge from the Temple would be silhouetted against the sky and appear to be much higher than the mountains behind. Accurate measurements like Everest's had not been invented.

One can easily understand how Abraham's men building an altar would use the only access up such a hill, and a poor goat could get stuck. But how could a goat get stuck on the one metre high rock the Dome on the Rock is now built on? The Moslems think t is Abraham's, rock because it is the highest point today. If the Chanujoth was destroyed a natural rock leaves no foundations.

All inventors of Gods know that they don't exist, but what could Sarah do? Lose her son, or deny her God and lose credibility. She decided to preserve her son and her God but surrender her female power to a male Abraham and terrorism ruled the world for thousands of years. She also died aged *63½* (127) before Isaac *was grown up 13½* (27) and before Abraham died *87½* (175*) and therefore had no chance to regain power.* We are right in thinking Abraham was the Patriarch.

Religious leaders seek power and food. By inventing a God they were able to make people want to sacrifice and bring them animals to eat. Altars were popular and ones on the top of pinnacles had good publicity. At the time of Abraham pinnacles represented

God's erect penis to the local non-Jewish people.

He had many names Moloch (Melak); sculptures were made of him such that first born babies put on his squatting knees so that if they moved they rolled into the fire in front of him so that he could inhale the spirits of children. He was a successful God because women who had lost their first born were so shocked and horrified that they realised there was no point in arguing with the male priests. The women therefore consented to become slaves to men. The Jews believed in this God rather than YHWH during the reign of their Kings Ahaz and Manasseh 692-638 BC. 11 Kings 21:6 . The Encyclopaedia Britannica explains how Yahweh and Moloch are probably the same God.

God said to Abraham, I am very important, I made you, Abraham said now Sarah is dead, it is I that am very important because nobody would know about you if I did not tell him or her. Abraham then thought of the biblical text "Blessed art thou, O Lord our God, King of the Universe, who has not made me a woman".

Abraham ordered his oldest servant to journey 1,000 miles back to Haran to find his nearest eligible female relation as a wife for Isaac aged 20 (40). He says the daughters of the Canaanites will not do, and implies the other 400 eligible girls in his tribe are not good enough. Isaac cannot marry his sister, as he has not got one. He can not marry his first cousin because she is married and a generation too old for him, so he marries Abraham's brother's granddaughter, - the most incestuous marriage that is possible.

Isaac *30* (60) and Rebekah have twins, - Esau who is a splendid hunter, and Jacob who is just a tent dweller. Esau marries Judith who comes from a very superior Hittite family, but it is not incestuous so he looses his inheritance to Jacob who jilts his Canaanite girl friend Heth to honour the Lord. He travels 1000 miles and serves as a bondman for 14 years in order to marry two sisters, Leah and Rachael who are both his first cousins. God doesn't punish Jacob for stealing from his father-in-law, or for impersonating his brother or stop him f***ing his wife's maids, he gives him Esau's inheritance, because he is pleased with him. *Esau realises that being non-incestuous is wicked,* and marries his nearest relation Malahath, granddaughter of Abraham and Sarah's Egyptian maid. This partially reinstates him in God's eyes.

There are about 30 states in Canaan and there are sufficient Olive trees for them to sell Olive oil to the rest of the known world.   But no pig bones have been found in the Israel or Judah area, though their neighbours the Philistines kept them. Archaeologists say they worshipped bulls and their ancestors who lived underground.

Jacob's 7 years of service to Laban for each of his daughters suggests matrilocal marriage. (Called "Beena" in the Bible). Genesis. 24 speaks of a man leaving his father and mother and cleaving to his wife; the marriages of Leah and Rachael.   Is this an indication of a transition from matrilocal to matrilineal family organisation?

Jacob's daughter Dinah makes an extremely good engagement with Shechem who is son of Hamor, the Hittite prince of the country in which the Hebrews are *trespassing*.

The Hebrews were labourers and goatherds who lived in four-foot high tents, on poor quality scrubland near some of the most civilised towns on earth.

Shechem could give Dinah a house to live in, in a lovely walled town with quite a few luxuries, and her Uncle Esau's children speak Hittite.   Shechem is so in love with her that he offers Jacob equality with his townspeople and suggests that the Hittites and the Hebrews intermarry, and being neighbours, live as friends.

Jacob says my grandmother started circumcision so we should be different and a tribe unto ourselves.   Unless you are willing not only to have your foreskin cut off but also have every townsmen circumcised, we wont allow any marriage, and we will kill Dinah for having looked at someone who had a foreskin under his robe. But this is one of the great love stories of history.   Shechem is so besotted with Dinah the unloved, landless, illiterate girl out of a dirty goatskin tent and a millionairess in cattle, that he is not only willing to suffer the pain of having his penis hacked about, but manages to persuade his father Hamor and all the men in town to also forego sex for several weeks and have their foreskins cut about with flint knifes, with the inevitable death toll that would result from gangrene, just so he could marry the girl.   A covenant is struck, (the Hebrews know about covenants -they have one in their Ark).   The Hittites not only agree to have their foreskins cut off, but actually have them cut off and they are so sore and in such pain that they stay in bed for two or three days. But the God-chosen Jacob *dishonourably, and it is one of the most dishonourable acts ever recorded,* sends his men, ostensibly to pay social visits to the invalid trusting Hittites who have opened the gates of their walled town.

But instead the Jews cold-bloodedly murder them with swords in the privacy of the Hittites homes. However they were too uncivilised to have any use for the town "for they spoiled all that was in the houses". So, although they stole and looted, I think the primary motivation was not greed but love of the purity of their seed (incest). Jacob sets up a stone penis and poured oil on it, and God said he was to be fruitful and multiply and called him Israel and gave him the land of Canaan.

Jacob's *low moral standards infect* his sons by Leah who are jealous of Joseph, the son of Jacob's favourite wife Rachael. They sell Joseph, of the multi-coloured coat, as a slave to some Midianite traders. As a result of being a bright lad c.1900 BC the Pharaoh promotes him out of slavery, into being a scribe who during the famine takes mortgages out on the peasant's land against issues of corn from the granary which stops them starving. As a result he dispossess the begging peasants, first of their flocks and animals, then of their land, and finally of their liberty. In this way, the Pharaoh acquires nearly all the land and a large number of peasants as slaves in a few years. Joseph's advantage is that he has no relations who can bribe him, while an upper class Egyptian would be subject to too much pressure from his family and friends.

Then follows the marvellous story of how he practices a little comeuppance on his brethren, during which he invites them to a meal but "the Egyptians might not eat bread with the Hebrews, for that is an abomination unto the Egyptians". *And I don't blame them; I should think the ancient Hebrews had quite disgusting table manners.* This prohibition is reminiscent of the Hindu caste system. Joseph gets jobs for about seventy of his relations looking after the Pharaoh's cattle.

Genesis chapter 38 is much loved by the Roman Catholics who have invented a word "Onanism" to mean masturbation and to show how God disapproves of it. *It is a very good example of the fraudulent misuse of the Bible by the church.*

Onan's brother dies before impregnating his wife Tamar. It was the custom in such circumstances that a brother should give his brother's wife some seed so that she could have some children. Onan doesn't fancy Tamar and spills his seed on the ground; the Lord God strikes him dead. Please note all masturbators; this is the one and only biblical instruction not to masturbate. *Presumably he died of the same disease as his brother, poor chap.*

Tamar still needs sperm from her dead husband's relations, so when it becomes obvious that Shelah the younger son is not going to be given to her as a husband. She dresses up in a veil and pretends to be a harlot, and gets her husband's father Judah to f*** her while wearing the veil. When Judah hears Tamar is pregnant, he orders that she should be burnt alive, but when she proves through his staff and ring that the twins are his, both he and God approve. *So I suggest that there is as much evidence here that God approves of prostitution, as there is that he disapproves of masturbation.*

In reality neither is of importance, the whole story is about inheritance rights. One baby puts his hand out first and the midwife ties on a red thread, whereas the other twin is delivered first. Which child is born first? Primogeniture has become an issue. Jesus is descended from her.

The story has nothing to do with masturbation; it is the Leverite law, which binds a man to marry his widowed childless sister in law in order to provide an heir for the deceased and to prevent alienation of family property.

MOSES' PHARONIC EDUCATION

Miriam, Aaron, and Moses are the children of Amran and Jochebed who are both of the House of Levi, *it could have been incestuous, but on balance I think they both belonged to a tribe within a tribe.* At a time when the Bible says there were 2 million Hebrews but when scientists say there were not more than 15,000.

Sometime between 1300 - 1250BC Moses aged 3 months was hidden in a basket in the bulrushes to avoid the death of all male children decreed by a Pharaoh who was practising a form of birth control *because he had more slaves than he required or could sell,* and he was possibly short of corn; almost the money of the time, to give them. The Pharaoh's daughter adopted him, and employed a wet nurse which she did not know was his real mother, and she brought him up with the Pharaoh's children. He must have been the first Hebrew to have a proper education and learn how to read and write not only in Egyptian, but in Sumerian with consonants and vowels. He was privy to all sorts of political and magical secrets. Such as the advantages in making the people believe that the Pharaoh was a God. Moses played with the Pharoah's children *and must have known he was not a God. Thus was born his desire to be a High Priest, to a make believe God.*

A logical and intelligent Pharaoh called Akenaton reigned 1379-1362 invented a single God -the Sun- and denied the many other Egyptian Gods. Despite the overthrow of his monotheist ideas, *this could have given Moses the idea that you can invent a God, and that one God is better than many.* I have shown how Sarah's cooking pot made this idea unsurprising to Abraham's Israelites. Moses was an important prophet in the development of the father figure - an old man with a beard who knew what you were doing, not as an individual but as a tribe and punished or rewarded accordingly. Zoroaster developed this God later. It was also the start for the Hebrews of the concept of a lawgiver, where you could see marks on a scale of good and evil. Even if it was nothing like as developed as the ancient code of Hammurabi.

Moses crystallised the concept, *of an unseen, unpaid police force that could punish after death and extend the misery of beatings into eternity. Moses invented a single God; whose will, he alone could interpret. All power hungry rulers ever since have wanted to preserve this God. He could make superstitious people like Jews and Christians do exactly as he wanted and he is still doing it in the 20th century. But the original Israelites had some excuse, for believing in an underworld, with a real live God,* because the richest man on earth, by a thousand fold, the Pharaoh, spent most of his money and power including their work, on making sure his life in the next world was going to be good.

The pen is mightier than the sword. It is improbable that the Hebrews could read and write sophisticatedly before the ancient Egyptians.

Sir Isaac Pitman published his shorthand at the age of 24. *Moses could have invented writing in Hebrew as a young man. Everyone who ever wanted to write anything later would have to read his writings;* for there were no dictionaries.

As a result of being believed in by Moslems, Jews and Christians; he has become one of the top ten most influential men in history and only second to Jesus in the Bible. As a result, his writings although no longer in existence may have lasted several hundred years and therefore his reports may be more accurate than the stories about Robin Hood who never wrote a book. All his numbers are hopelessly exaggerated, like Methuselah's age. Mud bricks in bulk were not used in Israel so some Jews must have been in Egypt or Mesopotamia; and in both places they would have had to cross a desert.

THE MURDERER MOSES

As a young man Moses saw an Israelite being beaten by his Egyptian overseer. According to his own rules, which he laid down later in life [Exodus 21 20-21] he says that if a master beats a slave to death he should go unpunished providing the slave lives for a day or two. Therefore he had no moral or legal right to kill the Egyptian. When he realised that his own people knew what he had done and were not particularly pleased with him for doing it, the Murderer Moses who said "thou shalt not kill" fled from Egypt to a Midian town. He married Zipporah the daughter of the High Priest who befriended him.

The Midianites were descended from the patriarch Abraham and his second wife Keturah and they worshipped Yahweh (YHWH). The Midianite name for God is the cleverest title, the world has ever known "I AM THAT I AM". It is so abstract; he has no location, no name. Written as YHWH it is unpronounceable. You must not speak the Lords name, *or you might, by magic, get too much power over him.* Jehovah is a German mistranslation for 'unknowable Lord'. Moses borrowed their God's name, for the God of his own people; *because I suspect living in Egypt so long they only had very faint memories of his existence. Moses soon learnt how to manipulate Him.*

Many tribes in the Bronze Age looked upon their early ancestors as Gods. *Moses must have wanted to aggrandise his God with the family tree of Abraham,* when he said his God was the God of Abraham. Abraham's Lord favoured incest and racial purity. His wife Sarah was his half sister. Moses' God (Leviticus 18, 11) said death was the punishment for uncovering the nakedness of your half sister. Abraham tried many times to give her babies and in the end succeeded in giving her Isaac. *The simple explanation is that the two Gods are not the same God.* Was Moses a liar? Christians say Moses did not lie because she never took her clothes off.

Baal was The Canaanite's God of storm and rain. In biblical English Baal, Abraham's God is called "Lord God". And Lucifer whose name means light and fire was his right hand executive officer, the messenger of light. In contrast Moses' God was called YHWH and Lucifer was the devil.

My view of Moses is that he was a short tempered bully who desired to kill and capture the peaceful rich villages (called towns inaccurately in the Bible) which about this time usually had Lucifer as their chief God of light, so by turning Sarah's chief executive officer into a Devil he could justify attacking them. For example the contemporary king of Ugarit, together with his soldiers, wore horns on their heads, *memories of female cow goddesses with cloven hooves?* Theologians later invented a convoluted and complicated story to explain how Lucifer changed sides. They said there had been a fight and the angel Lucifer was driven out of heaven! Since this happened in a literate period, why did no one write about it? But no one has attempted to explain the change of attitude regarding incest. I believe this lack of clarity is exasperated by the later use of fig leaf phrases like "You must not uncover the nakedness of," *to mean 'f***'.* This phrase must date from the time of the Babylonian captivity, when they had three room houses. In King David's time they lived in one-room houses with no privacy for sex, and Abraham and Moses probably lived in tents.

WAS MOSES A GOD?

The Jews believe that Moses wrote every word of the first five books of the Bible, so if I attack him, I am not using the abuse that ancient enemies wrote against him, only re-interpreting his own confessions. Exodus 4..16 says, "and thou (Moses) shall be to him (Pharaoh) instead of God". Ex 7, 1 "And the Lord said unto Moses, see I have made thee a God to Pharaoh: and Aaron thy brother shall be thy prophet. Jeremiah 1. 10 "See I have this day set thee over the nations and over the kingdoms to root out, pull down, to build and to plant." Did Moses make his slave relatives see him as a God and Emperor like the Caesars. *If only the school boy doggerel were true* "The Lord God said unto Moses come forth [fourth] and he came first, so God sent him to the back of the queue, for barging."

Later he went on his own to Egypt, *with his stone law tablets, which he found so heavy, that he hid them on a mountain where he could find them miraculously on his return. Is it possible that the purpose of this trip was to collect an army so that he could murder his wife and her relations?*

The Murderer Moses, as God's servant, could do anything he liked and did, because only Moses could contact his invented God. In front of the Pharaoh he turned a snake into a stick and then back again. So that the Pharaoh and his court knew he was a proper magician *but instead of keeping to the civilised safety rules of using harmless snakes because of the watching crowds,* his snake killed all the others.

The Exodus dates are uncertain but are between 1677-1207 BC which puts him after Hammurabi and the break up of the Indus culture and 700 years before the religions of Zoroaster, Jain and Buddha, and Classical Greek culture.

The Nile produced a host of frogs, then flies that carried plague, followed by locusts that Moses *was able to pretend to his people* he had prophesied. As a result of the famines, the Pharaoh was acquiring slaves too fast; Egyptian farmers were selling themselves to him in return for food. The granaries were dangerously low; the responsibility for feeding all these slaves was becoming a nightmare. *Although the Hebrews thought their mud bricks were important, I would describe them as occupational therapy, without straw they were quite useless. There was such a glut of slaves he couldn't sell them to any one else. Could we sell our unemployed to the Japanese?* The Pharaoh says the Israelites are becoming "more and mightier than we: come, let us deal wisely with them lest they multiply". *So the Pharaoh discussed letting all 600,000 of them go, but both*

Moses and the Pharaoh knew that they would soon drift back when they saw the desert and got hungry, so together they planned to cut off their retreat. The Pharaoh arranged to give a mock chase with 600 chariots, of course he could have caught them if he chose, but Moses' idea of an apartheid homeland did not displease him. Finally they did a deal satisfactory to both sides. Moses publicly asks the Hebrews not to damage Egyptian property, at the same time as he told them to borrow as much gold and silver as they could from their Egyptian neighbours, *when he knew that they would be unable to return it. The majority of the Israelites at this time were still living in Canaan not in Egypt (not all the Israelites had come to Egypt to be slaves), which explains why they thought the locals might accept them.*

The copper mines in Sinai, were very important big mines in those days, but because living conditions were unacceptable, they were only used for six months a year. *Did Moses plan to enslave his people by taking them there? These mines possibly explain the casting of the calf and why they lived in the Sinai for 40 years. But it must have been impossible to stay longer, because of the depletion of the vegetation by the goats.*

The Koran written 2,000 years after the event and 1,000 years after the Jews wrote down the story reveals that Allah's records are in a muddle. Not only does Allah muddle up Miriam the sister of Moses with Mary the mother of Jesus, but says "We led the Israelites across the sea and Pharaoh and his legions pursued them..... But as he was drowning, Pharaoh cried". *Really, how absurd, there is no record of a Pharaoh dying in this way; the mere idea that he would be that interested in a gang of Hebrew slaves defies belief.*

Moses marched the Hebrews down one side of a major channel in the Nile delta, which was called the Sea of Reeds (mistranslated as the Red Sea. Reeds grow in fresh water), which was dry due to water conservation. As soon as Moses heard that the soldiers were close behind he ordered his tribe to cross on a wide front through the dry water course bed *and told his men a dozen miles back to open the sluice gates. The water came down the channel like a raging sea, a wall of water.* I myself have seen a wall of water 4' 0" high consisting of dancing Coca-Cola tins after a flash flood in Montego-bay, -it's very frightening as you run out of the dry wadi to escape it. 3' 0" would sweep a man off his feet. It could have been 6' 0" so boats could use it. It would have the force to toss a chariot and the horse into the air. The flood could have stopped the Egyptians in an area where there were no bridges. Most Bible maps nowadays show Moses missing out the Red Sea. Their flocks would have died of thirst if they had gone that way. The eastern bank of ancient Egypt had trees and was not so much of a sandy desert as it is now. *As for the East wind blowing the water apart, tell that to Father Christmas, wind powerful enough to hold up water in a wall at right angles to it's direction of flow would stop a tribe with all their possessions crossing against the blast.* Having been shouted at by soldiers and with a river behind them they could hardly go back and ahead was the Promised Land.

The Koran says of Moses, "I may become impatient and stammer in my speech". "Free my tongue from my impediment that men may understand my speech". This stammer could be the reason why he wrote so much and why his elder brother Aaron had to do the talking. *So it's not surprising that while Moses was away collecting the stone tablets he had dropped off on his journey from Midian to Egypt,* Aaron casts a golden calf *with all the women's generously given jewellery, which they had borrowed from their Egyptian neighbours and they have a nice sexy party dancing naked round it.* The Hathor [golden calf] temple excavated in 1969 and 1974 at Timma in Midianite country shows that this was the religion of Moses' wife. *Moses broke up the party, pretending God was angry; he promoted the chief perpetrator his brother, to the rank of High Priest instead of executing him according to his own laws. He achieved financial power by melting the statue down and keeping the gold, because it could no longer be reformed into the original jewellery.* Had they continued to worship the golden calf they could have settled down in peace with the Canaanites. *But Moses has murder in his heart. He temporarily satisfies his blood lust* by killing 3,000 Israelites who have been in his absence following his brother's instructions. Moses did not like female cow Goddesses like Hathor. At Zalmonah he erected a *phallic* **brazen** serpent with healing powers. *Was he too niggardly to use the gold from the calf?*

Moses' Ten Commandments:-

1   No other gods. (Notice by implication there are other gods)

2   No sculptures.

3   No blasphemy (i.e. no free speech)

4   Be idle on the Sabbath (trade union rule for slaves)

5   Honour your father and mother. (Similar to Confucius' filial piety)

6   Don't kill

7   No adultery.

8   Don't steal.

9   No false witness.

10 No coveting.

Notice there is nothing about love; with the exception of 5 they are all negatives.

Moses' laws, which follow in the Bible, are appallingly muddled compared with the earlier Hammurabi code c1792 – 1750BC and a modern Christian *should be ashamed* to implement any of them. *He preaches the vendetta, and Moslems follow his teaching.*

THE MIDIANITES

The numbers of Israelites over 20 years old following Moses are said to be 603,550 not including the Levites. Moses *by being so dictatorial nearly lost control*, so his father-in-law, Jethro the High Priest of the Midianites, came on a short visit and taught Moses how to delegate authority. The Moslems take Miriam his sister to be a saint, and report that she complained to Aaron that Moses' second wife was not racially pure because she was an Ethiopian. So, the *Mass Murderer* Moses has his own sister locked up under the trumped up charge that she has Leprosy. Miriam learnt quickly that women have no voice in the affairs of men; suitably terrified she changed her opinion and was released after seven days. But she is still having her revenge, because Moslems still think it their duty to punish the Jews.

An Israelite brought a Midianitish woman who worshipped YHWH back to his camp. Moses had them both killed. Yet Moses is still married to a Midianite called Zipporah! Surely it is surprising that a Christian God of Love should choose an unrepentant active murderer to make into "a God for Pharaoh" as the King James' version puts it. The Israelites start mixing socially with the local people. *Moses pretends God is angry. He is full of hatred for the Midianites because some of them teased him about his stammer years ago, he does not want to live peacefully. So, he satisfies his blood lust* by killing 23,000 of his own people for daring to speak to his wife's tribal group, there is no mention of a trial. Certainly they did not have a fair trial like Jesus had.

Moses prayed on a mountain while Israel fought against the Amalek. If they won, Moses could say his prayer was the cause, if they lost Moses could escape.

The Israeli army conquered the Midianites and killed their King and all the men, *which presumably included Moses father-in-law and two sons Gershom and Eliezer and burnt their city.* They marched the captured women and children to *the MASS MURDERER* MOSES' tent. In Numbers 31 the chapter heading in the King James' version of the Bible says, "Moses is wroth with the officers for saving the women alive". Verses 17 "now therefore kill every male among the little ones and kill every woman that hath known man by lying with him". *This presumably included Zipporah his wife and her relations.* The numbers killed are not clear, but 32,000 virgins were kept. *This is genocide; - the Nuremberg trials would have found Moses guilty of mass murder. Did Hitler with his chosen Aryan race and belief in genocide, model himself upon the Jewish hero Moses? When the people of Jericho were exterminated it was described as a holy war.* It was somehow a good clean war because every one was killed and God was pleased. Deuteronomy 5 9. "I am a jealous God visiting the iniquity of the father upon the children unto the third and fourth generation".

Thomas Paine at the end of the 17th century in The Age of Reason doubted that God really told Moses to slaughter all Midianite males and married women, while the maidens should be preserved. The Bishop of Llandaff indignantly retorted that the maidens were not preserved for immoral purposes as Paine had wickedly suggested, but as slaves to which there could be no ethical objection.

Seneca 8 BC-65AD "We are mad, not only individually but nationally. We check manslaughter and isolated murders; but what of war and the much vaunted crime of slaughtering whole peoples?" *Male dominated societies seem to me to be unbelievably awful, they invent Gods of revenge, and they murder women and children. The whole idea of slavery was to avoid killing the conquered. The followers of Moses smash and burn all art works; i.e. the golden calf, and prohibit sexual enjoyment, calling it a sin.*

'Moses took the blood and threw it upon the people'. Before the invention of soap this is a nasty thing to do. Yet today he is honoured as if he were a good man. How can Christians who profess to believe in a God of LOVE, hero worship a man who believed that might is right, and racial prejudice leading to genocide is good? Some say he is mythical like King Arthur so it doesn't matter. Arthur stood for chivalry and the **Round** table despite carrying *a shameful* patriotic sword. But real or myth, Moses persuades believers it is the word of God.

The Essenes who lived at the time of Christ even wrote a book about how Moses had assumpted to Heaven. Orthodox Jews are certain that Moses wrote every word, even when he records his own death, or says things like, "Moses wrote this law and gave it to the priests". Historians think that something might have been written in David or Solomon's time 10th cent BC, but most was written in Babylon or on their return to Jerusalem in the 5th century BC. The 10 commandments are comparatively innocuous to what follows in Leviticus. The Christians I have met have seldom read Moses' disgusting laws. Nearly everything is punishable by death. In his defence; unbreakable chains and concrete prisons had not been invented. But his teachings *are responsible for millions of deaths in wars, for the murder of girls for unfaithfulness and men for homosexuality.*

Notice how in the after verses his God is immaturely "jealous" and slavery is mentioned with no disapproval. Immoral earnings made by sending your slaves out as prostitutes, may be used for having a good time but not for making vows in the house of the Lord. Is this the reason why the British government was reluctant to tax prostitutes' earnings?

Remember I am judging the Moses by the books he wrote himself in order to make himself out to be a hero, *he is likely to have been much worse.* Isaiah said Cyrus the Great, a non-Jew was Christ [the Messiah] because he released the Jews from slavery in Babylon a thousand years later and told them to rebuild their temple. In its ruins they found a book by Moses that told them that they had been slaves before, naturally they also made Moses into a hero. *I do not believe they were given a promised land by a loving God. Both times I think they were thrown out because they were uneconomic to keep. In Babylon the conquerors must have captured too many slaves.*

Christians say Moses preached love and indeed there are six verses tucked away amongst the 5,845 verses in the five books of Moses which do so. But they are out of keeping with Moses and his teachings, which are mainly about sacrifices and food taboos. They stand out like a sore thumb, they do not relate to the verses before or after them.

I am convinced that someone who wanted the authority of Moses for his own ideas, a thousand or more years later added these verses. Maybe Hosea, Hillel or Annas. It must have been quite an easy job if you were high priest to alter the text. All you had to do was call in all the ancient copies note a spot were they were all illegible and insert your new verse in all extant copies.

It is the religious who are responsible for war, and terrorism. Either Moses must be eliminated from all religions, (Jews, Muslims and Christians) or all religions must be eliminated not by war or murder but by educated people scorning and laughing at them. We must refrain from giving to Christian charities or we will mislead the uneducated. Giving to charity must certainly be encouraged, but we must not give to religious charities, for they will use our money, as they give, to pretend we believe in the chosen peoples of God, and terrorism.

SAMSON & DELILAH

Moses was followed by Joshua who went on killing to steal property, but after a succession of Judges they quietened down and even had a woman as a Judge, Deborah.

One of these judges, Jephthah selected his soldiers on their regional accents, and he murdered 42,000 because they said sibboleth instead of shibboleth, he also burnt his daughter alive, in order to say thank you to God for letting him kill a lot of Ammonites. God was very pleased with him.

Palestine is named after the Philistines, who were probably the Sea Peoples, so it is sensible to see the Samson and Delilah story from their point of view. Samson's father says "is there not a woman among the daughters of your kinsmen....that you must go take a wife from the uncircumcised Philistines".

Notice how women are still important; Samson goes to live with her rather than vice versa. Samson marries a Philistine and to avoid paying up on a debt of honour concerning some bees in a lion cub he has killed, he murders a lot of people and burns the Philistine's fields of wheat and olives. He deserts his wife for having told her kinsfolk the answer to his riddle and goes to live in a cleft in a rock.

His own people realise he is a liability so they bind him with loose knots and take him to the Philistines, but Samson broke the bonds and slew a thousand men with a jaw bone of an ass. (The Hebrews didn't have iron implements at this time and still were not very accurate with numbers.) For doing such a good deed he becomes a judge for 20 years. He is nearly caught in a Philistine town when he visits a harlot (*Goddess?*) but escapes by uprooting the gateposts (*only temples could afford gates*). But he won't learn and visits another girl called Delilah *a temple prostitute? Who doesn't like his fleas* and so cuts off his hair. *He is caught while drunk and sleeping off a good f**** and puts down his loss of strength to the loss of his hair, because he is a Nazerite he must never shave. They blind him and put him in the temple, the ceremony is very popular and thousands come to see it including 3,000 who go on the roof which collapses under their weight, *afterwards the Jews pretend it was Samson who did it.*

The temple at Tel Quasile which is now said to be Samson's temple has only two pillars and measures 7.5 x 5.5 meters much too small to house so many people, but people at that time were not encouraged to enter temples in the way Christians are encouraged to enter churches. *But I am suspicious that it has been chosen simply because one man could knock it down.*

The God of Israel WHWH had a female consort up till the 7th century. *I think this makes the Holy Ghost the goddess of Wisdom. (Sophia)*

Both these sculptures are by
MICHAELANGELO

Desc: MOSES, c.1513-16, San Pietro in Vincoli (Church of St Peter in Chains), Rome
Artist: MICHELANGELO Buonarroti : 1475-1564 :
Italian Credit: [The Art Archive / Dagli Orti]
Ref: AA367676

Moses:

The horns on Moses head are said to be rays of light. *I cannot believe Michaelangelo could depict light so lumpily. I believe it is a humorous way of saying he is the Devil.* Had he said so openly, he would have lost his job, and maybe his life. He cannot have loved Moses for inventing the law that said Michaelangelo should be killed for his homosexuality.

Desc: Italy: Michelangelo's Statue of David, Galleria Dell'Accademia Florence,
Tuscany
Credit: [The Art Archive / Neil Setchfield]
Ref: AA408866

King David:

This is one of the best known and most valuable sculptures
in the world, loved by women. Jesus, a Christian God, is proud to
be descended from David the man that danced naked, exposing
his genitals, round the Ark of the Covenant. However it is very
odd, because David cut off 200 Phillistine foreskins, and yet he is
shown with one! To quote Joseph Heller "No, what we have from
Michaelangelo, I'm afraid is not David from Bethlehem in Judea, but
a Florentine fag's idea of what an Israelite youth might look like if he
were a naked Greek catamite."

Because the Merovingians found records in the temple of
Jerusalem showing they were descended from David. They were
elected kings of Jerusalem, and then the Pope made them Holy
Roman Emperors. My name is David in his memory. Charlemagne
and his father married Merovingian Princesses, so I am descended
from King David.

DAVID AND SOLOMON ETC.

The Philistines very sensibly would not sell iron swords to the impoverished Hebrew nomads who lived around their towns as goatherds and beggars. So when the Hebrews needed disciplining for too much thieving they sent an army out, not like Moses would do, to commit mass murder but as a sporting event. They said let us have a fair, fight, between your champion and our champion. So they sent out Goliath, dressed in bronze armour with an iron tipped spear. They hoped he would either kill Saul, the king of the Jews, or so shame him, that he would lose control, so that the nomads might be disunited. While he was still issuing the challenge with his helmet off, a small cheeky young goatherd took a pot shot at him with his sling, this stunned him, David ran forward stole his sword and cut his head off. The Philistines according to the rules of the game withdrew but *with typical bad manners* the Israelites rushed forward and killed some of them.

Saul's son Jonathan gave David his sword, robe and belt that he is wearing, remember he has no underclothes, and his love for David exceeds the love of a woman. Saul told Jonathan that he was 'a confusion' to his mother's nakedness, whatever that may mean. Saul is very jealous of his fresh-faced harpist's success, and invites him to marry his daughter Michal providing he can collect 100 Philistine foreskins; he hopes that he will get killed while getting them. The High Priest Samuel anoints him King secretly, and David collects 200 foreskins by unprovoked murder, and marries Michal. Later he sings a song which *'goes to the top of the charts'* about how Saul with his 3,000 men slew 1,000s of Philistines, whereas David with 600 men slew 10,000s. While unarmed he plays the harp to Saul, who tries a couple of times unsuccessfully to kill him with a Javelin. Twice David secretly invades Saul's camp and cuts off some clothing to prove that he could have killed him, but Saul is still unfriendly though his son Jonathan is very friendly.

So David ran away to become a Philistine vassal and they gave him a town in the Negev as a feudal holding. He marched against King Saul but was sent back by the Philistines in case he changed sides yet again. Dr. Dothan says the Philistines had a highly sophisticated culture, which was superior to that of the Israelites.

When Saul dies his illegitimate son Ishboseth rules Israel for 7½ years, while David rules Judah from Hebron. His great grandmother is the very respectable prostitute Rahab who had hidden the spies in Jericho. David is made king 1,000-962 BC. And has an army of 30,000 men with iron weapons, he conquers all Canaan which Joshua is said to have done 300 years ago. This kingdom stretches from Egypt to Lebanon and the Mediterranean to the Arabian Desert. He slew amongst others 18,000 Edomites to obtain it.

David loves his handsome son Absalom, who murders his elder brother Amnon because his sister Tamar alleges that Amnon raped her, although she did not bother to shout out, until Amnon threw her out for not being a virgin. *So it is quite likely he got his sister to allege rape, to cover up for her lack of virginity and justify his murder.* Absalom then drove his father out of his newly founded city of Jerusalem, but David's generals defeated and killed him, and to celebrate David danced round the Arc of the Covenant exposing his genitals.

David after enjoining Solomon to walk in the ways of the Lord, told him not to spare the son of a man who had cursed him, [and who had been forgiven on oath], saying "but his hoar head bring thou down with blood". Yet the gospel writers are very keen to show that Jesus is descended from so great a man. The prophet Nathan said that David is the Son of God and that his sons shall be the sons of God. Etienne Charpentier says, "Isaiah was a Judean, for him the king was the son of David/Son of God."

David made God static and monarchical by locating him in Jerusalem. Solomon inherited this kingdom and built YHWH his first temple.

Yahweh's wife is called Asherah in 8th cent BC. *(I think this makes the Holy Ghost (Sophia) the Goddess of Wisdom. But Christians say Jesus' God did not have a wife). Oh, what a muddle. The Holy Ghost's sex is not clear.)* Previously they had had a tabernacle, which is simply a pompous word for a tent.

Solomon is famous for his 'wisdom'. In his Proverbs the word 'wicked' is synonymous with 'fool', and 'just' with Wise'. An example of his wisdom is his judgement concerning two harlots who quarrel over a live and a dead baby, both of them claiming that the live baby is hers. He orders that the baby be cut in half; this reveals the real mother.

Solomon rules this large land area for 40 years. As a result of his wealth the Pharaoh gives one of his daughters to Solomon as a wife. The Lord said you must not marry Moabite, Egyptian, Ammonite, Edomite,

Zidonian, or Hittite women or they might lure you away from me. Solomon marries 700 women including all these; plus 300 concubines. This was thought to be far worse than killing people, and is given as the reason the kingdom breaks into two parts, on his death. The Northern half, called Israel, with it's capital at Shechem, where Golden bulls were worshipped; and Judah in the south, where they worshipped YHWH, till Maacahah the queen regent introduced male cult prostitutes, who were disbanded by Asa King of Judah 913-873 BC.

Ahab 874-853 BC King of the Northern Kingdom, in order to cement a peace treaty, to keep out the Assyrians, married the beautiful non-Jewish Princess Jezebel. Elijah denounces her *because she has introduced her civilised* Gods *and naked priests so they could have nice sexy parties, in the exquisite ivory covered temple she built which was architecturally far superior to Solomon's. Jezebel's civilised set pretended not to notice Elijah, who was dressed in dirty old thick robes.*

Polytheists rarely attack other Gods it was YHWH who attacked them. Elijah, in the Northern Kingdom, was a member of the international priestly guild who chewed soma a hallucinatory drug and while under the influence, made ecstatic remarks, which he pretended, came from God. The God he worshipped was the green-eyed god of Jealousy but he called him YHWH who was the God of parochial nationalism.

They agreed to have a religious competition and both set up altars. Baal and his sexy sister were much more popular. *Elijah decided to cheat and flooded his altar with clear inflammable liquid,* he called it water and ignited it with a crystal, but the 'water' in the surrounding trenches burnt! This conflagration so distracted the people that they were too late to stop Elijah's men murdering the *possibly naked* priests and priestesses of Baal.

Little children mocked Elisha a follower of Elijah, so he got two bears out of the forest to tear 42 children to pieces. Later he inspired others to have Jezebel with her Mary Quant makeup (painted eyes) thrown out of a window and trampled by horses and eaten by dogs, and some more Baal priests murdered. 2 Kings 9.30-37. Her mother continued to rule for another six years, until she was killed, by Jehu a general, who God elected to become King. He founded a one hundred year dynasty the longest in Hebrew history. It is remarkable how *God is always on the side of uncivilised killers providing they are fighting for national identity.*

In 786 Amos stood for social justice, and later Hosea for the covenant of love. The Assyrians wipe out the Northern Kingdom of Israel in 722 BC, but Judah carries on and Manaseh c.651 rules peacefully for 55 years forgetting about the *nationalistic terrorist God YHWH*. They worship the fertility goddess Asterah and her temple prostitutes and her priestly buggers. The temple congregation was now mainly men, the women had to stay at home.

Archaeologists find small figurines of Astarte (Asterah was her Jewish name) in a plentiful supply throughout the whole of Palestine, right up to 586 BC. The ordinary people never forgot her; *YHWH was most probably never worshipped except by a small number of literate powerful families*. The Caananite religion centred round a Phallus [a symbol of a male penis] and a female symbol for a cunt. These symbols can be seen all over India today. Christians call their God "Lord"; the locals worshipped Baalim [means Lords], and Baalot [means Ladies]; *presumably he was one of them*. However, Goddesses were more usually called Asterah in the singular or Astereth in the plural.

The church services were a revitalisation of the sacred marriage ceremony [hieros gamos], which contained sexual imagery as well as actual sexual acts between male members of the agricultural community and the Goddesses. However Manasseh also goes in for the nasty god to whom one has to offer ones first born son, he gives him his own. It is likely that the story of Abraham was first written at this time. The Assyrians "came down like a wolf on the fold, their cohorts were gleaming with purple and gold" and brought Israel to an end in 720 BC. Sargon II says he deported 27,290 Israel captives and relocated others in Samaria [Samaritans]. The only known portrait of an Israelite king shows him kissing the ground in front of an Assyrian one. *No wonder nobody mentions Moses in history, who would want to chat about a slavish people?*

In 586 BC about 20,000 of the cream of the Jews are led off to Babylon as slaves by the order of Nebuchadnezzar and their temple is destroyed. In Babylon they learn about Zoroaster and the idea that truth is important, the concept of the Holy Ghost [Sophia] and rewards in an everlasting heaven and hell.

Daniel 12.2 a minister of Darius the Mede introduces to the Jewish religion the bodily resurrection of the dead.

Later Cyrus the Great conquers Babylon, and builds tunnels to irrigate the land. He releases 50,000 Jews plus 4,000 priests and

7,000 slaves after 56 years of slavery and tells them to go home and rebuild their temple. He says, "The God in Heaven is called Ahura Mazda by his Iranian subjects, Yahweh by his Jewish subjects, and Marduk by his Babylonian ones".

In the ruins of their temple the Jews find hidden a book of the law believed by scholars to be Deuteronomy, with the help of this, in the next 100 years, they write more or less the whole of the Old Testament. The Old Testament is not as old as the times it tells about.

The story of Jael murdering a sleeping man with a tent peg is the oldest bit of writing in the Bible. In 444 BC they pass a law forbidding marriage with foreign women because the *Mass Murderer* Moses who had married a Moabite and an Ethiopian wrote in his law book racist prohibitions on marriage. This law irritates their neighbours the Samaritans who were captives imported by Sargon the Assyrian King in 746-721 BC to live amongst the remnants of the Jews. The logic behind this racism is amusing if the results were not so tragic. God gave the land of Herem – by holy genocidal war - and He might become confused if they gave away small parts of it by marriage.

After this there is a long gap in their history. However, it should be remembered that although the extremely civilised code of Hammurabi is already more than 1,000 years old; it is still very early. Buddha [5th cent] is teaching, but in Rome Romulus and Remus are yet to be fed by wolves in the 4th cent.

Judaism invented, and Christianity preserved the male kinship system. Male ownership of the family name and family property; and the divine right to the throne for males only; could not exist without virginity for unmarried females and strict sexual restraints on married women. "Blessed Art thou O Lord our God, King of the Universe, who has not made me a woman" is a male Hebrew daily prayer. St. Paul said "For man is not of woman but woman is of the man". He presumably thought as his contemporaries that men's sperm contained homunculi (fully formed tiny babies).

Mohammed stated "When Eve was created, Satan rejoiced". Polygamy was outlawed in the 11th century amongst Jews and women had to consent to divorce. And in England it wasn't until 1884 that a wife could no longer be imprisoned for denying her husband his conjugal rights.

Fear of Everlasting Hell fire, is a valuable social encouragement to good behaviour. But it has no powers, over the majority today, who no longer believe in it. Punishment may be desirable for those that frighten small children with stories of Hell fire, or who steal or murder. But is it right that those who have never heard of Jesus should be sent there when they die? It is inhuman to give punishments that do not allow the recipient to repent and change and therefore come back from a perpetual Hell. *It is mere vindictiveness.* "Vengeance is mine", sayeth the Lord. *God is obscenely wicked to permit a perpetual Hell, and it makes his talk of mercy hypocritical, unless of course the All Powerful is so weak that he has no control over the Devil.*

*If there is no Hell or God is weak, wicked or non-existent mankind must create a merciful alternative rule through the "'**God' card**" (A book I hope to Publish) or other means.*

CHAPTER V
EARLY RELIGIONS AND SNAKES

SACRIFICE

In the days before people had money, priests liked to be rich and idle, so they had to devise a way, to make people bring them food and goods as gifts. This had been no problem when the goddesses were beautiful and loved by everyone. But now men had the power they could only get it through trickery or fear.

One of Charles Dickens characters invents a non-existent partner in his firm. If any of his customers ask him to lower his prices or grant them favours, he agrees with them and says he wishes to do so but his hard partner would punish him. The partner was his invention. The people were gullible. The priests said they had just such a partner, an awful, terrible jealous God who would punish them if they didn't feed him and please him. Sacrifice was the centre of religion and the priests grew rich on the leftovers. Some times they suggested that if you had nothing to give you should bring your children to be murdered. This had the effect of letting the people know that the priests were not joking and they quickly found the odd gold bracelet instead. In India the Brahmin priests had become so selfish that they sold the animals rather than sacrificing them.

Cannibals slowly realised that sympathetic magic does not work; one does not acquire the skills or looks of the eaten person. Therefore the essential spirit must disappear like alcohol, which evaporates. This essential spirit got called the soul. Logically the only way to send the soul to a sky God was to burn every little bit as a sacrifice; this is called a Holocaust. The original word had nothing to do with the murder of the Jews by Hitler. *The Priests may well have cynically known as I do that there are no Gods and thought it best not to waste too much food on the altar fire.* A compromise was found, the blood, [life's blood] was burnt sending the essential or soul of the animal to God and the rest of the animal which God was not hungry enough to eat was shared out among his worshippers with the priests getting the lions share. Incense and flowers had to be used to cure the smell in the temples, which often became little more than slaughterhouses, and this sacrifice slab, called an altar, is the central attraction in Christian churches to this day. The Roman Catholics priests perpetuate this memory by drinking *pretend* blood at the Mass.

The Jews and thus the Christians could not eat blood, or strangled animals that had not lost their blood. The blood had to be properly drained, if need be with salt. In Nepal to day blood is poured on the altar. Despite the fact that many people are dying of under nourishment. Blood today is still not a popular drink in the West, because of these superstitions. We have much to learn from the Masai in East Africa who live substantially upon this excellent food source. St. Paul said it was all right to eat meat dedicated to Idols and then sold in the market, because Idols were nothing; but many Christians did not approve.

Christ did not denounce the contemporary customs of the priests, and therefore tacitly approved of them. The priests got the first fruits from the trees; [i.e. the fourth years supply from a new tree]. Also the first born of all animals, [they were entitled to keep the skins, and the rest of the meat], but they had to burn the fat which covered the bowel liver and the kidneys, and sprinkle the blood on the altar. Every time an animal was killed the priests had to be given a shoulder. The first born of impure animals, and human first born, were redeemed for money. Modern Jews never sacrifice because it was made impossible for them to buy any legally pure sacrifices as a result of the destruction of the temple in Jerusalem, by the Romans, in AD 70.

LITERACY

The workers on the tower of Babel like the Jewish slaves would all have come from different countries, with different languages, and like the migrant labour in the African gold mines today, they could not band together quickly, because they couldn't talk to each other. But this coming together of peoples encouraged development and competition in languages and styles of writing.

The Sumerians were the first people to write phonetically, they had 4 vowels and 16 consonants, the verbs and nouns were the same but there was a present and a future tense.

Syllabic writing was invented in Mesopotamia 3,100 BC, there were seven other systems: -

1) Sumerian in Iraq,
2) Elamite in S. W. Iran 3,000 - 2,200 BC. Still un-deciphered
3) Indic in the Indus valley 2,200 BC. Still un-deciphered
4) Chinese 1,300 BC to the present day
5) Egyptian 3,000 BC - 400 AD
6) Cretan 2,000 - 1,200 BC (not linear 'B') un-deciphered
7) Hittite in Syria 1500 - 700 BC.

The ancient Semites must have had an opportunity to be familiar with all the logo syllabic systems excluding the Chinese. Aramaic the language of the Persian Empire superseded Assyrian and Babylonian.

The story of Adam and Eve and Abraham is written in Aramaic not Hebrew, Jesus is thought to have spoken Aramaic not Hebrew or Yiddish [*Yiddish was probably spoken by Jews in Germany before the Germans migrated into Germany from the east.* Hebrew was not spoken as a first language for a millennium until it was revived in 1881 as part of the Romantic Movement. Today over half the Jews in the world speak English.

In the Near East, writing was developed mainly for priests to write about the magic secrets of Gods. Ethiopian and Sanskrit come from the Semites. Conquest helped to knock out special signs out of the old languages and systems of writing. Greek was the first language to be used widely for every day trade, and they took their consonants from the Phoenicians.

Writing is one of the most important inventions man has ever made, and only unusually intelligent individuals were able to use it, especially in the olden days when it was much more difficult.

THE FERTILE CRESENT

The civilised Hittites appear c.2000 BC at the time of Abraham, from Russia via Turkey and they were powerful from 1700-1200 BC. But the Sea Peoples a group that includes the Philistines, who had access to iron, through trade, defeated the Hittites. The Iron Age is from 1300 BC to 550 BC. It fits between Moses and Buddha. Iron was a mixed blessing it brought with it an age of fighting and male terrorism, men owned iron implements; women did not. Peaceful people and women became socially inferior.

The Phoenicians, were Semites who called themselves Caananites who had settled on the coast of Israel, as seafarers, in the towns of Tyre, and Sidon, & Byblos, [the Bible is named after this publishing centre]. The Phoenicians traded with Cornwall, England. They rounded Africa from the Red Sea to Gibraltar taking 3 years and growing crops on the way in 3 places as recorded by Herodotus who thought it must be a fairy story because they said the stars changed and the sun came up on the other side, i.e. they twice crossed the equator. The Assyrians 1630-612 BC, who were also Semites, were much more brutal than the Hittites and collected tribute from the Phoenicians. This resulted in their colony at Carthage becoming more important than their hometowns, but they allowed their Goddess Astarte to deteriorate into Anat and then Tanit who collected the ashes of cremated live babies. Carthage almost ruled the Mediterranean but Rome defeated Hannibal and his elephants and sowed their fields with salt.

The Fertile Crescent supported many civilisations. As soon as they became established, a nomadic *non-entity* like Jacob came and murdered you in your beds and destroyed your town because nomads didn't know how to live in towns, or if like Moses they had some use for your land they murdered the people. There was plenty of 'New blood' but precious few new 'memes' (ideas).

Even Solomon in all his glory, never exceeded the civilisation under Hammurabi 750 years earlier. Our laws in the West did not exceed Hammurabi's until we abolished slavery and passed the Married Woman's Property Act in AD 1870. But the Nazi German treatment of slaves in the 20th century was worse. *Surely if there was a God, he would have nursed one of the civilisations, instead of putting the boot in every time.*

At the time of Hammurabi, the ruling classes believed in a battle between Good and Evil, an after life, and a Saviour incarnated in human shape. When a King is born, they thought a divine star appeared in the sky, which could be seen by shepherds from a hill. Mithra, their chief god, the God of light was born on December 25th. It is almost uncanny how Jesus fits the bill coming almost as long after these beliefs as we are after Jesus. They were interested in the calendar. His birthday is the beginning of the New Year?

According to Homer, not only craftsmen were in guilds but also priests, potters, physicians, architects and minstrels. These guilds had no national basis, so the culture spread quickly. The priestly trade union was strictly hereditary; they called themselves Magi [from which comes the word magic]. They had to relate to differing geographical conditions. In the dry lands, rain was praised, and could be obtained or encouraged by filling the temple dancers with sperm (moisture). In Mesopotamia the floods were a disaster, and the story of Gilgamesh is the first recording of the 'Noah type' flood story, and the supreme importance of the sacred prostitute.

ZORASTER

Zoroaster 628-551 BC or 660-583 BC or earlier *is the greatest religious inventor the world has ever known.* He championed monotheism, man's free will and the rewards and punishments of an everlasting heaven and hell. Ahura means 'lord'; the old religion had several Ahuras, and several Devas. He preached worship Ahura Masda only; forget the other Ahuras and fight the lying Devas [The word devil is derived from it] whose leader is Ahriman [Satan]. However his ideas were too advanced for polytheists, he never wrote anything and his religion got in a muddle and his language was killed when the locality was conquered. He preached "good thoughts, good words, good deeds"; honesty, righteousness, and generosity are the cardinal virtues. "If in doubt that an action be just, abstain". The settled herdsmen and farmers, caring for their cattle and living in a definite social order were on the side of the wise Lord, (Ahura Mazdah). The "follower of the lie" (Ahriman) is a thieving nomad, an enemy of orderly agriculture and animal husbandry.

My view is that Moses' YHWH is Ahriman, for it is YHWH who is proud to break a covenant with Dinah's fiancée of foreskin fame, it is Samson, the beloved of YHWH, who burns olive trees. It is YHWH who is the mass murderer, cynically breaking his own law not to kill. We have seen how Abraham's wife's cooking fire detached YHWH [the Lord] from his alter ego Ahura [the Lord]. In the older parts of the Old Testament, Lucifer (another name for Mazdah, God of light) is the chief executive officer of the more abstract nameless LORD whose main tasks are judgement, executions, and death. However the Hebrews regularly attacked their civilised neighbours who worship Lucifer/Mazdah as their God; they are embarrassed at being less civilised, so they call him the Devil. Often the best way to learn about religion is to listen to the abuse that later religions give it. Isaiah XI 6 tries to explain away the problem, "O Lucifer son of the morning [star] how art thou fallen from heaven". The Jews and Christians become tongue tied if you ask them how in the early Bible Lucifer sits besides God and for no apparent reason or crime becomes his enemy in Hell later on in the Bible.

In the Yasna ceremony; a yellow plant, called Haoma (Soma in Hindu) which is now extinct; presumably because it was difficult to cultivate like mistletoe; was pounded to death to produce a mild narcotic or alcoholic juice which when consumed gave ecstatic immortality. The juice was regarded as the incarnate son of the God Ahura Mazda. The Roman Catholic mass might be a joyless descendant of the Yasna ceremony, just as the Brahmins sacred cord also comes from Zoroastrianism.

If you have ever tried lighting a fire in a hurry by rubbing two sticks, you will appreciate how vital it was to keep one fire that all the villagers could rely on perpetually alight. It also provided lighting for the main square because there was no street lighting. *This fire, thousands of years later was to change into the Zoroastrian God of fire. And the Ark of the Covenant was a similar mobile fire.* Mazda (think of the light bulb) another name for the God of light, fire or truth was the one and only God, but because the common people wouldn't abandon the old Gods, they describe him as Chief God. Mithra was his twin, who very nearly ousted Christianity from the Roman Empire. However far more important than the residual Gods and Goddesses believed in by the ordinary people, was the God of Darkness, who was a force for evil, which he endlessly had to fight. This battle remains today as the battle between Heaven and Hell. This battle was so important that the religion became dualist [two Gods], though, originally and today, the followers of Zoroaster call themselves monotheists. The most brilliant idea of all time arose out of this battle. If you do what God wants (you are good) and you go to Heaven but if you disobey or are bad you go to Hell. So the rulers (providing they maintained the superstitions) could reward good people (Those that did what they said God ordered) and frighten the bad without having to pay money or maintain spies, a police force or social services department.

Zoroaster thought in terms of abstracts, things like the seven deadly sins, his adherents turned similar abstracts into demon gods, and good abstracts into the bounteous immortals, who then picked up the names of the old Asuras or Ahuras.

JAINS

The killing of animals revolted Mahavira the most famous Jain leader, together with his younger contemporary Buddha, especially as neither of them was foolish enough to suppose that there was any sort of God that would appreciate it. They were both against the Brahmin priests who demanded too much in cattle payments for their religious services and in memory of this view, cows still wander unharmed amongst the motors in the streets of India. By persuading people not to eat meat they struck at the root of priestly wealth.

Mahavira the famous Jain, that sits cross-legged, is often mistaken for Buddha [5th cent BC] sitting in his identical cross-legged position. You can tell he is Jain because he has no clothes on. Nirvana cannot be obtained except nude, *(even in the Artic?)* Buddha is always fully dressed though Westerners can't see his clothes; they are transparent - "the Emperor has no clothes" - all the folds in his garments are shown as thin raised lines across his body. These statues reveal an ancient debate about nudism; baring all on the beach is not a new idea.

Mahavira 599 - 527 BC who was a Ksatriya [warrior caste] was reared in idle luxury; but as a younger son, inherited nothing. His parents voluntarily died of self-starvation. He joined the same group Parsvanatha and revamped it. He laid down guidelines for monks, nuns, and lay people. The Jains believe in non-violence, vegetarianism, *dirt* [in as much as they do not wish to kill small living organisms], and prohibition of sex. Mahavira was the last in a line of 24 prophets, the 23rd was in the 9th century BC, the 19th, had been a woman who lived before Abraham. Jains do not believe in a creator God, or a jealous God of war like YAHWEH. They believe that atoms have souls and all life is to be respected, which explains why they cannot eat meat. *I expect his parents couldn't even eat vegetables, which is why they starved to death.* You sometimes see Jains today with some gauze over their mouths to prevent them accidentally swallowing a gnat and so eating a living animal, or reincarnation of their grandmother.

In AD 80 under Digambara there was a big split, half believed monks should be naked and I mean naked, and the others who believed that women could not obtain salvation and should never be seen. These Southern Jains often marry their daughters aged 10 or 12 to boys of 19 or 20.

There are two million Jains today. They have beautiful carved white semi-translucent marble temples, which put St. Peter's and St. Paul's cathedrals to shame. They are honest traders and much richer than the average Indian, they are not atheists but do not believe in a Supreme Being.

BUDDHA
563 - 483 BC

Buddha was a prince brought up in a garden, like Eden, who being idle like myself, had time to think about abstractions like God and found he didn't exist. He was an ethical atheist. Aged 29 he deserted his wife and newborn child and his mother, and father who was a Rajah, to search for Nirvana [perfect peace]. His 250 million Mahayana adherents today have turned Buddha into a God. He was really a very nice gentleman who practised gentleness; his teaching contains all the love, peace and kindness that modern Christians *on the slenderest of evidence* believe is Christian. Buddhism is monastic, and crimes are punished by expulsion from the order, but monks are not shut away in monasteries they teach lay people to read and write. However he was against images, and although they are allowed in his temples today they are frequently boring because they consist of endless representations of himself, *but Buddhist buildings are far superior aesthetically to Mohammedan's ones.* Like Jain he was horrified by bloody sacrifices of the sort practised by Hindus, Jews, and Greeks. Buddha would not kill animals but would eat meat if offered it.

Buddhism does not acknowledge the individual immortal soul. This means that man does not reap the consequences of his own good or evil behaviour and receives no punishments or rewards. This upsets the other major religions that believe that self-interest (punishments and rewards) is the only motivation for a moral life, and the preserving of social cohesion.

Ashoka 274-232 BC re-established the Indian empire; after Alexander the Great's 326 BC invasion of India; and expanded his empire and captured Kalinga (Konarak). However Ashoka was so horrified by the war that he was converted to Buddhism, which he spread by erecting 84,000 stupas to the memory of Buddha. His son and daughter peacefully conquered Ceylon with Buddhism. Later it swept the whole of the Far East carried by peaceful traders. Buddha left no written instructions and so was forgotten about in India because the ancient Aryan texts were being written for the first time 320-550 AD and with them Hinduism returned. Jesus must have heard of him and how he converted people by performing miracles, Buddha was the first one to walk on water. Buddhism taught Christians to preserve relics.

However there are 28 million Hinayana Buddhists who retain the original atheism in Thailand [Siam] today. The majority Mahayana are not atheists.

SNAKES AND DOVES

Jesus says "be ye as wise as serpents and as harmless as doves". The gospel of Thomas Log 39 says – become as wise as serpents and as innocent as doves. But biology shows that serpents or snakes are not very wise, and doves are not gentle, is this proof that Jesus was ignorant? *I think not, and I think you will see why in my fiction of his life. In the meanwhile I wish to dismiss any other possible interpretation.* Fashionable Roman ladies kept doves for amusement and brought them to parties; because they discovered that if doves are hand-reared they try to copulate with the human hand. Leda was more ambitious. This is because bird Love is as a result of imprinting, doves that are reared by pigeons will try to mate with pigeons, and doves that do not see a female dove in the first 70 days of their life become permanently homosexual. Chicks will follow an orange balloon rather than their real mother, if it is the first moving thing they see. *Could he have thought doves harmless because they rubbed their sex organs on girl's hands?*

Why did he say that snakes are wise, now if he had said Dolphins that would have been different. A hundred years ago the Greek legend of the boy who rode on the Dolphin would have appeared as fanciful as flying carpets and unicorns. Today we see riders on Dolphins in many aquariums, and know they have a great brain capacity. When man domesticated the dog, cat, horse, bullock, elephant, chicken, and dove did he also try to domesticate other living species such as dolphins and snakes?

You may think Jesus' remark about snakes is not important because it is not stressed in church, but the Gnostics believed it, and had it not been for St. Paul, Gnosticism would have triumphed over Christianity. The charming of serpents was a Palestinian speciality about the time of Christ. [Jeremiah 8 17] The Lord threatens the Jews, "behold I will send serpents among you which will not be charmed". There are a lot of snake charmers in the streets of India today. As snakes are deaf, they follow the charmer's movements not his piping, which is for humans. Today several thousand people are killed annually in India by cobras.

When language was very primitive; there were fewer words. A piece of string might be said to be a snake of wool or fibre. A mathematical line has no thickness but if you chisel a line on stone it has quite a lot of thickness and I can imagine some one striving to explain in an inadequate language, a motif on a plaque with a line around it. He could say the motif was bordered or wrapped by a snake with its tail in its mouth. When Michelangelo speaks of 'figura serpentinata' he is really admiring the movement in a spiral line, not a snake. *So are snakes, clever mathematical lines, props for dancers, symbols for seals, representing societies and persons?*

So far I don't seem to have come up with much of an explanation for Jesus' remark. For this, you will have to wait for my chapter about him. In the meanwhile I shall continue to lay the groundwork. *Could the snake have been the house logo or a symbol for a society of extreme importance and learning in very early history? If we could find one this would excuse Jesus from making a meaningless statement.* Snakes are ubiquitous in all the

125

early religions.

West Africans might think of the snake whose egg created the world, or of Bosomuru a river snake who descended from the sky to encourage the first woman to bear children, or is this simply the Eve story garbled? Buto the goddess of Lower Egypt was a cobra twinned round a Papyrus stalk; she became one of the most important Pharaohonic titles and appeared as a diadem upon his head. The snake is also the symbol of kingship for the Zulus.

Ancient Americans might think of Quetzalcoatl a feathered snake connected with lightening rain and fertility, or of underwater evil snakes.

Snakes shed their skin every time they grow bigger and therefore might seem immortal. The snake in the Babylonian Gilgamesh story appears as the one that knows the secret of rejuvenation like Eve's snake.

Asians might think of the Nagas [Sanskrit for serpent] in Hindu and Buddhist mythology, a class of semi-divine beings, represented zoomorphicly as hooded cobras with one to seven heads or as human beings with snake characteristics below the navel and a canopy of hoods above their heads. They are a strong handsome race, superior to men, who live in resplendent palaces beautifully ornamented with precious gems. They are associated with underground rivers, lakes, seas, and wells. They are pre-Aryan, from the Bronze Age and Brahmins are proud to be descended from them. The Nagis are serpent princesses of striking beauty. The dynasties of Manipur in N.E. India and Palaras in S. India and the ruling family in Funan ancient Indo-china trace their origin to a man and a Nagi. Manassa is a popular snake goddess in Bengal. Nagalkals are stone tablets with an entwined serpent pair, or a half snake half-human mother, supporting children, which are often set up under trees as votive offerings by couples desiring children. Tirthankara [the Jain saviour] Parsvanatha is always shown with a canopy of snake hoods above his head.

Demeter, Athene, Hermes and Asklepios [Asculapius] all had snakes. Instead of hair, Medusa had writhing snakes; she had a flat nose and her tongue lolled out of her round face. Modern anthropologists believe it was a mask used as a protection against the evil eye. Not much wisdom here. Snakes hang around tombs, are they the souls of the departed? They live in caves, which might be ventilation shafts down to the underworld and therefore represent the devil.

In Plutarch's life of Alexander the Great, Phillip of Macedon observed that Olympias, Alexander the Great's mother, kept company with a serpent while she slept, *I would have guessed it was a live dildo,* but the Delphic oracle informed him that it was Jupiter Amon [Zeus] in the form of a serpent that had consorted with his wife. Zeus was a snake before the imagery of the gods was modernised so that they looked like men. Snakes live in holes in mother earth and might on account of this seem phallic; *may be Zeus started life as a penis God.*

Snakes seem to be connected with the priesthood and doctors but it is not very clear why. But the connection is so ancient that it goes back to the time of the goddesses, matriarchy, and the agricultural revolution.

The Ophites [from the Greek word, ophis 'serpent'] reinterpreted the mythological theme of the fall of man in Genesis, According to the Ophites, the serpent of the Garden of Eden was the good messenger, helping man to know his identity, from the good God that sent Jesus. The bad God of the Old Testament was trying to stop men having knowledge [gnosis]. They flaunted their freedom from the Ten Commandments by extreme sexual licence. They were called Gnostics and inherited the Zoroastrian dual good and bad Gods.

SNAKES

The snake features in most early religions on every continent for example the Nagas in the Far East, Bosomuru in Africa, Quetzalcoatl in America, the cobra in Hindu. Only the Jews regard Eve's snake in the Garden of Eden as bad. Being a new religion they enjoyed being rude about pre existing religions.

Before the domestication of the cat, women may well have protected their granaries with mice eating snakes. They could have put snakes in their baskets to stop thieves rummaging in their clothes to find jewels, because locks had not been invented

ATHENA has a SNAKE

Desc: Athena, marble, 2nd century AD Roman copy of famous original by
Phidias inside the Parthenon
Credit: [The Art Archive / National Archaeological Museum Athens / Dagli
Orti]
Ref: AA388200

2nd century Roman copy of Phidias' Athena in the Parthenon

The original statue was in gold and ivory. Before Zeus was promoted to being chief god on Olympus, he was called a snake. **Jesus said "have the wisdom of serpents". Biologically speaking snakes are not wise, was Jesus referring to a house logo sign and if so whose?** *His natural father's?*

In the early days of the domestication of animals, women might have preferred non-poisonous 18" snakes to wild cats, about the house. Snakes could reduce the number of insects and mice, and thus guard the grain store. It may be cruel but snakes are able to live for many months without eating. If they have not eaten for a day before being given their guard duties, they would not shit, and they never piss, they shed uric crystals. They would not eat the wheat, or unduly mess it while guarding against rodents. Poisonous ones could be used in baskets of fine raiment and jewels as a deterrent to thieves. Since only priestesses could afford such finery they would be the only people who could handle snakes, and being in such close propinquity they would quickly learn that snakes like cuddling under the bedclothes on cold nights alongside their warm bodies.

A pretty girl might prefer the effect to a man just as some girls today prefer electric dildoes. Their religion was wise, and the snake became their house logo sign. *So I will tell a possible fiction.*

A POSSIBLE FICTION

In the idyllic days of peace and plenty when men lived in a matrilineal matriarchy ruled by prostitute goddesses from the temple on the hill, where they kept the granary for bad years. People were joyous and relaxed and sang and danced and made love, but everything had to be organised according to well-known tradition so that things did not get out of hand. There is nothing that requires more organisation than a peaceful orgy, and none of the girls wanted to be treated roughly or loose their dignity.

One day a scar faced pirate captain came in with his sailors and started to behave disrespectfully to the Goddesses. The Head Goddess realised that she had to stop this. She could not understand the coarse badly pronounced alcoholic language of the captain but she guessed that he was boasting that she would be begging for mercy by the time he had finished with her. In short she feared he might treat her and her well-trained staff of dancing girls, with the modern manners of a Moslem.

So before the floor show was finished, seductively wriggling her hips she stood in front of him, then with her eyes she led him to the back of the temple stage, into the womb like darkness of the heart of the building, an area archaeologists would describe as the Holy of Holies. It was a small richly decorated room with rich carpets, knotted by the tiny fingers of children. Lit by one oil lamp in front of the statue of her mother, it was reeking of incense. She divested him of his sword and clothes and she lay back on the raised cushions cooing sweet nothingnesses at him. He jumped roughly on her, he aimed his penis between her legs and something sucked his penis in. She backed gracefully away, blew out the light, and rearranged her elaborate dress. How can she be over there he thought when I can feel her cunt take more and more of my penis tightly. He put his hand down and he felt scales. The Captains erection died on him, as he realised that a snake was eating his penis, screaming with fear he pulled it off and ran naked from the room on to the stage to the laughter of his own men.

The Goddess emerged fully dressed and posed languorously against the door jamb, smiling and flicking her made up eyelashes she cooed "next please", but there were no takers. The following morning the captain saluted smartly when he collected his sword, he looked longingly at the closed wicker baskets but dare not shake their possible golden contents on to the carpet for he feared the snakes in the baskets might be poisonous.

When he returned home he told his wife of the cold maiden who had scales where her cunt should have been, the children half overheard, so his wife told them it was a mermaid, because she was a fig leaf philosopher.

This is why Brahmin priests are proud to be descended from snake goddesses for they were truly diplomatic priestesses. Is this why mankind with a five thousand-year emotional memory calls Satan 'that old snake', and Eve with her snake the temptress?

Some readers of my book feel that my remarks about snakes are shocking and should be covered with a fig leaf. Is this because their powerful unconscious floods their less powerful conscious mind with ideas for which they have no pigeon holes? And thus they panic. Clive Bell, the art critic, said 'unshockableness was the sign of the civilised man'. Similar goings on may have been extremely rare, but shocking things are memorable, and I believe this could be a contributory reason why snake/penises became the sculptor's symbol for both prostitute Goddesses and carnal knowledge/wisdom.

Desc: Goddess holding serpents, c. 1500 BC from Palace of Knossos, Crete
Credit: [The Art Archive / Heraklion Museum / Dagli Orti]
Ref: AA367491

A Minoan Priestess.

A middle Minoan faience statuette from Knossos The Goddess or priestess holds a snake in her right arm, the other arm and snake is an expert's guess.

Why should Minoan Goddesses bare-breasted and dressed to seduce, hold two small snakes in the air? Was it just a *cabaret act?*

CHAPTER VI
CLASSICAL AND EASTERN RELIGIONS
T H E   G R E E K S

'The mother is not the parent of the child which is called hers. She is the nurse who tends the growth of the young seed planted by its true parent, the male.' Says the playwright excusing Orestes murder of his mother at the time of Troy.

Peter Levi, Lecturer in Classical studies at Christ Church Oxford says «The dominance of war and male athletics, is most people's notion of Greek civilisation. This is partly a mistake projected backwards from our own world. From remote prehistory the Greeks had always shown a particular interest in a goddess.»

Hilary Evans in «The Oldest Profession» says «The Greek Aphrodite was a fertility deity, feted at orgiastic festivals and honoured by temple prostitution». From Crete via Mycenae, they took their Goddesses who were loved till the very end by the lower classes.

Cecrops was the first King of Attica in the 13th cent. BC he promoted Zeus who had incestuously married his sister, to being top god and abolished matriarchy.

Homer in the 8th cent. BC describes events 500 years earlier, ie about the time of Moses. He describes Olympian Gods which are like distinguished guests with whom one shares the sacrificial meal. Honour is paramount and wealth is equivalent to honourable prestige. In the Homeric odes women had a free and dignified status "which degenerated into child bearing slaves. Wives were secluded in their homes, had no education and few rights." They became chattel. Although Homer is very early, his religious beliefs are so sophisticated that he is of no use in detecting early religious beliefs. In Homer when you died some went to the Isles of the Blest but most were gibbering ghosts.

The Dorians brought to Greece, in 1200 BC male Indo-European Gods. They conquered the Myceneans in 1100 BC whose goddesses had no temples but shared the palace. The new male Gods were frequently said to be the Goddesses babies, but when women turned out to be just 'old bags' the Gods grew up quickly.

The Original Goddesses did not have husbands or lovers. They choose a local hero whom they inspired and protected, they did not ask him to love them but to do great deeds. Hera has Jason; Athena has Perseus, Herakles [Hercules], and Theseus'. Demeter [the grain mother] and Kore [Persephone], a mother and daughter, have Triptolemos. Kore the maiden when she is local to Athens is called Athene, they both wore snakes but later the snake acted like a guard dog for the house. Aphrodite's behaviour is not virginal, by taking a bath, symbolised by her arising out of the sea [she was an island queen], she gets back her virginity every time. *Is Christian baptism a memory?* When she was worshipped on land she was earth born. The older goddesses were always served honey and cakes because their well established rituals preceded the discovery of wine. The priestesses of Artemis and Demeter and the oracle at Delphi were symbolised by bees, slaves serve the queen bee and males die for her. The Greeks like the Myceneans before them were constantly at war. Matriarchal societies were not effeminate; Aristotle said "Most of the warlike and belligerent people were ruled by women". Theseus destroyed the Amazons (women) and founded Athens; so the male father principal triumphed early. Achilles kills Penthesilea the Amazon princess. As she dies in his arms, she falls in love with him, thus power passes from woman to man, she realises her natural calling is love and fertility, not fighting.

Gaia a woman gave birth to Kronos who married his sister Hera and gave birth to Zeus on the island of Crete. Zeus f***ed his aunt Metis and then ate her; which is why Athena came out of his head. Athena's statue was housed in the Parthenon on the Acropolis in Athens.

Ancient Greek religious beliefs can be detected in their rituals, the rites of Diasia a nocturnal festival of curses and imprecations though ostensibly in honour of Zeus, are addressed to an underworld snake. *Snakes live in tombs could they be underworld ghosts?* Heroes and Zeus Melichios are represented as snakes sometimes bearded, Jane Harrison fellow of Newnham, Cambridge in her Prolegomena can not understand why the Greeks chose a snake as their symbol of a Hero but she is a woman and writes in 1903 when syphilis and 'fig leaf' philosophy reached its apogee.

The first Olympic Games were held in 776 BC. The Lydians invented stamped coins 700 BC. Thales in the 6th cent BC considered water and fire to be the first substances.

The Olympian Greeks made their god Zeus in the image of man, he is a barbarian conqueror, and he laughs at lame blacksmiths, and hurls thunderbolts because he is also a northern sky god. His title is 'blameless one'. The conquered peoples did not think their Heroes bad, although they were now described as bloodthirsty. This was because when one sacrificed an animal to a hero on his burial mound the blood passed through a hole to the skeleton below. Demons were both good and bad spirits, angels were messengers. In Islam angels are good, demons are bad and genie can be either. Hesiod in 8th cent. BC made an attempt to systematise the Greek myths and traditions in his Theogony. He believed Zeus had ordained justice and punishment for the unjust.

Zeus married his sister Hera to gain her female power, she thought he should be faithful to her, but he hung her up by her wrists and added weights to her feet.

Hades was the abode of the Gods, immortals and heroes, good and bad. With the coming of the sky Gods - Zeus - all the old gods were turned into baddies by being in Hell [Hades], all the new ones were in the sky on Mount Olympus [heaven]. Xenophanes in the 6th cent. BC puts the case for anthropomorphism:-

"One God there is greatest of Gods and mortals;
Not like to man is he in mind or body.
All of him sees, all of him thinks and hearkens......
But mortal man made gods in his own image
Like to himself in vesture, voice and body.
Had they but hands, methinks, oxen and lions
And horses would have made their gods like fashioned
Horse-gods for horses, oxen-gods for oxen."

The Greeks regarded their bodies as temples of God and circumcision as a desecration of these temples. Their Gods lived in the world; the Hebrew God lived outside the world. Jesus' knowledge of his own resurrection depends upon the assumption that like a Greek he referred to his body as a temple.

The Greeks believed in an ultimate discoverable order in

the universe, whereas Western religion holds that science can only explain it.

Aphrodisias is a Greek town in Turkey which had more than a 100,000 people in c600 BC. It grew from an ancient Temple site of a near eastern goddess attended by sacred prostitutes, to become a major provincial capital of the Roman Empire.

Critias 5th cent BC a Sophist considered that religion was invented to frighten men into adhering to morality. *As I do.* The Sophist Protagoras c 481-411 BC questioned the existence of the gods. *As I do.* Plato 427-347 BC says the Cretan term "beloved mother country" is stronger than "fatherland"

Plato was a noble scion of an Athenian family that was descended from a king, b.428 BC he thought leisure and independent means or a state pension was essential for the growth of wisdom. *I agree.* He also assumes God is a 'she'. "The Universal nature which receives all bodies must be always called the same; for while receiving all things she never".

Plato and Aristotle pushed the idea of a head God who was leader.

Aristotle 382-322 BC. in order to illustrate his arguments about cause and effect a subject that greatly interested him. He chanced to say that the purpose of f***ing was to produce children, any f***ing that didn't produce children was 'bad' f***ing. (which includes women after the menopause). Aristotle obviously had odd ideas, for he said the glance of a menstruating woman could tarnish a mirror. Medieval Christian scholars literally translated this 'bad' to mean morally wrong, and constructed our Christian sexual beliefs on his words, because Aristotle was even more respected by them, than the Bible. If Aristotle had believed in Christian sexual taboos, he would never have allowed Phylis to ride him like a horse. St.Thomas Aquinas writing in 1258-73 AD brings this anti-sex idea into official Christian philosophy. The result is that the R.C. church disapproves of sex for fun, and the use of the condom and the pill. As a result menstruating women in many parts of the world are considered unclean *and lower middle class women still refrain from intercourse during their periods.*

Athens was a democracy with 45,000 voting male citizens and 70,000 to 80,000 slaves, who did not have to step aside in the street and who dressed in normal clothes. The total population was 250,000 including the secondary vote less *slave force* of women. The Athenians exposed new born babies in pots on the hillside, for a few days especially girls, strangers could take them, many weaklings died.

Demonsthenes says "we have hetaerae for our pleasure, concubines for our daily needs, and wives to give us legitimate children and look after the housekeeping." The Hetaerae were beautiful and witty courtesans who were knowledgeable about accounting and literature; some of them exerted intellectual and political influence. They ate at the supper table, wives ate in the kitchen. Plutarch says a woman must appease Aphrodite (Venus) by a period of free hetaerism and purchase the chastity of marriage by the previous lack of it. To avoid having children they usually insisted on anal intercourse. The temple of Aphrodite at Corinth had more than a thousand Hetairae, *were they the echo of the temple goddesses?* The Naditu priestesses of Babylon were selected on the quality of their minds. Sparta was more puritan than Athens, maidens stayed within their rooms, matrons within the house. Old men and boys had affairs which were approved of by society. Dildoes were used by Lesbians or Tribads (women homosexuals) - the word is not derived from Latin 'homo' = man, but from Greek 'homos' meaning 'the same'.

An Athenian thief would be sent as a slave to work in the mines. Theft was not recognised in Sparta because all property was communal. To steal from a miser was to return his money to the common pool, avarice was the crime. This Spartan military state gave Hitler an historical precedent to steal from the Jews.

The Greeks were bubbling with philosophical and religious ideas I will but briefly touch on some. Epicurus lived in retirement in a garden and believed in pleasure and happiness, he believed in gods but did not believe they should be feared as they cared not about men but that man could occasionally in dreams pick up emanations from their talk like radio waves. He did not believe in dissolute pleasure.

Pericles in his funeral oration hints at nothing more than the immortality of fame. Socrates b 470-d 399 BC discovered the immortality of the human soul, he was killed by democrats.

Wine in ancient Greece was said to be sweet, this is because wine had not been invented and it was mead, made from honey. The Greeks later regarded the drinkers of alcohol made from cereals [beer] as socially inferior. Northern men could not grow grapes and when they imported wine they drank it like we do today undiluted and in the same quantity as the beer it replaced as a result they drank too much, and behaved like animals so they were called Centaurs. Large wine pots were despised as barbarian and suggestive of drunkenness; the Greeks mixed their wine with water. The Romans always had 3 parts water to 1 part wine, this made the water safer to drink and quenched ones thirst. Demeter and Zeus had a son Dionysos [Bacchus] who represented moisture in trees, bulls, and wine, and his priest Orpheus who became a God symbolising intoxication.

Orpheus the priest is slain by the Maenads [the musical female muses] whose ancient power he has usurped. Orphics believed in the transmigration of souls; they taught that the soul hereafter might achieve eternal bliss or suffer eternal or temporary torment according to its way of life on earth. The orgy allowed the soul to escape from the wheel of birth [re-incarnation]. It was an extremely sophisticated religion which came from Minoan Crete and has suffered from the abuse of later religions. Orgy means Orphic sacrament, and Bacchanalia means a drunken party. Their chief gods were Eros [Cupid God of Love] and Dionysus [Bacchus]. Orphics were an ascetic sect; wine was diluted by two-thirds water, to them it was only a symbol, as later in the Christian sacrament. *Orgies in my opinion are the most difficult event to stage manage; there are always inadequates who do not know how to behave. So it in no way surprises me that critics can point to events that went wrong. Today you cannot get a dance going unless you give your guests alcohol.* Both the beauty and the savagery of the cult are set forth in the Bacchae of Euripides, in Bacchanalias, respectable matrons and maids in large companies would spend whole nights on the bare hills in dances, which stimulated ecstasy and in an intoxication partly alcoholic. The Bacchic ritual produced 'enthusiasm' the god entered the worshipper; it is the antithesis of prudence. When one was drunk with Dionysus or his God priest Orpheus; a mystical communion was created by eating the body of God, one became God. This rite slipped into the R.C. mass. Pindar says strive not to become a God it is insolence.

Orphics churches founded religious communities to which anybody without distinction of race or sex could be admitted. Because most religions were nationalist they excluded traders or slaves that were far from their homelands only Orphism and Christianity accommodated them and this accounted for their popularity. Christianity imbibed a lot of Orpheus in his role as the sober, gentle musician, and monotheistic "Good Shepherd". Orphism is a return to an earlier religion, but with the female element made male, it is a forerunner of the martyrdom of Christ. The Christian, Father Clement in his 'Exhortation' to Greeks who have experienced the rites of the Orphic mystery, (which is a marriage with the universal mother goddess), disapproves of the abominable wickedness of Zeus who becomes the husband of his daughter in the form of a snake. In the initiation ceremony a gold snake is passed through the bosom of the initiate. A six inch piece of gold must be fabulously valuable, *the priest would hardly want it out of his hands,* and the snake must at least ceremoniously visit the c*** of the girl who is either naked or wearing a chiton, in either case the holy hierophant must see the pubic hair of the hieron with whom he had sacred congress. This mimetic marriage which the Christian fathers thought was unbridled license, takes place on the bridal bed in the bridal chamber. The first marriage took place in a cattle shed [Jesus' generic birthplace] where once a year a highborn blameless woman re-enacted the dread and sacred rite of being married to a bull. This was the basis of the Eleusinian rites together with a ceremony representing the birth of a child held to the breast in the familiar pose of the Virgin Mary. The phrase "Unto us a child is born, unto us a child is given" come from these rites.

Empedocles of Sicily 440 BC, like Jesus, believed he was a God and could heal people. He said there had been a golden age when men worshipped a Cyprian Aphrodite and love was in the ascendant. Christopher Kinnimouth said "Before there were Gods there was only the Goddess....the wind impregnated women.... parthenogenetically.... Slowly as masculine 'superiority' was asserted here below, so in heaven it became necessary for a God to usurp the Goddess's throne. A male deity had to be created to mate with the Goddess, so she bore herself a son to be her lover."

The Greeks conquered world culture not by democracy, but by coin, trade and language. The silver mines at Athens worked by naked slaves provided them with coins. By meeting foreign traders they so improved their language that they were amongst the first people who were capable of abstract thought. With knowledge and an alphabetic language, they were respected, and their language became the international language of trade.

Their [Roman] numerals were so cumbersome; they found geometry quicker than arithmetic and this is why their buildings are so beautiful, the parts are always in geometrical proportions instead of arithmetical ones.

CHINESE CIVILISATION

Tool makers lived in China half a million years ago. In Neolithic times 7,000 BC to 1,600 BC they made fine pottery. On the broad river valleys of the Yangtze and Hwang Ho the soil [loess] is sometimes 200' deep and is good for pressed unfired bricks. They had wild horses, pigs, deer, sheep, and rhinos during the Bronze Age or Shang dynasty which had a slave society ruled by a God king 1600-1030 BC who went in for human sacrifices. This was followed by the Chan dynasty 1030-475 BC and the warring states 475-221 BC. The Great Wall was started in the 4th century BC and completed in 259-210 BC and extended in the Ming dynasty 1368-1644 AD. This wall; which is still the largest engineering work ever undertaken by man; is a fitting monument to the greatest cultural divide in the history of mankind, the divide between Cain and Abel, the divide between private property and communal ownership of land, between those who believe in a money economy and law and order and those who believe that right is might, between settled agriculture and nomadic herders.

The Taoists believe in a Western Paradise [a Middle Eastern wonderland] where the Royal Mother of the West rules all in perfect joy. They also said "let me be glad of suffering that redeems the world from suffering", three hundred years before Christ. Christians however destroy Taoist manuals because they say they are pornographic. It has been suppressed in China but still strongly influences the Japanese.

'Clouds and rain' is their poetical way of saying 'f***'. Men should "push on slowly, like a snake entering its hole to hibernate". Tao means 'the way' and one way is to f*** as many women as one can. "If in one night he can have intercourse with more than ten women it is best". A typical middle class householder would have between three and twelve wives and concubines, the lesser nobility thirty or more. A man usually married his principal wife and all her sisters and maids at the same time, so she would not feel lonely. Confucian men never talked seriously to wives, only to prostitutes. The longer the man can keep his penis inside the woman the more Yin he can absorb, a woman's orgasm is no less important to the man than to the woman. Yin essence is the moisture lubricating a woman's sexual organs and Yang essence is male semen. They are opposing yet complementary forces. Tao is Yin, Confucianism is Yang.

K'ung fu-tsu c.551-479 BC the man the Jesuits called Confucius was an impoverished descendant of the Sung royal family. He preached at a time when iron was being used extensively and the Chinese had invented breast harness for horses. In 124 BC the imperial university was set up to study Confucian classics it had 30,000 students by 220 AD. About 100 BC local governors were selected by examination rather than by hereditary.

Confucius teaches in his book the Analects, service to God is meaningless if one does not serve man. Courtesy, loyalty, unselfishness, good manners, gentlemanly behaviour and filial piety are what matters. He said we are not all intellectually equal but we are all equal in moral capacity. Gentlemen should cultivate themselves so that they bring tranquillity to all whom they rule. A meritocracy drawn from the upper classes is what he seeks with promotion by examinations in morals. Government must have the confidence of the people. There is equality of opportunity to become a sage. "Humaneness is to love others" analects 12.22 "Courtesy, generosity, good faith, diligence and kindness" " Do not do to others what you would not like yourself". Almost Jesus' message, but centuries earlier. He changed belief in good and bad luck to a system of right and wrong. "If you lead them by virtue and keep order among them by ritual, they will have a conscience and reform themselves". *Ritual is status quo known behaviour with a dash of pageantry.*

Meng Ko 371-289 BC [called Mencius in Latin] was a social and ethical teacher, who also did not believe in God.

But despite filial piety the name for a father and an uncle are the same, whereas the name for mother and aunt is different, revealing that patriarchy must have been preceded by matrilineal kinship.

In Japan matrilineal inheritance must have once been common, because the Imperial family ancestors are descended from a Goddess called Amaterasu who is a female Sun.

INDIA and the HINDUS

Reincarnation is the great thought that the Indians excel in, rather than have heaven and hell as reward and punishment for good and bad behaviour, they have a system whereby one's caste or animal status when one is reborn on earth after death, depends on the record of ones previous life or Karma.

At this point I do a chronological gear shift, for two reasons, first because Indian culture having folded in the Indus valley, their development was a thousand years behind the Mediterranean people, and secondly they had a revival of ancient religious beliefs, these of course are as different as a 1920 Tudor pub and the real thing but they still have some influence. Solomon's *scruffy little* temple was 1,000 BC, the Parthenon 450 BC but there were no temples in India until after the second century BC and then it was nothing much more than a lingam [a standing stone representing a penis] in the open air.

The principal Hindu icon is the white lingam [phallus] set in a red Yoni [vulva], sometimes the yoni [c***] is worshipped on its own.

Tantras are manuals of sexual ritual and magic from which the world was born. They recommended action and ecstasy not study. They were transmitted by female power holders from the Palaeolithic mother goddesses. These women are outside the caste system because they pre-date it. They proclaim everything, the crimes and miseries as well as the joys; they are the active play of the female creative principle. Shakti the female force is the dominant one but .the Goddesses take many forms, and are sexually penetrated by an invisible, indescribable seminal male. They are still believed in to day, but high born Indians pretend that the sexuality is only in the mind, but the male's erections are physical. The Brahmin's dire warnings recommending sexual miserliness of sperm, prove that orgies did in fact take place. The poor believed that the more copious the expenditure of pleasure and sexual juice the better.

"In spite of the protests of some authors Phillip Rawson writes in 'Tantra'. "Much Hindu Tantra welcomes orgasm, provided it is recognised as being the analogue to ancient Hindu sacrifice. This sacrifice consisted essentially of pouring oil, fat or butter on to an altar fire, on which other things may also be consumed. Tantra equates the male ejaculation with the oil poured out; the friction of the sexual organs with the rubbing of the sticks to light the fire; the vagina of the female companion, who should, for extreme 'left hand' ritual, be menstruating so that her own vital energies are at what is believed to be their dangerous peak, ... But at the human level, since sexual excitement is felt to indicate the presence of divine energy, some orders of yogis worship their own erect penises, performing full puja to them; and numerous icons represent sadhakas inflamed with desire for union with the Yoni. The lingam in the yoni is the jewel in the lotus".

Yoga is the right hand road, the path of contemplation and denial of flesh. Bhoga is the left hand road, the path of action and acceptance of flesh. But Christians pretend the left hand road does not exist. Every Hindu temple glorified both simultaneously. Hinduism embraces all religions it does not war among its sects like Christianity, it therefore embraces Sahaja, which is the path of spiritual evolution and ultimate emancipation through the adoration of young and beautiful girls, originally created by Tantrick Buddhists, its great exponent was the Brahmin poet Chandidas who loved a washerwoman in the 14th cent. Sex was a religious duty, it improved one's Karma.

Vratyra was outside the Vedic religion, he was an ascetic who wandered in a bullock cart with a woman who was used for ritual prostitution and an apprentice, and he indulged in flagellation and self mortification.

One constant emblem for this inner libido, sexual and cosmic is the snake, whose symbolism is known all over the world in many modifications. Kundalini is a subtle female snake. Through yogic postures, muscular actions and sexual intercourse the sadhaka hopes to vitalise Kundalini so that she enters the bottom end of his Susumna nadi. Nature worship and snakes and Kali are worshipped in obscure villages suggesting these religions are the more ancient. However offerings of flowers and fruit are much more popular than the ancient menstrual blood sacrifice which is represented today by red powder.

Bliss can be obtained in a single lifetime, by meditation, the cult of extreme feeling, aesthetic experience, sex, drugs, magic and social action. Coomaraswamy said of the village masses that they "worshipped not abstract deities of priestly theology, but local Genii [Yaksas and Nagas] and the feminine divinities of increase and mother goddesses.

Long before Jesus, Muni [Wizards] or Shaman were capable of supernatural feats such as healing and levitation, they are in the Regveda and were active from 2,000-600 BC

Was Jesus original? :-
"To injure none by thought or word or deed
To give to others and be kind to all-
This is the constant duty of the Good."
"Treat others as thou wouldst thyself be treated. Do nothing to thy neighbour, which hereafter, thou wouldst not have thy neighbour do to thee. A man obtains a rule of action by looking on his neighbour as himself." Also "A good man who thinks only of benefiting his enemy has no feeling of hostility towards him even at the moment of being destroyed by him." These look like Christian sentiments but they are combined with "A son, a brother, a father, or a friend, who present an obstacle to one's interests are to be slain" and all these quotes are to be found in the Mahabharata c. 300 BC.

The heroine of this poem, Draupadi is the wife of five husbands [polyandry]. "Women were formerly unconfined, and roved at their pleasure, independent. Though in their youthful innocence, they abandoned their husbands, they were guilty of no offence; for such was the rule in early times".

However she would have been guilty if she had crossed the caste barrier. The Hindus today still punish the raped woman, if she is raped by someone in a different caste. Katherine Whitehorn explains the logic "which made the Saxons execute a woman who was raped - for if you look on a woman as a source, as a well, then polluted is polluted, and the question of whether the well had any choice in the matter is beside the point."

Hsiuan-tsang in the 7th century AD was shocked by the crude tribal group-marriage customs on the lower middle Indus. Brahmins [1,000-500 BC] had to marry Brahmins, ie the same caste but only from another racial group [exogenous]. Is this an incest memory?

The Mahabharata records events from 1400-1000 BC, *according to my time scale this is after the male takeover*, and was written 400 BC - 200 AD. Uma the sweetly human Queen of Heaven says to her husband Siva, not her rights as a modern socialist woman would do, but her duties. "The duties of woman are created in the rites of wedding when in the presence of the nuptial fire she becomes the associate of her Lord, for the performance of all righteous deeds. She should be beautiful and gentle, considering her husband as her god and serving him in fortune and misfortune, health and sickness, obedient even if commanded to do unrighteous deeds or acts that may lead to her own destruction. She should rise early, serving the gods, always keeping her house clean, tending the sacred fire, eating only after the needs of gods and guests and servants have been satisfied, devoted to her father and mother and the father and mother of her husband. Devotion to her lord is woman's honour, it is her eternal heaven; and Oh Mahesvara, I desire not paradise itself if thou are not satisfied with me"!

From the 1st century laws of Manu. "Though destitute of virtue, or seeking pleasure elsewhere, or devoid of good qualities, a husband should be worshipped as a god by a faithful wife.... If a wife obeys her husband, she will for that reason alone be exalted in heaven".

The practice of suttee [throwing oneself upon one's husband's funeral pyre] is no more foolishly superstitious, gallant or brave than the behaviour of the Holy Christian Martyrs we call saints. For example Sir Frederick Haliday had to concede the right for a widow to be burnt alive because she resisted all dissuasion and finally proved her determination by asking for a lamp, and holding her finger in the flame until it was burnt and twisted like a quill pen in the flame of a candle; all the while giving no sign of fear or pain whatever. Is suttee different from "my country right or wrong"? Conscripts were made to die by social pressure. In the west our greatest love story is Romeo and Juliet.

In the 1st century AD, sacrifices were done away with and self denial and penance were popular, together with the idea of a loving God and being devotional. In the Bhagavadgita, Krishna tells Arjuna "Whenever there is a decline in righteousness and a rise in unrighteousness then I send forth myself. For the protection of the good, for the destruction of the wicked, and the establishment of righteousness, I come into being from age to age". This philosophy is contemporary with Jesus. Krishna was a sun god, he f***ed 16,000 women and had 18,000 children, *this means he f***ed 10 times a day for 50 years providing he was clever enough never to f*** the same girl twice and choose their ovulating day. Radha was a married woman who did the right thing in being unfaithful to her husband in favour of Krishna. A woman can easily f*** that number of times, but of course can not have as many children, could the story originally relate to a goddess, and the children be a word for adherents?*

The Cakrapuja is a five fold Eucharist involving wine and sexual intercourse. It is very ancient. The Aghoris [ascetics who are regarded with horror because they cultivate customs which break social convention] sometimes eat bits of corpses as part of the Eucharist, and have sexual intercourse with corpses, they are obsessed with the crematorium. There are icons showing Lord Siva carrying his drug jar of bhang or ganjam under his arm, this is another way besides sex to gain religious experience. Ascetics sometimes dress as girls and retire a few days each month to represent menstruation, because all souls are feminine.

In India the mudhras or hand signs are still in use, *and this is why their Gods have so many arms in order to have many hands to make many signs and carry as many attributes as possible.* Because, of course they still speak 225 *not very adequate* languages 15 of which are accepted by the present government and often signs are more easily understood.

The hand sign of Christian prayer is also the hand sign of the Japanese and Thais together with a bow for showing greetings and respect today. Hindus were taught to show respect to all forms of life, *which made Europeans assume that they thought trees were powerful Gods like Allah, because they bowed to them with their hands in the Christian prayer position.* I would think it more likely *that it was a misunderstanding, because Hindus have a tendency to agree with their questioner or say what they think their questioner wants to hear.* Nowadays we have people who join clubs to save trees, butterflies and wild life from extinction, not much different from bowing to a tree you do not want your neighbour to turn into fire wood, thus letting him know politely you would be offended if he cut it down. However, I could be wrong, and this could be a left over from the days when language had no future or past tenses only the present tense.

The Aryans [the word comes from Iran] were nomads *from Southern Russia,* and while passing through Persia in repeated waves they learnt Sanskrit which they brought with the horse and chariot and Vedism to India. The Aryans introduced the custom of having their Queen f***ed by a horse, which was then allowed to go free for a year before being killed, should any tribe molest the horse one had to fight that tribe, this custom gave success in war. This may explain persistent but improbable stories of how Catherine the Great died in a protective basket while being f***ed by a horse.

They wrote their Vedic texts in AD 320-550 but had forgotten Sanskrit by the time the English had arrived *although it is a more sophisticated language than any they now speak.* They had to re-learn it from the English.

Vedism is pre Hindu. The Vedic householder was expected to maintain his household fire into which he made his offering. *They obviously came from a cold climate.* This fire was related to Abraham's Ark of the Covenant. They also borrowed from the Zoroastrians, the Brahmin's sacred cord, soma the hallucinatory drink and cremation of the dead but the Hindu Devas were good and the Asuras were bad; the exact opposite of the Zoroastrian Deavas who were bad, and the Ahuras who were good. The way Gods can change sides should not surprise Christians because Satan the prosecutor in the court of God's justice in the Old Testament Book of Job became the chief antagonist of Christ and of man in Islam. *Hindus learnt about Yoga, and ritual washing from the Harrapans.* They divided themselves into 3,000 endogamous castes [castes that do not intermarry]. They feared chaos if the good God fought the bad ones. Most of the Vedic gods are sky gods. You can force the gods to give, by giving edibles to the sacred fire Agni.

These Aryan conquerors became higher caste than the conquered, a very much more civilised scheme of things than Moses who mass murdered his captives in order to steal their land, and is preferable to slavery. The word caste comes from the Portugese 'casta'. The Aryan Sanskrit word 'Varna' means colour. So the original people were dark skinned and their conquerors lighter. The small people of South India are Australoid or Veddoid. A well known saying, shows how the top class maintained their importance "The whole universe is subject to the Gods; the Gods are subject to the spells [mantras]; the spells to the Brahmins, therefore the Brahmins are our Gods".

In the Ramayana the hero is helped by Hanuman king of the monkeys, *since monkeys do not have kings this needs some explanation, the monkeys are obviously non-caste hunter gatherer forest people, who the superior town folk call monkeys and when they become friends they forget that the original nickname was insulting and later generations interpret the name literally.*

The congregation frequently ate its own offerings after it had been ceremoniously offered to god at the temple. Certainly early Christians argued over the ethical position of buying leftover meat that had been offered to idols.

Shiva is now the principal Hindu deity, in 1,500 BC he was a storm god, he is worshipped as a phallus [penis] his mount is Nandi the bull. A Harrappan seal shows him seated in the yogi position with an erect penis.

When the devotees of the mass murderer Moses deny the possibility of sexual acts taking place in the temples they show that they have not read their hero's books for he describes a visit to the civilised Phoenician Temples 'as a Fornication'. And I am forced to show you Indian temples, because Moses and his adherents have smashed the architecture of the past, leaving only virgin temples, without their sculpture, for he said sculpture was a greater crime than theft or the killing of a woman.

The temples at Khajuraho were built for male priests not popular prostitutes as of old. The pageantry and ritual revolved round serving the statues of Gods as if they were great Kings and Queens, they were woken in the morning, dressed, fed, entertained by dancing girls, and put to bed with the dancing girls. The courtiers their priests were also served by the Devadasis (dancing girls). The Devadasis were privileged girls dedicated to the temple in childhood, or the daughters of Devadasis. They could pass divine energy by sexual intercourse as a result of being trained by divinised Tantrik men. In the eleventh century one temple in Tanjore was supported by the earnings of the 400 women. The religion partially survived the iconoclasm of the Moslems, only to be closed by the hypocritical Christians, on bogus public health grounds, claiming that because they were prostitutes, they spread syphilis, when syphilis was a Christian import. Even today when syphilis is cured, big American money is devoted to the cause of religious intolerance, and the prevention of Devadasis schools being set up. Polygamy and child marriage was the norm so dedication to the temple in childhood was no different. But South Indian temples besides being brothels served as schools, dispensaries, poorhouses, banks, and concert halls. Vedic mass sacrifices were abandoned, but occasional theatrical sacrifices were practised and very rarely even human ones.

It is said that the Christian Empress Catherine the Great, one of the most civilised Russians, used to murder secretly the guard-officers who slept with her, in the same way the male actor having f***ed the goddess had to be disposed of, but dramatically and in public.

The followers of Moses have brainwashed the Hindus into thinking all sexuality sinful, so sadly they no longer dance in temples or discos. But the high moral tone of Indira Ghandi is worthy of Jesus "Do not shed blood, shed hatred". Unfortunately the same can not be said of the Sikhs whose religion is just a cover for *wicked* nationalism which is revealed by them having to carry five 'K's one of which is a sword.

Photo DHH

One of many Indian Goddesses dancing on snakes.

The names of Shiva's female consorts are Uma, Sati, Durga, Parvati, and Kali. I am not allowed to show Kali because my chosen image was too pornographic for English Christians. Kali is the destroyer, her name is feminine for time, and she dances on Shiva's corpse which despite being dead still has an erection. To increase the horror she creates she is said to be 'pregnant with a child of incest'. Her priests make statements as Gods, having sucked blood from a goat's throat. Calcutta is named after her and 'thugs' are named after a Moslem sect who worshipped her. Indians who come to England do not speak of her because they know that to do so would offend the middle class 'fig leaf' philosophers.

Desc: Relief, Laksmana temple, 11th century Candela style, Khajuraho, India
Credit: [The Art Archive / Dagli Orti]
Ref: AA394984

KHAJURAHO

Although the temples at Khajuraho were built from 950 -
1150 AD the carvings catch the spirit of an earlier age. Twenty
temples survive, out of the original eighty three. The sculptures were
plastered in white marble dust to gleam in the sun, so we can only see
the broad outlines of the poses in the un-plastered stone. Photographs
somehow fail to convey the exquisite beauty, only the moving camera
could possibly hope to convey the pleasurable, peaceful, loving,
deeply religious emotions that these small temples convey. In their
time they must have been the greatest architecture upon the earth. In
them were performed ballet, opera, and audience participatory sexual
acts accompanied by scents.

Desc: Relief, Laksmana temple, 11th century Candela style, Khajuraho, India
Credit: [The Art Archive / Dagli Orti]
Ref: AA394984

STONE CARVING on a TEMPLE at KHAJURAHO.

These stone carvings originally would have been covered with plaster made of marble dust and then painted. They have survived a thousand years of wind and rain. So you will have to imagine the original details of jewellery and facial expressions. Maithuna figures represent two or more figures in the more interesting positions in the Kama Sutra.

It is a miracle that 20 of the 85 original temples have survived the iconoclastic destruction of Moslem and Christian rulers, who *ignorantly* regard sex as dirty and shameful *because it is fun and pleasure is sin.* Sexual carvings, both inside and outside, the temples reveal *that sex was thought to be fun.* In this era men were dominant but the women are not all crushed in the 'missionary position'.

ROME

Romulus and Remus the founders of Rome who organised the rape of the Sabines were the sons of Rhea Silvia, the daughter of a Queen. Because she was a Vestal Virgin she had to hide her babies. They were adopted by Acca Laurentia whose land was situated on the Tiber. The house was named 'Lupercal', a word in Italian still implying a brothel. 'Lupa' in Latin means 'she wolf', but it also means 'prostitute'. Literal minded sculptors and Fig leaf philosophers, would rather have us believe that Romulus and Remus were suckled by an animal, than by a rich prostitute.

It is slightly irelevent but the Encyclopaedia Britannica Vol X says "St. Valentine's Day as a lover's festival and the modern tradition of sending Valentine cards have no relation to any saints but seems to be connected to either the Roman fertility festival of the Lupercalia (February 15) or with the mating season of birds.

There were eight kings of Rome, and the last five were not mythical, not one of them was succeeded by his son, yet many left sons and grandsons. One was descended from a former king through his mother; three kings were succeeded by their sons in law who were foreigners. Inheritance must have been matrilineal, exogamous and beena [the rule that the man must leave home and live with his wife's people.] The Queen's first daughter's foreign husband would become king, the other daughters would be Vestal Virgins whose duty was to tend the sacred oak wood fire and if it went out, they could be whipped by the Pontifex Maximus.

Rome, the world's largest city with three quarters of a million people, did not add much to the culture of the world. Their religions were borrowed from the Near East, mainly Greece. For example the ritual flogging of boys on the altar of Artemis became a show for Roman tourists after 181 BC. To defeat Hannibal they imported a black meteorite statue of Cybele from Mount Ida, and when Hannibal was defeated, her priests said, Cybele had defeated Hannibal. Her priests and adherents danced round her naked and castrated themselves, afterwards they dressed as women. These ceremonies were being practised on special occasions as late as the 4th cent AD. St. Matthew mentions them, "There have been eunuchs who have made themselves eunuchs for the Kingdom of Heaven's sake".

Roman philosophy and law was mainly borrowed from the Greeks. Their law, however, was clear; it was published 450 BC to please the plebeians, and they honestly adhered to it. They thought that Justice was a virtue, and Mercy (Sentimentalism) a Christian fault. In the early days the administration of the law was a family matter. The vendetta was a system whereby a family took the law into its own hands. Ancient priests tried to stop this vile practice by saying "vengeance is mine sayeth the Lord". Draco [from whom we get the word draconian] in 620 BC in Athens abolished the family vendetta and substituted state punishment for murder. The Romans codified the law worldwide.

In Pompeii a 300 BC Samnite temple has been found were girls from good class families worked briefly in "sacred prostitution" as a rite of passage to full womanhood.

In the 3rd century BC marriage usually consisted in living together in mutual consent, and women could divorce their husbands for almost no reason at all and frequently did. Augustus accidentally introduced statutory penalties for both male and female adultery; increased to death in the 4th cent. AD. Unless his wife was a prostitute, a man could be prosecuted if he did not divorce his wife for adultery. As a result huge numbers of patrician ladies registered as prostitutes. Roman law makes a big fuss about the substitution of 'the patriarch's dowry' for 'the harlot's marriage portion'. This is because in respectable Sabine and Etruscan families girls had bought their husbands with what we call immoral earnings, where as after the Roman conquest it became fashionable for a father to provide his daughter with a dowry. The laws of Romulus required parents to bring up all male children, and first born girls. The Lactaria column was set up so that deformed, illegitimate, or extra girl babies could be left to die of exposure in baskets.

Moneta was a Goddess in whose temple at Rome money was minted, she gave 'money' its name. Publus Syrus circa 42 BC said "Money alone sets all the world in motion". It was the widespread availability of money that gave the world it's huge improvement in life style.

Deus the Latin for God derives from the Zoroastrian Devas [bad or foreign Gods] which is also the root for the word 'the Devil', which encouraged the Christians to be rather disrespectful of the established Roman Gods.

Latterly however, as long as the divinity of the Emperor was accepted once a year, other divinities were tolerated and contrary to Christian propaganda there was little persecution of the Jews or Christians. Vespasian who had a sense of humour, feeling his death agony, exclaimed "Oh dear, I am afraid, I'm becoming a God". Many religions competed for popularity. Cleopatra claimed she was the Goddess Isis and Anthony became Dionysos-Osiris, and their children became the Sun and the Moon. Juvenal in his Satires says the priests of Isis were pimps. Strabo says there were 1,000 prostitutes living in the temple of Venus at Corinth and the principal ceremonies were sexual. The priests in Rome made money from sacred prostitution. It was a male world. The God Priapus had an enormous penis and was said to be jealous of the ass because he also had a large one.

However Mithras the twin of Ahura Mazda, the Iranian God of contracts, so appealed to the Romans that he nearly became a state God in 60 BC. *As a result the state undertook to enforce private contracts through law and this may have been their greatest cultural achievement.* Excluding his adherents belief in Haoma [a drug] his ceremonies also influenced Christianity. There was a myth that a star would lead the Magi to his birth place and pictures of his birth show him with sacrificial cattle which remind us of Mary's stable. His ceremonial communal meal of wine and bread is preserved in the R.C. Holy communion. St. Augustine condemned and Polybius [Greek] praised the Roman aristocrats for using religion as the opiate of the people.

Unlike the Greeks their wealth did not so much depend on trade as on booty taken by their armies. They defended the known boundaries of the world against the frightful thieving nomads, and kept the peace. [Pax Romana.] The legal position of women was one of complete subordination. Husbands held paternal power [patria potestas] over wives. Women were unfit to sign a contract or will or act as witnesses; they were treated as imbeciles and could hold no public office. Christianity did not improve matters. Although women were credited with a soul equal to men's in the eyes of God, they were regarded as temptresses, responsible for the fall of Adam.

The plebeians and slaves were descended through their

mothers; the Patricians through their fathers.

About half of the population were slaves. The government did not have income tax they depended on special duties payable when one freed slaves and customs duties. Why they built aqueducts instead of underground pipes I will never understand. But cheap slave labour reduces the profitability of invention.

Finally the civilisation of pagan Rome was overthrown by Alaric the Christian barbarian, but a worthless currency was contributory - all the gold had gone to China to pay for silk and china -.

S L A V E R Y

As a result of the Agricultural Revolution, men learnt to capture and break the spirit of wild animals and turn them into beasts of burden. It was only natural that this skill should be extended to enslaving other humans, and having them as private property.

Ordinary learning has to be repeated regularly and maintained, so it was found as it had been with animals that it was much quicker to teach slaves by traumatic learning processes; these are burned in, in a flash but difficult to adjust if the wrong lesson is learned, defeat in battle is an obvious example, and buttock caning a very successful method because it is reinforced with sexual messages. Oscar Wilde said "Nothing succeeds like excess".

When two groups of hunter gatherers quarrelled over hunting rights or drinking water, each side might consist of 50 people of which only ten on each side were adult males. Frequently one side would back off as a result of a shouting match but even if they did throw stones or hit each other with sticks, they very seldom killed each other, though both sides might suffer cuts and bruises. But with the coming of metal, first bronze, then iron, the death rate in battle increased rapidly. But because of the Agricultural Revolution the overall population increased dramatically. With over crowding, the only satisfactory way, was to kill your enemy, then he never came back to plague you. If you simply killed some; bruised others and let them escape, in a month's time, they were back again fiercer than ever, and then if you didn't kill, you were killed. All the good pacifist tribes died out. *Hunter gatherers never took slaves only settled agriculturists had slaves.*

It is fashionable today to think that slavery is uncivilised but it is *better* than the previous system which was to mass murder every one in the village, just to steal the temple treasure, like the God of Abraham ordered Jacob to do.

But for the Babylonian captivity there would have been no descendants of King David to rear Jesus. Christians should be grateful to the polytheists who were more generous than their beloved *Mass Murderer* Moses who by ordering the murder of women captives, whom his soldiers believed should have been sold as slaves regressed to behaviour that had been outlawed for more than a thousand years in Iran and Egypt. Slavery was not punishment and the conditions of the domestic slave, though terrible to modern man with his high expectations, were similar to the conditions that the owner's wife and children had to put up with. Women were the first slaves. Men were killed. Women can easily reproduce and thus maintain or increase the supply of slaves. For the protection of their children they will cling to slavery. Many fighters decided to surrender when attacked, especially if they were already slaves, true you changed your master but he might be no worse.

The Sumerian word for slave means "woman from a foreign land". I think Mary Astell's exaggeration contains a kernel of truth "If all men are born free, how is it all women are born slaves?"

The most usual way of becoming a slave by capture *seems the most unfair.* But punishment; sale for non-payment of a debt, birth to a slave, or sale by ones parents or a chieftain were other methods of becoming a slave. Hammurabi prescribes death for harbouring a runaway slave and release after three years, for a slave becoming a slave, through debt. The slave is not a human being he is a head like cattle, if you hurt a slave, you owe compensation not to him, but to his master.

Slaves in order to avoid the slave master having the right to kill them said all men are the slaves of God. *This clever trade union trick however still prohibits us from committing suicide because we are not free men who belong to ourselves.*

Tribes *or individuals* who own no property are almost bound to be thieves. Money by metal weight did exist; but there were insufficient coins for slaves to be paid weekly wages. Increases in the money supply did more to stop slavery than Christian love and sympathy. Slaves could find a place in society doing boring repetitive work in the fields which were local and easy to supervise and men when starving could sell themselves for life to a landlord for the promise of food. Slavery may be bad but death is worse. It does mean today that there are still genetic descendants of those loving mothering people who first created languages and writing and civilized the world with their ideas of private property. But it was this very idea of private property that helped the idea of slavery. The strong seized the goods of the weak and less capable and instead of killing them, made a disarmament or slave contract with them. Both sides gained by the reduction in effort required for defence and predation. *But though I approve of contracts, even when they are between people of unequal wealth, I do not approve of the slave contract because of the element of coercion through violence.* Working on galleys, on plantations and particularly down mines are particularly in-human forms of slavery. The Pharaoh of Egypt owned all the slaves in Egypt. In the silver mines in Athens, slaves worked naked and chained. In some mines they never saw the light of day they simply exchanged excavated silver bearing rock for food at the gated entrance to the cave. There were forty thousand slaves in the silver mines of New Carthage.

Roman slavery was very organised. In the unlikely event that a slave was needed in the army, he would be freed. Roman slaves could own property and purchase their freedom. A Roman slave engaging in business e.g. banking had to pay his master for the privilege. But who ever heard of an American negro slave owning a bank! Classical slavery was much milder than Christian Ante Bellum American slavery where ownership of property and learning to read and write and get married were all prohibited. Classical slaves wore no special form of dress and often did the same work as free men. In general craftsmen were not slaves but could be. Greek architects and sculptors often were slaves and it did not stop some of the finest architecture in the world being built.

There were very few slave revolts. Lots of people die when armies fight but the death toll through slavery was minimal. 73 - 71 BC a Roman army deserter who was enslaved for punishment, called Spartacus led a successful revolt but his army of slaves did not want to go back to their homelands and leave Italy so they were captured and six thousand were crucified along the Apian way but this is minor compared with the number of harmless children Moses murdered. Later in more stable times when prices for slaves rose because they had to be taken from beyond the Rhine, it became sensible to breed them and treat them better.

Florentius a 2nd century Roman lawyer reflecting the view of Stoics and Cynics said that slavery was against natural law, but nobody especially the Christians wanted to stop it. Antonio Pius 138 - 161 AD ruled that killing a slave was homicide but Constantine the Christian Emperor 306 - 337 AD absolved the master if it was due to flogging. In latter-day Roman law, there was no slavery for debt. But debt bondage including third persons left as security for debt was common in S.E. Asia until quite recently.

Russian serfs were not slaves, it was merely to avoid theft and nomadic vandalism that serfs were restricted to one parish and were not allowed to travel outside their village, this no doubt worked alright when they had a choice of employers, say ten different farmers, but when all the land belonged to one large land owner they were trapped in a monopoly.

Corvée is a better system; they had it in ancient Egypt. It meant that a free citizen had to do a sort of National Service, unpaid labour on the roads say for three weeks a year. It had to be unpaid because there were insufficient coins in the world to pay him.

Black slavery in America, from Africa, was started by a petition from Bartolome' de Los Casas, Roman Catholic Bishop of Chiapas to the Spanish King Charles I in 1517. Colossal numbers were being transported by the 1690s. Slavery in North America started in 1619 with a Dutch boatload; by 1681 there were a total of 2,000 slaves and 6,000 indentured Europeans. In 1754 there were 263,000 slaves and in 1860 4,441,830. In all 15 million blacks were taken to the Western Hemisphere. Countries ruled from Europe were not as gentle as classical slavery, but were much gentler than independent colonies which loved their own freedom. The Protestants in North America were *beastly*, they prohibited marriage and some States made manumission [freedom for good service] illegal. But despite the average new slave committing suicide within seven years, some must have liked it for they served in the confederate forces, and did not shoot their own officers but shot the Yankees who were trying to free them!

Except in Haiti, which is not notable for it's economic or cultural success, slaves have never thrown off slavery, their freedom has always been returned to them by the super rich. *Thus if we are to learn from history, we must increase the wealth of the super rich, rather than redistribute wealth equally, if we believe in moral improvement.* Wilberforce lived on unearned income all his life. *Trade Unions would never have freed the slaves.* Quakers [Society of Friends] started a campaign in 1783 against slavery, and a society for the abolition of slavery was founded in 1787.

Louis XVI wished to tax his aristocrats (2% of the population who were exempt from tax and owned 1/3 of France) to pay for the American war of independence, they forced him to convene the Estates general in 1789. The workers were organised by the aristocrats to start the revolution and to abolish slavery, but the revolution got out of hand, and Napoleon reintroduced slavery so the French did not abolish it until 1848. The trade across the ocean was abolished in 1807. England and America abolished it in 1833, but 50,000 slaves a year were still being transported by international trade as late as 1850. Pregnant slaves when they were beaten in the fields had a depression specially hollowed in the earth under them so that the valuable master's baby was not killed, and grandmothers to this day in Jamaica, look after the babies rather than the mothers because the masters could not spare the young slaves. But awful as slavery was, the Jews must have preferred the Babylonian captivity to Hitler's Germany, and the abused American Negroes are now the richest group of Blacks in the world. Incidentally the use of the Latin word 'Negro' was introduced to show them respect, together with its derivative nigger, rather than use the English word 'black' which they now prefer.

In 1919 efforts were made to suppress slave raiding in Africa for slavery in a number of Moslem countries. The international Labour Convention of 1930 weakened it by allowing compulsory enslavement of conscientious objectors to National Service. Ethiopia was the last country to abolish black slavery in 1942. The third Reich had 9½ million slaves in 1943.

I personally hate slavery but submission is very popular, it is still retained for children, National Service, and marriage. People love quick reactions even if it is a beating, it is better than being unnoticed. The need to submit to something more powerful than ones self is a part of the human psyche whether it is to drugs like tea or a mythical God. The Moslem religion is growing because of love of the great slave master Allah with his scourge.

MOSLEMS

The Shalman Rushdie affair shows that Moslems are too immature to permit criticism. So if this is the end of this chapter, it shows that my publishers censored it in fear.

Islam is an Arabic word for "submission to God". There is no Islamic Pope.

Respectable God fearing Arabs were very backward and cut off from the news, even of Mohenjodaro 2,000 years earlier, which is why the Koran says "Henceforth you shall not marry the women who were married to your fathers. That was an evil practice, innocent and abominable" 4 22. The Jews, living at the trade cross roads of the civilised world benefited from Zoroastrianism and so had the best 'memes', but they restricted it to people who could prove that they were genealogically Jewish. *The Arabs in order to use their religion pretended that they were related,* but the Jews would not give them equality, so Mohammed born circa 570 AD waged Jihad against the Jews in Medina, beat them, decapitated their men folk (save one who converted) in the public square and divided women, children, animals and property among his followers and *stole their religious ideas. This shows that he was a murderer, and a thief who believes in slavery for women and children.*

The Moslems, Jews and Christians are very anti nakedness, whereas the Jains and Greeks were proud of their bodies and liked to show them. However the worship of Allah with his slave owner whip despite coming from a poor country is still growing. faster than Christianity which also borrowed the Jewish religion, *but the addition of Jesus got them in a muddle which is revealed by* the Koran saying that Jesus' says "Take me and my mother as two Gods besides God", *which summarises the Christian Trinity rather well.* Allah returned to the more logical and simpler idea of one God.

The Koran describes Allah as a *bullying* slave master with a scourge who *hypocritically* repeatedly tells one he is merciful. Ordinary Gods can live alongside each other, but when there is only one, *he gets so jealous that he encourages his adherents to murder the followers of other Gods,* this is particularly true of Mohammed who executed all the Jews, 800 of them, in Medina and married Rihana one of the pretty widows, later he executed another Jew to marry his widow. He allowed the Jews to live in foreign countries but made them pay higher taxes and prohibited them moving about. *Treating them this way, it is hardly surprising that his Koran is the most muddled repetitious book that I have ever read, with less order than my discarded notes. He muddles up Moses' sister with the mother of Jesus!*

Believing themselves to be descendants of Abraham, the Koran 6 84 says of the incestuous "Lot we exalted above our creatures". They are followers of the mass murderer Moses, and believe in the Jewish Talmud text "Happy is he whose children are male and woe to him whose children are female." The Koran teaches that "[for none is secure from the punishment of the Lord]; who {do not} restrain their carnal desire [save with their wives and slave girls, for these are lawful to them: he that lusts after other than these is a transgressor];"....."On the nose we will brand him" "You shall not force your slave girls into prostitution in order that you make money, *[O.K if you do not make money out of it?]* if they wish to preserve their chastity *[O.K. if they do not?]* If any one compels them Allah will be forgiving and merciful to them." *[No mention of punishment for their pimps].* "Men have authority over women because Allah has made the one superior to the other....Good women are obedient. They guard their unseen parts....As for those you fear will be disobedient, admonish them and send them to beds apart and beat them." Koran 4 34. "Women are your fields: go, then, into your fields as you please." "Keep aloof from women during their menstrual periods." Today Iranian girls mainly marry aged 13 & 15. No one can marry anyone who has had the same breast milk, ie adopted children. Children are produced by a prayer to Allah, intercourse is insufficient.

An Iranian acquaintance of mine travelling at 70 mph in a Jaguar through a village at siesta time hit a child which ran out, the driver of a passing lorry saw the accident on the deserted road, and seeing the child raise himself in a daze, took his starting handle and hit the child over the head and demanded money from my acquaintance for concealing the accident. *A society whose morals are such that one can be certain that one will be rewarded by a total stranger for such an act will take 100 years before it can join the human community. Is this the covetousness that Moses objected to? Which prohibited usury and there by delayed civilisation.* "Allah has permitted trading and forbidden usury". Allah is not above trading to have his own way, he knows Hell fire and the scourge are not enough. "Whatever alms you give shall rebound to your own advantage, providing you give them for the love of Allah. "He that does a good deed shall be repaid twofold, Allah will bestow on him rich recompense". "Retaliation is decreed for you in bloodshed: a free man for a free man, a slave for a slave, and a female for a female. Allah knows; you do not." A slave mentality encourages learning by rote.

In the Meccan period Muhammad aged 25 married the twice married widow Khadija, aged 40 whose wealth enabled him not to have to work until she died. She bore him all but one of his children. He had time then to dictate to a scribe (he could not write) the Koran. Aged 50 when she died he married another widow. In the Medinan period when he acquired his own city state, he took a young wife about once a year, and had nine when he died aged 62. The Angel Gabriel revealed an unclothed Ayesha aged 6 to Muhammad aged 50. When his third marriage was consummated, she was nine years old; his libido soared from the "least of men to the strength of 40". She teased her conjugal rivals that she was the favourite because she alone had been virgin, and the Prophet preferred "to eat fruit from trees un-grazed".

Because there was no law of primogeniture, Muhammad II issued the Law of Fratricide; Kings must murder their brothers in order to avoid civil war.

The Moslem beliefs make it easy for *evil* men to raise armies and start a war, which they say Allah has ordered them to do. "Fighting is obligatory for you, much as you dislike it, but you may hate a thing, although it is good for you, and love a thing although it is bad for you." *It appeals to people who like to be told what to do because they are too lazy to think.* The Moslem only has to say it is 'Jihad' and his soldiers know that providing they die with their wounds to the front they will automatically go to Paradise, where each man is allotted 72 black eyed Houris, to give him sexual pleasure when he is dead, their hymens are renewed each time they are f***ed, like the Virgin Mary they will remain perpetually virgin. Since these Houris are slaves who he may f*** at any time, this means that their hymens heal immediately after each session, so that they can dirty the bed linen each time with blood. It is a perpetually painful and messy business for them, *but who cares they are only female.*

The Koran has Mary the mother of Jesus brought up by Zacharias father of St. John. 3.36. Allah said 'be' and created Jesus out of dust like Adam. "You sometime see the earth dry and barren but no sooner do we send down rain upon it, but it begins to stir and swell, putting forth every kind of radiant bloom. That is because Allah is truth: He gives life to the dead...." Mohammed seems to think that this is proof that the resurrection will come.

I may not be as intelligent or have as good a memory as Buddha, Jesus or Mohammed, but because I am living more than a thousand years later, *I do know more about every subject than any of them ever did,* so *there is a good chance that my ideas are more likely to be correct.* By giving to Orbis (An international Charity) I have cured more blind people than Jesus ever did.

Waris Dirie an upper class Somalian girl has had published by Virago "Desert Children". From it one learns that 135 million females have suffered FGM (Female Genital Mutilation) i.e. they have had their clitorises cut off and many their labia as well; many just before they are given as brides in order to stop them enjoying sex. Two million female non-adults are operated on every year, and a quarter of them die of the operation. There are half a million in Europe and 100,000 in England. It was made illegal in Britain in 1985, but not one person so far has been prosecuted for it. After all Christians don't like talking about such things, so it is all hushed up.

I believe that this is a far greater crime than unloading under age pornographic images from the internet, on to one's computer. I am not recommending paedophilia, but putting a penis up an arsehole especially if it is lubricated is not very painful, some grown ups enjoy it. If the child is very small and it is done frequently it may make it difficult for the child to retain diarrhoea. And I believe even the circumcision of men, the cutting off of one third of the sexual nerve endings of the penis, which is legal is more wicked than buggery as it gives no pleasure to anyone.

I believe that all Muslims entering Great Britain should be made to swear by Allah that they will not only not practise FGM either in England or abroad, but report their fellow country men who practise it.

Moses coincided with the invention of writing, Mohammed with the invention of paper, and Protestantism with the invention of printing. What will IT, Information Technology bring us? The 'God' Card?

CHAPTER VII
JESUS' HISTORICAL BACKGROUND

WRITERS:- FARRAR, JOSEPHUS, SCHONFIELD.

I now comment on three very different writers versions of the events.

Frederic W. Farrar, D.D. F.R.S. fellow of Trinity Cambridge, Chaplain to Queen Victoria, wrote The Life of Christ, a bumper best seller, built on years of scholarship, in which he gives a literal interpretation to every phrase in the Gospels and refuses to admit a single lie or inconsistency.

For example because the gospel stories do not exactly correspond, he has Jesus suffer seven separate trials! He rails at the pomposity of the Pharisees *but his own exceeds theirs.* He is THE ultra conservative Christian. He is very erudite and pro Jesus, but says "letters he has never learned". *Yet Jesus wrote one word in the sand, so I think he could write. He might have been too lazy to write a book, or his hands might have been damaged on the cross.* Since Mary could read; after all she had been brought up in the Temple, *she would have been a slut if she had not taught him.* However elsewhere Farrar says Mary had read the scriptures and goes on to agree with me in the following passage. "Now, the acquisition of writing by a young Jewish woman, adds to proofs already suggested, that Mary was in respectable circumstances, and had received a liberal education; for we are not to attribute to those times, and to that country, the same diffusion of knowledge as obtains among ourselves. Writing and reading were rare among men, much more rare among women; the possession of them seems decisive against the poverty which some have unwittingly attached to our Lord and his parents."

Farrar is naive he thinks that because evil befalls a man, this is proof of his wickedness, he will not allow Annas to be a good man despite the historian Josephus's good report, but says he is a bad man because his family is punished decades after his death by Zealots. But he is inconsistent for he says Nicodemus, who helps bury Jesus, is a good man despite the following quotation. "If he is Nakdimon in the Talmud; he outlived the fall of Jerusalem and his family was reduced from great wealth, to such horrible poverty, that whereas the bridal bed of his daughter had been covered with a dower of 12,000 denarii's, she was subsequently seen endeavouring to support life by picking the grains from the ordure of cattle in the streets".

Farrar says pages 146-9 "'Destroy' He said 'this Temple, and in three days I will raise it up'. ....'But he spake' says St. John, 'of the temple of his body',....when Jesus lay dead....they came to Pilate....'Sir, we remember what that deceiver said, while he was yet alive, "After three days I will arise again." Now there is no trace that Jesus had ever used any such words distinctly to them;....for over the slow hearts of the apostles these words of our Lord seem to have passed like an idle wind. ....How came these Pharisees and Priests to understand better than his own disciples what our Lord meant?" See my fiction for the answer.

The following will also be interpreted later in the book. "To the viper brood of Annas" and his children who make one of the great Roman fortunes by owning a monopoly of all the four shops approached by the bridge over the Kidron to the two cedars of Olivet. He says their prices are 250 times too much, especially the selling of doves. Farrar & Taanith IV.8

JOSEPHUS

Flavius Josephus was born in Jerusalem in 37/38 AD, a few years after John the Baptist's execution and Jesus' crucifixion. All his writings are pre 93 AD and he died in 100 AD. He was a Roman citizen and a very devout Pharisee, who was abandoned by his first wife, divorced a second one with three children and married a third. He was a very reliable historian; *in my opinion much neglected because Christians are embarrassed at the way early Christian liars altered his text.* He was originally a Jewish nationalist but when captured he told Vespasian the local commander in chief that he would rule Palestine and be the Messiah and, in a very short time this prophesy became virtually true. Vespasian became Emperor of Rome conquered Britain and built the coliseum in Rome and was regarded as The God. He remained friends with Josephus, but this may make his very accurate history occasionally distorted in order to protect nationalist identities and flatter Rome. While in Palestine Vespasian left the Christians alone but ordered the arrest of all royal descendants of David. Josephus approved of Herod the Great having

10 wives, against Roman Law, but was against pagan customs. He wrote a lot of long histories; everyone is there Pilate, St John the Baptist, Annas, his sons, James the brother of Jesus and numerous prophets who claimed that they could call down divine intervention and had considerable followings, such as Theudas 44-46 AD. He also reports on some impostors and deceivers who pretend to have miraculous talents when Felix governed 52-60 AD; he includes St. Paul amongst them.

He confirms Matthew's report of the census in Bethlehem. "Quirinius had now liquidated the estate of Archelaus; and by this time the registrations of property that took place in the thirty-seventh year after Caesar's defeat of Antony at Actium were complete *[6-7 AD]*. Since the high priest Joazar had now been overpowered by a popular faction, Quirinius stripped him of the dignity of his office and installed Ananus the son of Seth as high priest. Meanwhile, Herod and Phillip." *[Note how Herod Antipas is simply called Herod, because his father is dead], it could be this Herod that is responsible for the massacre of the innocents.*

Jesus is there too, but the bits that relate to him are obvious forgeries, there are three versions in different languages. All the other parts of the book can be translated from one language to another with no difficulty, but not so the passages about Jesus, they are different in length and content and are all out of keeping with Josephus' Pharisaic beliefs which are obvious throughout everything else he has written. Origen an Alexandrian scholar explicitly states 280 AD that Josephus did not believe Jesus was the Messiah. However, Eusebius a bishop in 324 records a glowing worshipful passage about Christ.

R, Eisler in 1931 AD through a linguistic tour de force comes up with this probable translation of this paragraph that has been altered by three different glosses. "Now about this time there arose a man [an occasion for new disturbances] a certain Jesus, a wizard of a man, if indeed he may be called a man [who was the most monstrous of all men, whom his disciples call a son of God, as having done wonders such as no man hath ever done].... He was in fact a teacher of astonishing tricks to such men as accept the abnormal with delight....And he seduced many Jews and many of the Greek nation, and [was regarded by them as] the Messiah.....And when on the indictment of the principal men among us, Pilate had sentenced him to the cross, still those who before had admired him did not cease [to rave]. For it seemed to them that having been dead for three days, he had appeared to them alive again, as the divinely inspired prophets had foretold - these and ten thousand other wonderful things concerning him. And even now the race of those who are called "Messianists" after him is not extinct." Nearly every scholar writing since 1931 includes this quote, if they are Christian they tuck it in a footnote but it seems generally approved.

Josephus [XVII] says in the time of Herod; *before Jesus was born.* "And so Judea was filled with brigandage. Anyone might make himself King as the head of a band of rebels whom he fell in with, and then would press on to the destruction of the community but causing trouble to few Romans and only to a small degree, but bringing the greatest slaughter upon their own people."

Varus a Roman governor of Syria 6-4 BC crucified 2,000 people. So a generation later Jesus plus two Zealots hardly makes news, and a generation after Jesus 70 AD a million people are killed in the destruction of Jerusalem.

DOCTOR HUGH J. SCHONFIELD

Doctor Schonfield in the Passover Plot argues that Christ did not die on the cross and gives good background information on Christ's time. He regards the fact that the Jews believed they were 'chosen people' as their most important belief, and that the Messiah was due about 46 BC. Christ is Greek for Messiah and means no more, and earlier he says it means anointed one. If Jesus had said he was God the punishment would have been stoning not the cross.

He says "Scholars have noted the dynamic purposefulness of Jesus.... confidently following a formula set down in an authoritative text book.... He says and does things quite unexpected by his intimate associates, which take them by surprise or which they are unable to fathom.... His visualisation of the role of Messiah was highly theatrical, and he played out the part like an actor with careful timing and an appreciation of what every act called for."

He thinks, that John 'the Beloved' disciple, is the only one that knows what is going on, he knew about Judas Iscariot and where the trials were being held. After the arrest, John who was a kinsman of Annas, followed Christ to Annas' palace and admitted Peter who was hanging about outside denying Christ. Stories in the gospels show that Jesus makes secret arrangements, which were so vital that he did not disclose them to his closest disciples, i.e. in Luke, Peter and John the sons of Zeberdee, are to follow a man with a water pot to the house were Jesus would celebrate the Last Super *before the Passover*. "It is difficult to avoid concluding that the omission in the synoptic tradition of all knowledge of the mysterious disciple was intentional". "But it would seem as if the sources did not wish to disclose why JESUS had turned to others rather than the twelve".

In the following fiction I intend to bring all these strands of information together and make non-miraculous sense out of the gospels, and give a raison d'etre for the birth of Christianity, by finding the natural father and promoter of Jesus.

ITEMS IN JESUS' HISTORICAL BACKGROUND

ALEXANDER THE GREAT.

Alexander the Great conquered the known world because his officer ranks were predetermined so that if a leader was killed in battle everyone knew who replaced him; the Persians did not have this, so if their commander was killed their troops deserted. Alexander turned the hordes of precious metals that he captured into coins stamped with his Godhead on. He used it to pay his soldiers and buy from the local farmers the food they ate. Darius just let his troops steal their food. The new money re-circulated quickly and made trade everywhere possible, thus reinforcing Greek culture. With the result that many of the people he conquered preferred him to their rightful leaders. He also left behind a superior alphabetic language, which superseded the local vernaculars to such an extent that the Five Books of Moses were translated into Greek in the 3rd cent. BC. It is called the Septuagint because 70 scholars translated it.

In 322 BC Alexander the Great, conquered Israel where he created 29 cities in Palestine [the land of the Philistines]. He then went on to conquer Egypt where the God Amon told him that he was the son of Zeus and therefore a God, because his mother kept a snake in her bed [which the Delphic oracle had said was Zeus]. The official virginity of his mother, was helpful in proving Alexander's divinity, [despite Olympia's reputation of not behaving like a bashful virgin and having a husband.] There is a body of literature showing how Hercules and Alexander were both 'wonder workers', [a contemporary phrase for one who cures the sick and the blind]. Historians writing about Alexander the Great never take the fact that he miraculously cured blind men and was a God very seriously. Jesus was another, virgin born, wonder worker, descended from a king. *What's the difference?*

After his death Alexander's empire was split, first the Ptolemies a Greek family ruled Egypt and Palestine and then in 198 BC the Selucids extended Syria to include Palestine. They converted the temple in Jerusalem into a shrine to Zeus Olympus complete with ritual prostitution, and abolished the Sabbath and the Jewish religion in 175 -168 BC. Death was the punishment for mothers who had their children circumcised and for owning any of the books of Moses. *After all the Mosaic message is only a licence to plunder cities.* The priests did not mind, they preferred the Gymnasium to the temple. 28 cities in Palestine remained independently Greek.

THE MESSIAHS

In 166 BC Judas Maccabeus who believed he was the Messiah, foretold by Daniel. His father thought of himself as the High Priest, despite the abolition of the Jewish religion. In the Passover Plot on page 28 it says that during this period several thousand Sadducees, Pharisees and Essenes claimed to be the Messiah, Alexander Janneus 104-78 BC grandson of Judas Maccabeus crucified 800 Jewish prisoners at an entertainment and killed their wives and children before their eyes, he was a Pharisee.

Maccabeus led a successful revolt against the Macedonian Selucids. In 164 BC he founded the Hasmonean dynasty. His success confirmed that civic rulers should be frightened of Messiahs and that he was "The Messiah". *The word Messiah must have had the meaning of 'patriotic murderer'*, but no Christian would agree with me. 'Messiah' when translated into Greek means 'King'. The

Messiah would be a new King and son of David.

The Jews still celebrate an eight-day festival, Chanukkah, concerning a miracle with oil similar to Jesus' miracle with wine. The Pharisees a new group backed the Maccabean revolt. They were very patriotic and against the spread of the world culture of Helenisation. John Hyrcanus 135-104 BC converted non-Jews and the people of Idumaea by force, killing those refusing circumcision. John Hyrcanus II appealed to Rome for help, against internal groups who did not want him as High Priest and King. Pompey was invited in and in 63 BC conquered Jerusalem and made it part of the Roman colony of Syria. John Hyrcanus II continued to rule as Ethnarch [High Priest] until he was executed in 30 BC for treason.

In Turkey Apollonius Tyana was a Messiah and God who healed the sick and wounded, some writers think Jesus modelled his behaviour on him.

In AD 135 the Jews believed that Simon bar Kokba who was descended of King David was a much more important Messiah than Jesus. He believed in patriotism *the most evil idea known to man, "my country right or wrong"*. He was offended by the Romans building a temple on the old temple mount to Jupiter, and raised a revolt; with guerrilla warfare he destroyed a Roman legion and temporarily drove the Romans out of Israel. As a result the Roman Emperor Hadrian killed large numbers of Jews and prohibited all uncircumcised persons to live in Israel in 138 AD. Don't forget that *Jews called* Christians by Nero had burnt Rome in 64 AD. *So the Jews have virtually no rights to return 1,850 years later.*

The Christians in order to avoid being killed had to make it clear they were not patriots, and since most Gods are local and patriotic; Christianity was able to spread throughout the world.

PHARISEES AND SCRIBES

The Pharisees [the translation of the word means separatists] were a pious group within the scribes and were supported by subsistence farmers, and small city traders. They favoured Moses' oral law, as opposed to his written law. They believed in providential guidance of the universe, in angels, in reward and punishment, in the world to come, and in the resurrection of the dead. At the time of Christ, they were in opposition to the Hellenised Sadducees who had all the ecclesiastical power and the Herodians and Romans who had all the political power. The Pharisees were not the establishment, they were the out of office opposition who despised the poor and were jealous of the rich and educated Sadducees. They were democratic but despised the rabble that did not know the law. *They were middle class, they could read and write* [scribe] *but they were narrow minded, legalistic, nit picking people who gave a very literal interpretation to the Old Testament* in particular to the prophetic books. Luke says Jesus dined with the Pharisees 7.36, 11.37, 14.1.

The Pharisees aimed at the sanctification of daily life by new rules. The Shammai Pharisees the majority were against Jesus, the Hillel ones more sympathetic. The Pharisees believed that one should do nothing on the Sabbath. No one must write, carry anything, not even a ribbon or a false tooth, the sick must die rather than send for a physician, so they told Jesus to stop his miracles, *but Jesus got a better class of observer on the Sabbath and the restrictions on travel meant that he was less likely to be found out.* Some Pharisees about the time of Christ shut their eyes in the street, so that they would not be defiled by seeing a woman, this was a frightful nuisance they kept bumping into things and had to be led around by small children. The Shammai sect was in favour of a literal interpretation of Moses, women could only be divorced for fornication or "a matter of nakedness" *only they did not know what that phrase meant.* Obviously if your new bride had spots, the first time you saw her naked, that would be a matter of nakedness. Whereas Hillel's school thought you could divorce your wife on the grounds that you had found a prettier woman provided you treated everybody properly.

After the destruction of the Temple the Herodians, the Pharisees and the Pauline Chritians were the only people the Romans were willing to live with. The Sicarii and Jamesian Christians (James was Jesus' brother) were cast out. Hillel's descendants became after the destruction of the Temple the leaders of Pharisaic or Rabbinic Judaism.

The Scribes were literate but uneducated, they were copyists and incapable of lateral thinking they were socially inferior to the Pharisees.

THE RABBIS

Rabbis are lay teachers who have studied the law, and they became important after the sack of Jerusalem and the abolition of the Jewish priesthood by the Romans in AD 70. Having no Temple, they did not continue with blood sacrifices, the expert priests were mainly dead. The Gospels were all written after this date and long after The Crucifixion. They represent the Pharisaic view, which is why Christians erroneously think that the Pharisees at the time of Christ were the establishment. Nowadays they have studied the Talmud and some are paid. The Mishna a legal interpretation of the Torah; was written by Judah 175-220 AD; he was the son of Gamaliel II, of the house of Hillel, a descendent of King David. The Mishna says, "Do not show kindness to gentiles." It became the Jews most important book together with two Talmuds, which are commentaries on the Mishna.

In general, through out history, the Rabbis were literate but poorly educated men *whose horizons were limited to the Talmud.* To be a Rabbi they have to marry, but all Holy men are only allowed to f*** on Fridays. *Their attitude is legalistic, bureaucratic and narrow-minded.* For example, today, they prohibit Jews marrying in Israel who have lost any of their written records proving that they are Jews in the last four generations, with the result that refugees have to marry in Christian Churches. If a Jew marries a Christian, or a Moslem, or if they marry in Cyprus; their children are illegitimate. They persist in the right of the brother to f*** his brother's wife when he is dead. Women do not own their bodies they are the property of their dead husband's brother. Jesus says that he is the Messiah to a Samaritan woman at a well, a Rabbi is shocked *not because he is claiming to be a God but because one shouldn't talk to women in public.* Under Jewish Mishnaic Law "an unmarried man may not be a teacher". Since Jesus is referred to as a Rabbi, *this means he was married.*

THE ESSENES

The mystic Essenes formed closed communities with simple living and rigid discipline [like Monks]. They shared all property in common and would not marry but kept their numbers up by adopting children. Journalists believe that the Dead Sea Scrolls c200 BC to 70 AD are the product of an Essene scriptorium, but the copper scroll reveals that they are simply part of the Temple library hidden at the time of the destruction of the temple. The final form of the Old Testament was created from many writings long after Jesus was dead. The Dead Sea Scrolls record two Messiahs, the priestly one, called the Teacher of Righteousness, of Aaron's line being superior to the royal one of David's line. *Nobody knows who the secretive Messiah of Righteousness was,* but every one is agreed that he lived in a different generation and was not Jesus. *The man, who I describe in the next chapter, was also secretive, showing that it was not unknown behaviour at that time. I doubt if these two secretive men were the same man, but it would neither strengthen nor decrease my belief that my hero was the natural father of Jesus.*

The Qumran faction that started in 150 BC, were Gnosticising Pharisees. Joseph with the child Jesus when they lived in *Alexandria,* Egypt might have become acquainted with the Therapeutae, who were a group similar to the Essenes but less nationalistic. The Essenes valued death, if it came with honour more than longevity; they despised danger and conquered pain by sheer will power. Some believed they could foretell the future. They taught about medicinal roots and stones and how to really hate the wicked, and to co-operate with the good. They believed rulers were especially good, because God conferred their power on them. *[The divine right of kings.]* Manaemus an Essene who said he could foresee the future prophesied that Herod would be king. As a result Herod gave privileges to the Essenes. *St. John the Baptist might have been an Essene.*

T H E   Z E A L O T S

The word in Greek means jealousy, enmity and rebellion. The names Galilean, Messianic, Sicarii and Zealot all refer to groups who shared many members. Judah of Galilee (Judas) founded the Galileans in 6 AD to protest against the Census. Jesus is said to be a Galilean. The Zealots and the Sicarii believed it right to kill people who refused to be circumcised. Because according to the Law of Moses you can not be saved if you are uncircumcised. *(Before the invention of paper it was your National Passport.)* The Zealots were against paying tax to Rome, on the grounds that God alone was master, they believed in the coming of the Messiah (the Greek translation is King) and plotted to overthrow Roman rule. The movement was partially responsible for Archelaus being exiled. This allowed the High Priests to greatly increase their power. It also explains why the Roman Emperors quickly became Gods and Vespasian worked miracles. Josephus describes the Zealots as a mixture of brigands and philosophers, who were undoubtedly religious nationalists. They were zealous, like the Pharisees for the Torah.

Barrabas; the robber leader who was arrested at the same time as Jesus Christ and then released; his first name was Jesus and this could have caused some confusion especially as Barrabas means "Son of the father". A 'robber' to a Roman, did not mean a house thief but was a pejorative word for a Zealot or nationalist disturber of Roman law and order. It is possible that, he had led a public protest and had damaged some public works as a protest against Pilate's illegal use of temple funds to provide a clean water supply.

The Sicarii murder the High Priest Jonathan, who was Chaiphas' brother-in-law and brother to Ananas the high priest who has James; Jesus Christ's brother killed. Robert Furneaux says that the apostle Mark conceals the fact that Simon one of the apostles is a Zealot; and that the two robbers crucified with Jesus were Zealots. The Sicarii [Assassins] so called because of the two daggers [sica] they carried became prominent in c.54 AD as a group of bandits who kidnapped or murdered those who had found a modus vivendi with the Romans. Because Jesus says two swords [sica] are enough, just before Peter cuts off Malchus' ear. He thinks that makes Jesus and Peter, Zealots. Iscariot he believes is a corruption of 'sicarii', which makes Judas another one.

Nero said the Christians burned Rome, he was probably partially right, they were led no doubt by Jewish Sicarii. The Zealots became such a nuisance that Rome had to kill more than a million people and totally destroy the temple at Jerusalem and move the capital, to Caesarea. Finally the Zealots committed suicide at Massada. 74 AD

The SAMARITANS

The Samaritans were a mixture of native North Israelites and gentile deportees settled by the Assyrians in the erstwhile Northern Kingdom, while the Jews were in slavery. The Northern Kingdom did not look on Jerusalem as the capital. In fact, the break with the Jews did not occur until the conquest of Shechem by John Hyrcanus 128 BC.

Jesus originally sent forth his disciples with *racist* instructions to confine their work to the lost sheep of the house of Israel and not to extend it to the Samaritans or Gentiles. The disciples were not to fear death because God would punish their enemies and reward them. Later, in the Parable of the Good Samaritan, Christians say he attacked racism. *I think he needed their support* because Galilee is separated from Jerusalem, by Samaria, and he had to walk through this foreign province. Like the Sadducees they refused to recognise the validity of the oral law beloved of the Pharisees, and *he hoped to encourage them to worship in the new temple at Jerusalem, because their temple was a small useless ruin.*

THE DIASPORA

[The spread of the Jews to other countries]

The following numbers are at the time of Christ before the Romans destroyed the Temple in Jerusalem in AD 70 which only added to the Diaspora. One tenth of the Mediterranean peoples were Jewish. There were 6 or 7 million Jews in the Roman Empire with another 1 million outside in Babylon and Parthia but only 2½ million in Palestine. There were more Jews than Greeks and probably more Jews were literate, but they were literate in Greek. For example the 8,000 to 50,000 Jews in Rome could not speak Hebrew they spoke Greek, there were 200,000 to 1,000,000 Jews in Alexandria in Egypt.

Now there are 3 times as many Jews in the United States as there are in Israel, and New York has more than there are in Israel.

HILLEL AND GAMALIEL

Hillel was born in Babylon 75 BC, came to Jerusalem in 36 BC and became Nasi [head of the Sanhedrin, the Sadducee ecclesiastical court] 30 BC. However he was a Pharisee. He died in 10 BC.

He taught "Do not do to others that which you would not have them do to you" long before Jesus Christ was born who revised the saying making it more positive. But the idea occurs in Isaiah LXI i 3 in the 5th century, who shows an interest in the poor. Other quotes by Hillel from the Talmud are "Love peace and pursue it at any cost", "Remember it is better to be persecuted than to persecute" Derech Erets Rab ii. Reenan and Geiger, Frankfort Rabbis describe Jesus as a pupil of good Hillel and said Jesus had no new thoughts. Hillel said "What is unpleasing to you, do not do to your neighbour, that is the whole law". Herod favoured Hillel.

His son was called Gamaliel, who spoke up for Jesus Christ during his trial. Acts 5 34. He also defends and obtains St.Peter's release before Annas, Caiaphas and the Sadducees.

His grandson, *who I will call Gamaliel 'II'*, was also his pupil and preached love. However he thought the Christians were heretics because they ran away from fighting the Romans but thought they should not be persecuted because since they were not divinely inspired their movement would die out naturally.

The Jesus who became the High Priest for a few months in 64 AD was Gamaliel II's son, *had he lasted longer the Temple at Jerusalem might never have been demolished and Christianity would have had a rival established religion of love, to contend with.* Another son was Judah who wrote the Mishna. The family are all highly regarded by the Jews today. They were a breakaway group of intellectual Pharisees who had very little power in their day, which was in the hands of the Sadducees. They believed in love thy neighbour and they thought of it before Christ did. The scholar rabbis who read their books in later generations respected them, long after the selfish children of Annas, the Sadducees and the hated conventional Pharisees had been wiped out, and the Romans had levelled the temple. One of Gamaliel's disciples, after both Jesus Christ and Hillel *were dead*, Rabbi Ben Zakkai foretold the destruction of the Temple in Jerusalem, before it happened in the Jewish war. He pretended to die and was resurrected and continued the Sanhedrin after the fall of Jerusalem and so managed to preserve the Jewish religion.

St Stephen was a Christian deacon, a Hellenised Jew who studied at the feet of Gamaliel. He *invented* the *idea of* the second coming of Jesus and was impertinent to the Pharisees. He was the first Christian Martyr. He is often depicted as a sort of Holy pincushion with arrows sticking out of him.

S T .   P A U L

St Paul [Saul] was also a pupil of the Pharisee Gamaliel. St Paul was commissioned by Ciaphas, the ex High Priest who condemned Jesus, to persecute the followers of Jesus. He was an onlooker who encouraged the stoning of St. Stephen, the first Christian martyr. Paul suffered from epilepsy, *which is probably why* he fell off his horse on his way to Damascus, *and to save his embarrassment he turned it into* a blinding light, *which helped him to explain his change of mind.* He announced that Jesus Christ and God the Father had commissioned him. *Was Jesus still alive?* Five years after Jesus' crucifixion.

In 39 AD he began his missionary journeys and visited Ephesus and Corinth several times. Paul told James the brother of Christ that Jesus was the Messiah; there is no record of disagreement. One might have expected an elder brother who knew how naughty his younger brother had been to object. Paul expected an imminent Parousia [second coming of Christ] so he preferred the status quo, why for instance abolish slavery, he had no time to get married, but conceded that marriage could prevent fornication. He said 'Let your women keep silence in the churches: for it is not permitted unto them to speak: but they are commanded to be under obedience, as also saith the law. And if they will learn anything let them ask their husbands at home.... It is a shame to hear them speak.' He found orgiastic ritual repugnant which was common in the Hellenic world. He may have started the fashion for early Christian Saints to have anorexia nervosa, especially the women so they would be clean of menstrual blood. *Jesus never said f***ing was for procreation only.* St.Paul praised celibacy, St. Augustine said, "Give me chastity - but not yet," but when old and passed it, thundered against, all kinds of lovemaking. Aquinas made homosexuality the worst sin. St. Jerome described unfortunate women who had died from abortion as "threefold murderesses, as suicides, as adulteresses to Christ and as murderesses of their unborn child". St.Paul said, "Do you not know that bodies are members of Christ? Shall I therefore take the members of Christ and make them members of a prostitute? Never! Do you not know that he who joins himself to a prostitute becomes one body with her? For, as it is written, 'The two shall become one flesh.... know ye not that your body is the temple of the Holy Ghost...and ye are not your own". This explains Jesus' remark about rebuilding the Temple; it was not the temple at Jerusalem but the Greek idea of his own body that he said would be rebuilt. At the council of Jerusalem in 50 AD, Peter and James confirmed St. Paul's idea that the gentile Christians did not need to obey the Mosaic laws of the Jews, or be circumcised. However Robert Eiesenman in "James the brother of Jesus" thinks they quarrelled because *silly* James was a vegetarian and could not sit down with a gentile especially one with a foreskin. Paul did not have a foreskin but he did associate with disgusting people who did. So Paul was arrested in the Temple at Jerusalem, but was rescued by the Roman soldiers who lived in the fortress Tower of Antonia, 300 cubits high, (a cubit is the distance from one's elbow to ones finger tips so it must have been 500 feet high). The tower had been built at the same time as the Temple and next to it, Herod the Great *paid for it* and named it after his friend Mark Antony. The priests had to release St Paul from prison because he was a Roman Citizen and having powerful contacts and relations, several hundred Roman soldiers protected him on the road to Caesarea. He was entitled to be tried in Rome. He died in 60 or 69AD.

S A D D U C E E S

The Sadducees believed in a single Temple and government by hereditary priests. They were mostly landed aristocrats and important priests who were often in the Sanhedrin [the governing ecclesiastical body]. They, not the Pharisees, were the establishment. They didn't believe in the oral laws of Moses, but stuck rigidly to the written laws and ethics, in the ancient books of Moses together with the Book of Decrees, which laid down a system of who were to be stoned, who burned, who beheaded and who strangled by way of punishment. This pleased the Romans, because it made it easier to operate a slave society, *because Moses is so pro-slavery.* The Romans were suspicious of the Pharisee's oral laws, because they could be altered so easily to be nationalist and anti-Roman. *This accommodation with Rome and belief in Quietism, had the unfortunate effect, that they could not add new ideas to their religion, and they therefore appear very old fashioned and stuffy.* They spoke Greek and were thoroughly Hellenised and rational. The Pharisees said they were greedy for gold. Farrar says "The Pharisees...... with their rivals and enemies the Sadducees, that sceptical set, half religious, half political to which at this time the two high priests [ie Annas and Ciaphas] belonged as well as members of the reigning family. The Sadducees were but powerful from wealth and position".

The Sadducees did not believe in angels, immortality, resurrection of the dead or rewards and punishments. They desperately wanted peace at any price but in 59 AD the Sadducees lost their power in the Sanhedrin, and were excluded from the Temple, by the Pharisees and Zealots, the civilised times of the building of the temple and the High Priest Annas were over, ten years later the Romans had to kill a million people, destroy the temple and burn Jerusalem in order to keep order. Because they were wiped out there is no subsequent historian to defend them. The Rabbis are basically Pharisees who altered and preserved the Jewish religion but vilified the dead Sadducee faction. Jesus was not a threat to Sadduceean authority he criticised the Pharisees. The Pharisee Josephus says the Pharisees were more popular than the Sadducees who lacked a popular following but that they had more influence with the rich. The Jews today think the Sadducees were heretics.

J E R U S A L E M   and the   T E M P L E

There were 3 routes across the land from north to south. One went along the coast of the Mediterranean; another went alongside the river Jordan. They both had the advantage that one could not get seriously lost, but crossing rivers with sheep and goats is difficult. Abraham chose the central route down the high watershed, and this became in antiquity the main route. In order not to loose ones way, any unusual geographic features must have been a godsend. Abraham's contemporaries were building stone penises to worship as Gods. He was a nomad so he would not want to build one, but he would be familiar with a large geographical area and be able to locate the best natural one, to attempt to sacrifice his son Isaac to God. *I believe there was a stone needle or 100 foot pile of rocks detached from the vertical cliff face adjacent to Herod's temple site.* This would have acted as a marker, so one did not get lost in featureless terrain, and marked the cross route to Jericho the oldest city in Palestine. *If there was such a vertical feature it would explain why a wild goat* (A ram) *got caught in a bush; the men climbing up and down to build Abraham's altar would have cut off its one and only escape route.*

I asked on the telephone, the official Church of England model maker who was making a model of the temple at the time of Christ about the four shops. He had heard about the Chanujoth reached by a bridge across the Kidron, but dismissed the idea of a bridge from the temple across the Kidron River to the Mount of Olives as ridiculous it would be the longest span bridge in antiquity, and serve no purpose. But the contemporary historian does not say 'Mount of Olives' it says, 'Twin Cedars of Olivet,' which sounds like a much smaller mountain, and it says 'Kedron' not 'Kidron River'. Alongside the base of the temple cliff face, the main north south road ran in Jesus' time parallel to the Kidron River, *where I maintain Abraham's pinnacle stood. And I think the bridge was across the Kedron Rroad, true the road is no longer named the Kedron road today but surely it is a reasonable name for a road parallel with the Kidron River.* A bridge across a road could easily be afforded. A rocky pinnacle would not be useful to a symmetrically and horizontally minded classical architect, building a huge temple, which covered 25 acres; for Herod on Mount Haram Esh Sharif. Abraham used the highest mountain in Jerusalem which was called Mount Moriah. Mount Zion 773 in Jerusalem is higher than a rock called today Mount Moriah at only 743 on Herod's Temple mound. The Dome of the Rock is now built on this rock. *I guess it is now called Mount Moriah because it is the highest point on the plateau,* but it is not a mountain it is only a rock barely higher than the surrounding plateau. *I believe that there was a penis shaped mountain detached from the main plateau which was demolished* when the temple was totally destroyed twice by the Romans. It would be the easiest bit to demolish, the Pharisees and Zealots would also hate it. I believe that if a goat got stuck it must have had steep sides; because those building Abraham's *murderous* altar used the only way of climbing it. However today there is no sign of a vertical feature but when demolished, being natural, it would leave no foundations for an archaeologist to trace. However there are traces of the foundations of a wall recently discovered around the area. This area is curious, as it has no access, due to levels, to any part of the walled area of Jerusalem in classical times. The temple builders would have found the bridge very useful to haul up with pulleys heavy stones and bulk timber from Nazareth, on ropes from the road below. As a result, during decades of building there would be no access across the bridge, so the sites for the four shops would be worthless. *Is that why Annas was able to obtain all four of them?*

Farrar says Jesus had cleared out the money lenders twice. The first time was 3 years earlier, this may be because two of the versions sound different, but it could be true, and this would show that Jesus regarded this as his most important work. The Temple was finished, or nearly finished about the time that Jesus turned out the moneylenders in c30 AD. *Herod proposed a new temple in 19BC. Could these 4 shop sites have just become available because the builders no longer required the bridge as their primary entry point for heavy building materials? If my surmise is correct it strengthens my Jesus Fiction but if it is untrue, it does not invalidate it. I would like a local Jew to check it out.*

Every male Jew had to pay ½ a shekel a year and visit the temple three times a year and each time sacrifice an animal, so that the drainage of blood was an engineering feat. The population rose from the normal 50,000 to 125,000 at the Passover, there were 7,200 Priests and 9,600 Levites [priestly servants] to look after them. The 100 door keepers, even allowing 3 shifts and annual holidays would mean 25 men on duty at any one time which should have been quite enough to keep Jesus and his twelve apostles in order. The temple was a bank for temple wealth, and a bank for private deposits. Roman coins had the God Emperor's head on them, this meant that they were sculptures of God, and that made the coins a God, so that Roman coins could not be given to the rival God YHWH (The Christian God with an unpronounceable name) who had a much smaller empire, *without making him jealous.* Judea alone of the Palestine provinces at onetime had Roman coins without the Emperors head. This is why there were so many moneychangers in the temple; one had to give YHWH shekels. Roman and Greek coins were in everyday use; shekels were hard to come by, as they were mainly used by the temple. Even if money changing was permitted on non-sacred ground the artificial platform was extremely high, and one would not want to walk up and down ten floors, with no lift, just to change a small coin at a better rate. *As a result the owners of the booths made a great deal of money and could pay good bribe money to the temple staff, and use slaves as the actual staff handling the transactions. Slaves would not have had much authority against Jesus a free man wielding a whip.*

Pompey desecrated the temple in 63 BC. Herod had to kill all the members of the Sanhedrin [ecclesiastical court] except two in 37 BC the first year of his reign. To atone for this he planned a new Temple in Jerusalem. c17 BC the site was acquired and the demolition of Zerubbabel's Temple which was already bigger than Solomon's was planned He started building a fine white marble classical one with Corinthian columns in c15 BC the basic main building was not opened until c30 AD but some minor decorative building work still continued. The temple mound was possibly the largest man made building excluding the Great Wall of China in antiquity.   It was 25 acres and the outer wall was nearly a mile in length.

Herod not being a priest was not allowed into the Holy of Holies, which was therefore kept simple and cheap, it just had ordinary beaten gold on the walls!   600lbs of incense were burnt per year, the recipe included frankincense [terebinth gum resin] and myrrh [camphor gum resin].

The Romans destroyed the Temple in 70 AD; no stone was left standing, as it had been a focus for nationalist activity. The Romans said it started with the Jewish faction fighting the Idumeans; *could this be the Zealots and Pharisees against Annas' children and the Sadducees?* Josephus says 1,100,000 people perished in Jerusalem and many more elsewhere. St. Paul was already dead. The destruction of the temple modernised the Jewish religion by putting a stop to bloody sacrifices, and made them study their Greek Septuagint (the translation of the Bible by 70 scholars) with the help of Rabbis.

The second Jewish revolt was related to a *silly* patriotic desire to be circumcised. Simon Ben Kokkba was defeated 132-135 AD. 985 villages were razed, 580,000 men slain, and the price of a Jewish slave dropped to that of a horse. Jerusalem became a Roman colony and no Jew could enter till the 4th cent. The Jewish centre moved to provincial Galilee.

THE SANHEDRIN,

The Great Sanhedrin ruled over all the Jews including those in the Diaspora. The High Priest was its president and its 71 members were predominately Sadducees

The Sanhedrin had had political and ecclesiastical power since 330 BC. Its importance varied but in AD6 and during Jesus' time it was supremely powerful. But only three years before Jesus' crucifixion and forty years before the destruction of the temple, the Romans took away their political power. It still had the right to pass judgement and recommend the death sentence. A majority of one was sufficient for acquittal, a majority of two was required for condemnation, but the right to execute that judgement, was now in Roman hands. Thus it was that all prisoners had to be passed over to Pilate. Pilate on the other hand in his own court could judge and kill a man, with out the approval of the Sanhedrin. Roman Law, was Roman Law, and it may have been harsh but it was not casual.

Jesus being taken to Annas' private palace at night was very irregular, especially on the eve of the Passover. The Sanhedrin by law had to be convened in the temple precincts by day. Likewise the Chanujoth cannot be on the Mount of Olives remote from the Temple. So the Mount of the twin Cedars of Olivet cannot as many people assume be the Mount of Olives. (Aboda Zara 8 b) Because long after Jesus' crucifixion the Sanhedrin did meet when condemning people to death in the Chanujoth on the Mount of the Twin Cedars of Olivet which *makes me believe it was attached to the Temple and a very safe location to withstand a group attack.*

The Sanhedrin had the right of taxation through tithes [one tenth of the profit from the land] and kept the money for their own purposes, they did not have to hand any over to the Romans. Tribute money was different it had to be paid in coin, and its collection was farmed out to the publicans, like Matthew.

ANNAS (HANAN, ANANUS) & the
HIGH PRIEST'S FAMILY

The Sadducee Annas is responsible for the arrest of Jesus. There is no doubt that Annas, Hanan, and Ananus are all the same person. The

Bible says he was the High Priest at the time of the crucifixion. This is untrue. He was appointed High Priest by the Roman Quirinus, legate of Syria and deposed by Valerius Gratus. However Luke's Gospel is resoundingly true in its non-scientific way. He was the power behind the priesthood and had been High Priest in Jerusalem. *He was second in command of the Sanhedrin at the time of Jesus' conviction.*

He was the son of a priest called Seth an Idumean (Arab) who two generations before at the point of a sword directed by John Hyrcanus had had to become a Jew. Seth chose circumcision rather than death. Herod was also an Idumean. The Idumeans had encouraged Nebuchadnezzar long ago to destroy the foundations of Jerusalem. All previous Jewish priests had been members of the Levi family whose most famous members are Moses and Aaron, one of whom was called Zadok. Before Annas, for a thousand years, every high Priest had been one of Zadok's descendants. *This suggests to me that Annas must have had exceptional personal qualities to have broken this succession, and successfully commanded the descendants of Zadok who were a majority of the Sanhedrin.* Farrar says Annas was 70 years old, when Jesus died, his dates are uncertain, but probably he was born in 30 BC and was aged 15 when the temple in Jerusalem was started, at 37 he became High Priest in Jerusalem in the year that St Luke and *I believe that Jesus was born in 6-7AD at Quirinus'* census at Bethlehem. At 44 in 15AD he resigned

Josephus the historian, a Pharisee who normally criticised the Sadducees strongly wrote in his Jewish Antiquaties XX 198, "It is said that the Ananus [Annas] was extremely fortunate. For he had five sons, all of whom, after he had enjoyed the office for a very long period, became High Priests of God.- a thing that had never happened to any of our High Priests." Farrar says, [2 Macc iv 13, 14], The Annas faction had introduced "Greek fashions and heathenish manners." *i.e. He was educated and not stupidly superstitious like an average Jew.* Farrar says of Josephus XVII 1§4 'and it is confirmed by the Talmud that the priest is Annas and the son is Annas the murderer of "James the Lords brother" in the following quotes. "All your life you teach without practising" bitterly exclaimed the Boethusian to the Priest his father. The reply was a humiliating confession that they could not practice their real theories, but were obliged to conform to the teaching of the Doctors. [Pharisees]'. John 13 42 says the chief rulers *[Sanhedrin]* because of the Pharisee faction cannot acknowledge Christ.

The Jews were the only people in the Roman Empire, allowed to preserve their religion, everywhere else you had to admit you believed in the Roman Gods. For Annas and his children to have maintained this privilege for half a century is an incredible feat. He managed to get Jews excluded from the state cult and military service and keep his own taxes because of Jewish dietary laws and Sabbath observance.

1,000 priests were employed in supervising the building of the Temple at Jerusalem. *He could have been in charge and persuaded Herod to pay for it by giving Herod the fame.* The family of Annas was well known for its large size, wealth and power. They made one of the greatest fortunes in the Roman Empire through the sale of "all things religiously and legally pure", because they owned a monopoly of the only four shops (Chanujoth) under the twin cedars of Olivet connected to the Temple in Jerusalem by a bridge over the Kedron where such things could be legally sold.   It was illegal to sell anything in the Temple at Jerusalem under the ancient laws of Zech. Because they were blessed they could be sold for many times their ordinary price. Every woman who gave birth had to offer a dove in the temple. The Annas family sold pigeons [doves] at 250 times their proper price. These huge profits caused a lot of jealousy at the time and the shops were sacked three years before the demolition of the Temple. There is no trace of the family or its wealth after the sacking of Jerusalem by the Romans and the zealots had scourged one of his sons. The Rabbis bitterly attacked 'their greed and the great wealth' which they had obtained through their monopoly 'of all things legally pure'. The Talmud refers to the viper brood of Hanan [Annas] and as a reaction to their behaviour, abolishes hereditary priesthoods and institutes celibacy, so that it can never happen again *and the Roman Catholics follow suit.*

C A I A P H A S

Joseph Caiaphas was the son in law of Annas [Hanan, Ananus] the famous High Priest and he became High Priest himself of Jerusalem in 18 AD. He and his father in law went on a friendly visit to see St. John the Baptist baptise Jesus. When Pilate freed Jesus with the words 'I can see no fault in this man'. It was Caiaphas who returned him to Pilate demanding his death. He said it was "expedient that one man should die for the people and that the whole nation perish not". Mysteriously he said, "ye know nothing at all". In Acts 4. 6 it says "And Annas the High Priest and Caiaphas, and John" examined the unlearned disciples of Jesus, Peter and John and released them. Yet when Annas is dead and Caiaphas is no longer High Priest Caiaphas commissioned St.Paul to seek out and arrest Christians. He wished to kill Lazarus for making a mockery of death. Those who believe Jesus was crucified after John the Baptist was executed think that the Christians had some part in Caiaphas's removal.

ANANUS II, SON OF (ANNAS, HANAN)

Ananus II, Hanan's son, was high priest in 62 AD. The death of Festus the Roman Procurator, made Pilate's old post vacant for several months while the message travelled to Rome and a newly appointed replacement Albinus sailed from Rome to Palestine. In this gap Ananus quickly got the Sanhedrin, the ecclesiastical court, to try James the brother of Jesus Christ and pass sentence of death on him which was all perfectly legal. But only the Romans could carry out the sentence. Ananus had James thrown down from the pinnacle of the Temple, stoned and finally killed with a fullers club. *(What pinnacle is this, the Chanujoth?)* When Albinus the new Procurator arrived, he deposed Ananus II after only 3 months in office. Ananus II was said to be rash in his temper and unusually daring, to be anti-Zealot, and pro-Roman. He is particularly praised for putting public welfare above his private interests and for his skill both as a general and as an orator. His bravery in opposing the Zealots is described at length with obvious sympathy, by Josephus who was a senior officer under his command. Thackery says he was "a veritable counterpart of Pericles".

Ananias who slapped St Paul's face was another unrelated High Priest.

A LIST OF HIGH PRIESTS

The numbers refer to their succession; there is wide agreement on the order but not always on the dates.

1 Aaron; Moses' brother.
11 Zadok every priest after Zadok was a descendant of his

until Annas No.63 broke the succession. He lived at the time of King David.

57 & 62. Two High Priests by the name of Jesus; who were
  unrelated to either Jesus Christ or Annas. *Jesus
  Christ could have been named in their honour.*

60 & 62a. Joazar 4 BC; and a second time when he was
  deprived of office by popular action. He was the son
  ofBoethus a powerful priestly house.

63 Annas 6-15 AD (Hanan Annanus) Son of Seth.
  The priest that tried Jesus. An Idumean Arab

64 Ishmael son of Phiabi c15-16 AD

65 Eleazar son of Annas c16-17 AD

66 Simon son of Camithus c17-18 AD

67 Joseph surnamed Caiaphas c18-37 AD or(24-37?)
  son in law of Annas, Crucifies Jesus.

68 Jonathan son of Annas. 2 months in 37 AD

69 Theophilus son of Jonathan, grandson of
  Annas 37-41 AD

70 Simon son of Boethus 41 AD

71 Matthias son of Annas 42-44 AD

72-76 Five unrelated priests 44-63AD. One
  of whose sons started the Revolt

77 Ananus son of Annas 62 AD deposed for
  killing James, the brother of Jesus

78 Jesus son of Damnaeus 62-63 AD

79 Jesus son of Gamaliel the famous Pharisee 63-64 AD
  related to Boethus

80 Matthias son of Theophilus; grandson of Annas 65-? AD

81 Phannias son of Samuel. Appointed by the people during the revolt 66-70AD, which caused the Romans to destroy the priesthood and the Temple in Jerusalem.

KINGS AND PROCURATORS.
HEROD THE GREAT

Herod was of Arab (Idumean) descent, ; he was not a Jew; born 73 died 4 BC. He owned a vast estate on the east side of the Dead Sea. . Under his rule 37-4 BC Judea paid no tax to Rome. He was a Hellenised aristocrat and a friend of Mark Antony.

He built many fine pagan temples in non-Jewish areas. He destroyed the scruffy temple in Jerusalem, which was being troublesome, and then built for the Jews, what may have been the greatest temple in the area ruled by the Romans, which he paid for out of his own personal wealth. His family became rich by finding an incredible treasure trove. *Could sick men have brought it from Mohenjodaro? I think this find was the second most valuable ever found in the history of the world.* Alexander the Great's 3,000 tons of *Zoroastrian* Gold at Persepolis sounds greater. As a young man he went to Rome with several gold plates which he gave to his friends who were sons of Senators, and by this means influenced the judgement that his family could keep their findings, the Roman judges of course had no idea how unbelievably vast the treasure was that he had found.

A later friend Caesar Augustus gave him a half share of the profits from the Cyprus copper mines. Herod the Great built by 22-10 BC a new deep-water port named after Augustus Caesar CAESAREA PALESTINAE Pilate kept his troops here as it was larger and more important than Jerusalem but it was not the capital of Roman Judea until after the sacking of Jerusalem. Eusebius 264-340 AD who tampered with Josephus's text concerning Jesus was the Christian Bishop; and at that time it was a more important bishopric than the one at Rome.

By taxing trade and dispossessing enemies, he increased his wealth. He rescued the Olympic Games and became their president; he set up welfare societies throughout the Diaspora. At the end of his life in great pain with worms in his balls he did become irascible, but historians do not think it probable or in character that he murdered the innocents at Bethlehem. Roman law was very strict, and Herod was not above the law. *It is reminiscent of the Pharaoh murdering the innocents at the time of Moses and could be Zealot propaganda. It makes it difficult to date Jesus' birth.* Josephus does not report it. Herod knew the date of the birth of the King of the Jews accurately; so an order to kill all children *of 2½ weeks old would seem more sensible than* the Bible's 2½ years.

Herod killed all the remaining Maccabeans including one who was his wife. Herod had six or nine wives, he makes Boethus the father of one of them High Priest. All the Herods were called Herod in the same way as all the Caesars were called Caesar. One of them had at least 10 gentile wives. After his death he divided his kingdom among 3 of his sons.

ARCHELAUS

Who was one of Herod the Great'ss sons receives half his kingdom including Jerusalem. Annual value 600 talents. [A talent is 114 lbs of gold, or the same weight in silver.] His mother Malthace is a Samaritan. He married his brother's daughter Mariamme.

He is called Ethnarch of Judea, Samaria and Idumea in 4 BC. I am ignorant and would like to know why the Romans confiscated his kingdom. *He has a bad reputation, and presumably broke Roman law.* He was banished to Vienne in Southern France. His kingdom became an imperial province in 6 or 7 AD governed by a Procurator named Quirinus (Cyrenius) appointed by Rome who organised the Bethlehem Census. Matt 2 22 says Joseph fled from Archelaus. Bethlehem was in his area.

PHILLIP

Tetrach of Iturea 4 BC-34 or37 AD.

His father was Herod the Great, his mother was Cleopatra [*a Greek?*] Tetrach means one-fourth part Annual value 100 gold talents. He married Salome, Herodias' daughter.

HEROD ANTIPAS

Tetrach of Galilee and Peraea 4 BC-39 AD. Annual value 200 talents. His father was Herod the Great

Nazareth is in Galilee which was his territory, and Pilate the Roman had no control over it, so he was consulted at the trial of Jesus, because he was in Jerusalem for the Passover and did not convict Jesus.

Herod Antipas' lawsuit to get the inheritance of Herod Archelaus his deposed brother, who had had the major share of his father's kingdom had been going on for six years at the time of the Bethlehem census To persist with the court expenses he must have believed he would win.

Rumours of a descendent of King David; being born to rule with magical signs, would have been incredibly irritating. For this reason he could have wanted to massacre the infants in Bethlehem even if he had no jurisdiction there. Much later another Herod, - Agrippa did inherit it proving that he had a good case at law. He could have felt the Roman census was to uncover his brother's deceits, rather than being the start of direct Roman rule, which is what actually happened.   So, though I doubt the massacre of the innocents, it could be this Herod not his father who gave the orders. Jesus called him a fox.

His mother was a Samaritan. He caused a war with an Arab king by changing the law so that he could marry Herodias the daughter of an Arab king while his brother who had divorced her was still alive. St. John the Baptist thought this wicked, so Herodias and her daughter Salome helped execute St. John.

R O M A N   LEGATES and PREFECTS.

QUIRINIUS (Cyrenius) in 6-AD was appointed, the Roman legate for all Syria of which Palestine was a very small part. He held a census for taxation in Bethlehem, as soon as he was appointed. Jesus was born in January so it must have been 7 AD. Luke Chap 2. He had no jurisdiction over the other Bethlehem near Nazareth.

PONTIUS PILATE was the fifth Prefect of Judea, Samaria and Idumea 26 to late 36 or early 37 AD. He commanded 3,000 mainly Syrian troops at Caesarea, which was 60 miles from Jerusalem. Nazareth was not under his rule so unless Jesus owned land near Bethlehem he was not likely to be under his jurisdiction.

FELIX Prefect 52-60 AD

FESTUS Prefect 60-62 AD.

AGRIPPA I. He was brought up with the Emperors Caligula and Claudius as a foster brother. He was a grandson of Herod the Great;

he was called Herod in the New Testament. He inherited Gallilee from Herod Antipas 39-41 AD when he was made king of Judea in 41 AD when all the prefects and procurators who superseded Pilate were withdrawn. This shows that Herod Antipas's hope of inheriting Judea and Bethlehem was not fanciful. His daughter Bernice was the richest woman in Palestine and married her uncle Herod of Chalcis 44-49AD. She knew St Paul and Josephus the writer, she was rumoured to be incestuous with her brother Agrippa II and became Mistress to Titus Emperor of Rome. The Jewish people declared Agrippa I a God shortly before his death. He allowed Ananus II to kill James the brother of Jesus and ordered St. Peter's arrest.

AGGRIPA II, the last of the Herods, King 50-100 AD, fought with the Romans against the Jewish revolt 66-70 AD and helped destroy Jerusalem in 70 AD.

THE   CAESARS

JULIUS CAESAR died 44 BC and was deified after his death. It was Cleopatra who taught the Romans the advantages of being a god in their eastern provinces.

AUGUSTUS 27 BC-14 AD Pontifus Maximus became a GOD and had his father declared one, he was the first Roman Emperor to do this.

TIBERIUS 14-37 AD

CALIGULA 37-41 AD ordered that his bust be set up in every temple through out the Empire, only the Jews who had unique special privileges for their religion objected to it, as much because it was sculpture, as that it was a God. The Procurator Petronius took a chance and delayed, he was ordered to commit suicide, this he avoided because Caligula was murdered. Caligula murdered men so he could sleep with their wives and then sold them into prostitution; he made his horse a member of the Senate. He may have intended to set up Kingship like the Pharaohs by marrying his sister Drusilla, when she died he made her a goddess. *I think his detractors put about the story that he ate the baby in her womb because he was jealous.*

CLAUDIUS Emperor 41-54 AD

NERO Emperor 54-68 AD. Said the Christians burnt Rome, *this could have meant Jews,* because most of the Christians in Rome were Jews.

VESPASIAN Emperor 69-79 AD victoriously campaigned in Palestine in 67-68 AD and was proclaimed Emperor and God by his soldiers in Judea thus fulfilling one of the Messiah *myths,* he miraculously cured a blind man and a cripple so that the whole East should know that the power of God was upon him. He was an Italian. He commanded that all the descendants of David be sought out, and that no one be left of Royal stock. *This could have fuelled the story of the massacre of the innocents.*

DOMITIAN Emperor 81-96 AD was addressed by Governors as "Our Lord" and "Our GOD commands". The Jews had to offer daily sacrifice for, rather than to, the Emperor.

TRAJAN Emperor 98-117 AD came from Spain, the first non Italian Emperor.

SAINT JOHN THE BAPTIST

The Mandeans were numerous in 350 AD. They believed that John was Christ and Jesus was his disciple because Jesus was baptised by John. There are about 100,000 alive today.

Zacharias an elderly childless priest who owned his own fishing boat and had hired servants was very upset emotionally when his wife became pregnant *because he thought he could not have any children,* he refused to speak until the child was baptised 'John' which was a non-family name, a name the local people were surprised he would accept. His wife Elizabeth [Elisheba] John's mother, who was showing signs of the start of the menopause, before she became pregnant, was closely related to The Virgin Mary and to Annas, who was to become the most important High priest the Jews ever had.

A MAP OF THE DEAD SEA AND GALLILEE AT THE TIME OF CHRIST

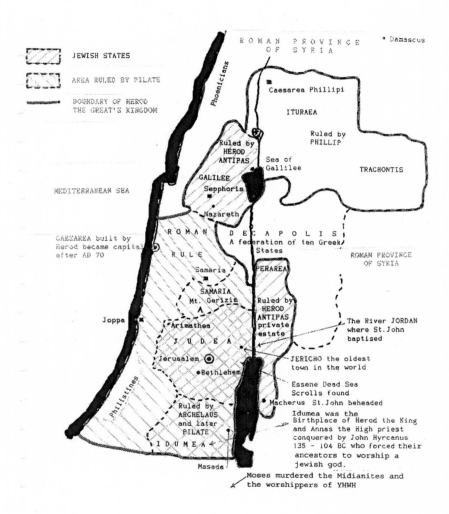

196

A MAP OF THE DEAD SEA AND GALLILEE
AT THE TIME OF CHRIST

Pilate ruled over a collection of provinces the majority of which were not Jewish. Along the coast lived civilized Greek speaking people who were under Roman rule, but had not been under the rule of Maccabeus. Patriotic Jews *have created a myth of a large Jewish state,* out of Herod the Great's Kingdom which was not wholly Jewish. Notice how Jesus coming from Gallilee had to pass through non-Jewish Samaria. The High Priest of Jerusalem religiously ruled over all the Jews in Africa, Asia and Europe. The only Jewish states were JUDEA, GALLILEE, and PERAEA and technically IDUMEA, but remember that the Idumeans had only been recently converted with the sword to being Jewish. Jerusalem remained the capital until 70 AD, when it had to be destroyed because of *outrageous* Jewish patriotism.

John was Jesus' cousin, Jesus was six months younger, but they were not neighbours. The Virgin Mary stayed for 3 months with Elizabeth his mother from her sixth month of pregnancy. John's preaching started in 28-29 AD, *he was probably an Essene.* He dressed like Elijah in shabby robes to make the point that he was a prophet and said he was unworthy to untie his young cousin Jesus' shoe. Only the super rich would have had fixings on their shoes. *He believed that cold water reduced sexiness.* He baptised people in the river Jordan *[shades of the Ganges].* Annas and Caiaphas the High Priests went to see him baptise Jesus.

He was against fornication, sex with menstruating women and incest which included marrying first cousins which Herodians believed in doing to keep power with in the family. He attacked Herod the Tetrach of Galilee's new wife Herodias by publicly saying her marriage was illegal and incestuous on the basis of some texts in the Old Testament prohibiting a woman marrying her divorced husband's brother, while he was still alive. Which was very irritating to civilised people who disregarded the old laws, they were rational and had Greek ideas even if to keep the peace they had to pay lip service to the old ideas. Salome, the daughter of Herodias and niece of Herod danced so well at Herod's birthday party that he promised her anything she wanted, she asked her mother and she advised St.John's head on a plate, Herod *was a bit shocked and tried to back out of it,* but having John in a prison below and not knowing what to do with him because he would not apologise, he acquiesced. Josephus says John called for a native Jewish King and was killed on the orders of Herod Antipas 35 AD. Matt 14 2 says he died while Jesus was alive. Nowadays we can sew back arms; Jesus did not sew his head on.

DIAGRAMS DEMONSTRATING THE PROBABILITY THAT JESUS WAS A VERY RICH MAN BECAUSE HE TWICE HAD HIS FEET DRIED BY WOMEN'S HAIR..

ORDINARY JEWS at the time of Christ sat cross legged round a mat spread with food and drink. Mary Magdalene and Mary (sister of Lazarus) would have to crouch in the middle of the food showing their bottoms and worse still the soles of their feet to the other guests. The impracticality of this suggests Jesus was not an ordinary Jew.

If Jesus ate in luxury like a Roman lying on a couch, it would be easy for him to have his feet dried by women's hair. The two Marys would be well away from the other guests. The candles being on the table with the food, would probably have cast dark shadows, so that a hand slipped up Jesus' robe would go unnoticed. Do Christians call Mary Magdalene a prostitute because they realise Jesus had no underpants? John 12 says the ointment used for his feet, called spikenard cost 300 silver denarii, say £5,000 today. Judas Iscariot said it should be sold and the money given to the poor. Jesus rebuked him saying "the poor are always with us I am here for only a short time" *an odd thing for an immortal God to say when the poor might die of starvation.*

Eating at a trestle table as drawn by Leonardo da Vinci, would have been most unusual. The Marys washing Jesus' feet and drying them with their hair would have been kicked under the table and had to put their hair on the dirty floor.

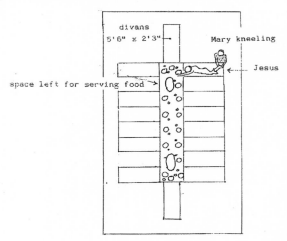

Rooms measuring 33'-0" x 18'-0" are not built today in houses costing less than one million pounds, especially an upper room. A plan showing the minimum size of the dining room in the houses of three of Jesus' friends; 'John the beloved disciple', Lazarus, and Judas Iscariot's father. The plan shows seating for Jesus, 12 apostles, and his host who might have two sons. Notice this does not allow any room for women but then women may have been too inferior to have eaten with our Lord.

He must have had a valuable robe for the soldiers to have played dice for it.

J E S U S   C H R I S T

Jesus was born on the 6th of January. In 375 AD at Antioch his birth date was changed to the 25th of December the shortest day of the year; to bring it into line with the birth of the Sun God. Constantine was the son of Sol Invictus (the Sun God). It helped to transfer worship of Mithras the Iranian God of light who was born several thousands years earlier on the 25th of December from a rock watched by shepherds to Christ. Astarte "the Virgin Goddess" brought forth a child, an actual baby every year to represent the rebirth of the Sun on 25th of December.

Scholars disagree on Jesus' dates. The majority say 6 to 4 BC because Herod the Great dies in 4 BC so he cannot massacre infants any later. Mathew chap 2 verse 1 and Luke Chap. 1 verse 2. All Herod the Great's sons are called Herod. Three of them being kings *could mistakenly be called 'Great'.* His son Herod Antipas had no authority over Bethlehem, but Nazareth was in his territory. But he had a legal claim in the Roman courts to be King over his brother's kingdom, which included Bethlehem. *So I prefer the Census date as it gives a serious motive for the murder of the innocents by Herod Antipas.* Luke says Jesus was born at the time of the Bethlehem census, the only recorded and important Bethlehem Census was in 6-7 AD. When Quirinus was appointed governor of Syria mentioned in Luke Chap 2. However, when I quote a date I simply repeat what the authoritative source from which I am quoting says, which you may find very confusing. The execution of John the Baptist was 35 AD. *Jesus was baptised in 34-35 AD.* The latest date for his Crucifixion is the Passover in 36 or 37 AD. I prefer this dating to the normal one, which says Jesus, died in 30 AD. Because Jesus says to his Apostles "whom do men say I the Son of Man am? Matt 14 2 and Luke 9.7 reveals that Herod Antipas's conscience makes him fear that he is John the Baptist risen from the dead. Luke 3 23 says Jesus is about 30 years old when John baptised him. This makes all attempts to date Jesus' birth a nightmare, everyone agrees he was not born on 1BC-1AD. There was no Zero. [0] was invented nearly 1,000 years later. AD is an abbreviation for Anno Domini, which means in the year of the Dominant Master.

St Paul says in Galatians 1:11-20 that Jesus commissioned him and he says he is not lying. *This makes it probable that Jesus as a sick man was living in Damascus after the crucifixion.* The usual depiction of Jesus as a blue-eyed blonde offends the blacks and is untrue. Eastern peoples, including the Jews prohibit portraits, so it is hardly surprising that the earliest surviving images make him look like a Gaul. In fact he probably had black hair, an olive skin, and quite possibly a hooked nose. It is only in the last two hundred years that people have thought of the Bible as history in a geographical location, in the past the painter depicted the characters as his contemporary locals.

Jesus said very little that was wholly new, but he did make the religion of love a bit more positive, than in the Old Testament, where it says, "You shall love your neighbours as yourself" *with the implication that you may hate your enemies.* This compares with Jesus saying, Matthew 5.44 "Love your enemies and pray for those that persecute you" and He gives this equal importance with loving God. To people living at the time, 'enemies' must have seemed to refer to the Romans. The Hindus and Buddhists believe in individual love but Christians are more corporate, and believe in one body of mankind through love.

Jewish Apocalyptic writings are a type of literature depicting the intervention of God in history to the accompaniment of sudden, dramatic and cataclysmic events and written in symbolic or cryptographic terms, which incorporate Zoroastrian traditions. Jesus can be said to be a Sadducee [render unto Caesar what is Caesar's] with strong Messianic, apocalyptic and eschatological [end of world] interests with a revulsion against Pharisaic legalism but a delight in the Hillel's doctrine of love [a High Priest and teacher of the same generation as his grandfather].

If the object of God was to obtain first hand experience of what it is like to be a man, it is odd that he missed out on human sexuality and paternity. The Gnostic Gospel of Phillip found in Egypt in 1945 says, "The companion of the Saviour is Mary Magdalene. But Christ loved her more than all his disciples and used to kiss her often on" (next word is missing as there is a hole in the text). Mary Magdalen came from Magdala the fish town with 230-330 small boats. She may have been Jesus favourite. The Pope in 591 AD declared Mary

Magdalen a prostitute. Another Pope 1969 AD said she was not a prostitute but a saint.

At the marriage at Cana his mother orders the replenishment of the wine *an odd thing for a guest to do. May be he married Mary Magdalen or someone else, at Cana because immediately afterwards he was referred to as a Rabbi and teacher* and at that time Mishraic law says all teachers and rabbis had to be married and celibacy was extremely unfashionable. The Bible never says that Jesus was single and there is no word for bachelor. The Roman Catholic teachings would not be invalidated if Jesus did marry.

Corinthians 8.9 says "Lord Jesus Christ rich as he was, he made himself poor for your sake, in order to make you rich by means of his poverty". Jesus' social class is not clear. At no time in history, have the peasants and urban proletariat been very interested in religion, or for that matter Christianity, they have regarded it as effeminate. In 1851 the first proper survey in England showed that only 10% of workers in towns ever went to church. In 1318-25 the Bishop of Paniers later to become Pope found that the peasants believed that to give alms for the salvation of souls was rubbish, and that Christ was created by f***ing like the rest of us [Raymond de L'Aire of Tignac]. Archbishop Grindal in 1571 said that all lay people should come to church 'especially householders: servants and the poor were another matter'. *The fact that Jesus was interested in religion suggests he was upper middle class. Today the poor are as rich and as frequently idle as the upper classes of old and being uneducated in science they are today the bulk of church goers.*

Mani in AD 240 referred to Jesus as the mortal son of a widow and said that someone else was substituted for him on the cross. In 276 AD Mani was flayed, skinned and decapitated; St Augustine had believed his teachings for a time.

Arius of Alexandria preached from 318 AD that Jesus was an inspired teacher who was wholly mortal and in no sense divine. By 360 AD it had all but displaced Roman Catholicism. When the Merovingians rose to power during the fifth century virtually every bishopric in Europe was either Arian or vacant. **Arianism** was condemned at the council of Nicea in 325 (which *promoted* Jesus from being Messiah into being God) and Arianism was declared heretical in 381 AD.

With the recent rise of democracy *it became desirable to get ordinary voters so Jesus became a poor man,* and it was as easy for a rich man to get into heaven as it was for a camel to enter the eye of a needle. *As always the working classes were so ignorant that they thought a needle was a sewing needle!* Cleopatra's needle stands by the Thames; she died before Jesus so the Gospel writers must have been familiar with what she thought a needle was. A needle is the entry symbol for a town and for safety's sake the entrance was narrow so thugs could not rush it. Every town and village had a high mud wall to protect it from robbers and they charged traders for seeking safety at night. To mark the position of the entrance a needle (*say 10 meters high*) was erected above the wall so one could see where the entrance was at a distance. Double gated entrance towers with portcullises had not been invented. There were no roads or trampled grass which by leading one to the entrance made its location obvious. But Jesus *was a rich man* so he knew that getting a camel into town, was as difficult as passing through an airport today, the luggage had to be searched for taxation. A thief or robber with money would be detected by God in the same way.

Another misunderstanding by the man in the street concerns 'gleanings'. In England if you eat an apple in your neighbour's garden you are a thief, not so in the Middle East even today, you are only a thief if you take it off his land. French cooking and restaurants had not been invented travellers fed on gleanings. This does not mean Jesus is poor.

The soldiers normally cut a crucified persons cloak down the seams. Jesus' seamless cloak was so valuable they gambled for it. The scented ointment Lazarus' sister Mary puts on Jesus feet would be worth £4,000 to £6,000 today. John 11:2. Judas Iscariot is disgusted he thinks Jesus should have given the money to the poor.

Jesus is a proper Jew, not a Roman Catholic he believes in making money. He is appalled by the servant who buries his master's money when he goes on a trading journey and gets no thanks for retuning it to him when he returns. He thinks the servants that double his money while he is away, are worth a small reward. Today excluding inflation it takes a lifetime to double one's money and interest rates of 100% over a few months are thought to be shocking, and are therefore illegal.

The Moslems respect Jesus but do not believe he is a God or that he could do miracles.

THE VIRGIN MARY

In a poll of 2,000 of the 10,000 Church of England clergy only half are convinced of the truth of the virgin birth. If Jesus' brethren are her children how can she be a virgin?

Contemporary non-biblical accounts say, The Virgin Mary's mother; Anna was barren and old enough to have her menopause. Was it her husband's or her fault that she could not have a child? She prayed to God, *this means she consulted the Temple Priests.* Now that she thought that she was too old to have a baby *she might have let one of the Priests have a go.* When she became pregnant, she swore that she would hand the baby to the Temple to be looked after. She said this was in gratitude to God, for giving her a baby. *She might have said it because her husband* Joachim thought to be of King David's lineage, *refused to bring up the baby, or it might be that a Priest [the real father?] said he would like to bring her up in the Temple.* The Gospel of James says Anna handed Mary to the temple for residential training aged three on Nov. 25th. She was the only temple girl. (The Qur'an).

Ancient temples all had girls; the priests lived on the proceeds of their sexuality and f***ing. The Jews did not approve of sex in Temples. *So I suggest Jewish temple girls had the title "VIRGIN" to differentiate them from normal temple girls.* The Romans had Vestal VIRGINS on the capitol. *"Virgin" was a title not a comment on their personal behaviour.* Temple girls like Nuns might be married to GOD. If today a married woman has a baby by a lover, the law says her husband is the boy's father not the lover's and who could prove it before DNA. *If Mary was married aged 3 to God, her child's father would be GOD regardless of some lesser man or husband. Jesus could have been born a God, with the right to be King because of his mother's marriage to God and her high office. I do not say that this is so; I simply say it could be true.*

There is no word in Hebrew that means 'Virgin'. The word 'alma' means a woman who has never been seen by men. However a few almas in the old testament have children. Isaiah, a highly respected prophet, who wanted swords beaten into ploughshares, said [7-14] that the Messiah would be born to 'alma', [a young woman], because most Jews could not understand Hebrew, their Holy book was translated into Greek [the Septuagint], and because there was no Greek word for 'young woman'; 'alma' became 'parthenos' meaning a virgin.

The Pope has the title of "Holy Father"; *this is not a comment on his personal private life. It does not mean he is a good maker of children. Why should 'Virgin' only mean unbroken hymen?*

Just as a father today, has to put his son down at birth to get him into Eton. It was de-rigueur for a father to provide supernatural signs at the birth of a great man. For example one of the Dead Sea Scrolls, the Genesis Apocryphon says that an Angel impregnated Noah's mother. A star appeared in the East when Abraham was born [Ref. Book of Jashar and Maase Abraham] and moved across the heavens and wise men went to King Nimrod and told him that this meant the birth of a child destined to be great. [The morning star = Lucifer = Astarte = Venus.] *The presence of a star, shepherds and Magi at the birth suggests either unusual forethought by a rich powerful man* or presupposes the existence of a God. From the word Magi we get our word magic.

Mr R.D.West of Chalfont St Giles said "Virgin birth is a technical term to describe a female who gets pregnant before her first [menstrual] period". This would make Joseph by today's standards a child sex abuser. Child brides f***ed before their first ovulation by older men are not uncommon in Moslem countries today. *I think a 'virgin' means an unbroken hymen.* It is statistically very unusual but not impossible for a girl with an unbroken hymen [virgin] to become pregnant, Jewish priests by law could only marry virgins, *which could be a reason why Mary became engaged to a carpenter.*

In 451 AD, at the Council of Chalcedon, 520 celibate Bishops attended, *and thinking if we have to be celibate why shouldn't Mary be,* they decreed that the Roman Catholic and Eastern churches considered Mary was perpetually a virgin. Chalcedon is near Ephesus where the council had legitimised the title of 'Mother of God' *and the Ephesian priests must have been desperate to preserve Artemis the Virgin Goddess under another name.* The town was in trouble it had no natural resources, its harbour was silting up and religion had made it one of the most prosperous towns on earth. However for Mary to have remained perpetually a virgin - virgo intacto - *her hymen would have to remain unbroken, if Jesus was within one per cent of the normal size of a baby, she would have had to have had a caesarean section.* It is called a caesarean because Caesar's wife had one, so contemporary doctors knew how to do it, so it is not impossible, but it would mean Mary was very, very rich, which makes the unplanned stable birthplace seem odd. But if the Hymen broke, then the Roman Catholic churches infallibility is also ripped apart and in a bloody mess because inflexible statements cannot be partly true.

I don't like the idea of Mary failing to keep her marriage vows and in colloquial language not being a proper wife to Joseph in bed. If she was just a nursemaid for his previous children, *why did she desert these children to journey to Bethlehem, her signature could not have been required as women were classified as imbeciles under Roman law; and later run away to Egypt without looking after them.* The Catholic church regards chastity very highly for instance Pope Pius XII in 1947 canonised Maria Goretti b.1890 a saint for being murdered while resisting rape at the age of 11.

Mary is Greek for Miriam, Jesus is Greek for Joshua, so she appears to be Hellenised and that most probably means aristocratic and possibly a Sadducee. Joseph is a Hebrew name but then he is proud of being a descendant of King David. "Mary went in haste," means she can not be in servitude, she had read the scriptures so she cannot have been illiterate, which must have been most unusual for a woman at that date. *Even the story of the stable would not be mentioned* if it was usual for her class and position, it was clearly an emergency. Luke 1 36-56. Her cousin Elizabeth was the wife of a literate priest; the mother of St. John the Baptist; and kinswoman to the aristocratic Annas who could only have been high priest if Luke's date 7 AD for the birth of Christ is correct. This shows that the Virgin Mary was kinswoman to an aristocrat.

J E S U S' L E G A L F A T H E R

There is a story that Jesus' father was Tiberius Julius Abdes Pantera a Roman archer who died in Germany, *but I don't believe it.*

Joseph was a carpenter. "Tecton" in Aramaic, the local language at that time, means builder or learned man as well as carpenter. It does not mean, as the socialists would have you believe a "chippy" or Victorian day labourer. It was a respected job like Atomic Scientist today. "Of Nazareth" makes him sound like the most important person in Nazareth. Nazareth was in the nearest area of old forest to Jerusalem that still had large trees. I expect the trees were cut to an exact size in the forest for their future use in the temple, to lighten the load, because it was sixty miles from Jerusalem. Joseph would have to pay his taxes to Herod Antipas who ruled the district not to the Roman Governor of Syria. Therefore his journey to Bethlehem was to be assessed for tax by Quirinus on land holdings near Bethlehem, which was two days journey away. *Everyone I know today who is taxed in two countries or has to journey two hours between their properties is very rich. When people are sleeping in the street Joseph goes to the only Inn; the equivalent of a five star hotel today and gets three star accommodation in the stable annexe. Probably under a lamp on a very high pole which had never been seen in the village before, and so was described as a star as it guided one by night, to Quirinus (Cyrene) and his taxation officials who were using the Inn as their offices.*

Through Joseph, Jesus can trace his lineage back according to Mathew 42 generations to King David 1,000 years earlier and Abraham even earlier. Luke says there are only 26 generations and his grandfather is Heli. Matthew says, His grandfather is, Jacob. There are only four names that are the same in each list until we reach King David. Since the Gospels are gospel truth, this is a severe embarrassment to Christians, for if there is one error as serious as this there can be many. Therefore either the Gospels were not inspired by God, or God can make errors. The word gospel comes from the same root as gossip; *could they be no more truthful?* I hope and believe there are no errors of this magnitude in my book, but if there are it does not disprove the rest of the book. Mary's tree would be of more interest, but both say they are Joseph's. Today in a literate society that keeps good records, you will not find many of your friends, who can trace their ancestry back before the Norman Conquest, and if you can, I am confident that the average person that can do so will be an aristocrat. This suggests that Joseph was an aristocrat.

The Bible clearly states Joseph is not Jesus' father, in the next chapter I reveal who I really think it was. The United Bible Society who publishes 500 million Scriptures every year says in their "Good News Edition" that Joseph was engaged to Mary at the birth of Christ; according to Victorian Law which was based on Roman law, this make Jesus a bastard. There is no record of Joseph marrying the Virgin.

THE BRETHREN

Not every body is agreed about JESUS' relations. The New Testament says: - Matthew 13.55 «his brethren James, Joses, Simon and Judas and his sisters are they not all with us». 1 Corr. 9.5 «as the brethren of the Lord». Galatians 1:19 «but other of the apostles saw I none save James the Lords brother.» Are these full brothers? The Roman Catholics say that the brethren are the children of Joseph by a previous marriage. But Mary the mother of James from non-Biblical contemporary sources was still alive at the passion! *Was she another Mary, Joseph's third polygamous wife? Or was the Virgin Mary not perpetually virgin only virgin before marriage?*

James disapproved of sex and never f***ed. He thought one went to hell if you had not lost nerve endings in your prepuce due to circumcision. *His disgusting sex ideas may be the reason why he pretended his mother was a virgin.* The Apocrypha a non-divine roughly contemporary book says Joseph had a previous wife by whom he had 4 sons plus several daughters, Judas and James the less were two of them. James was said to be the eldest brother, but one might call a younger brother the eldest when the oldest was dead. Since the elder brothers did not die young it is surprising Jesus' genealogical tree is so important. If Jesus was not the first born, Jesus could not be King David's direct heir, but he would still be of the line, providing he was Joseph's child, who we are told; he wasn't. This James was called Just and was probably an anti Herodian, nationalistic High Priest (probably not a member of the Sanhedrin) but a rival bishop in Jerusalem, he wore linen and had knees as callused as a camels from entering the Holy of Holies. James and Jamesian Christians would not allow Herod or Herodians, because they were foreigners and fornicators into the Temple. Despite the fact that Herod had paid for it! He might *I doubt it,* be the "Teacher of Righteousness" in the Dead Sea Scrolls

If Jesus was born in 4 BC, James being the eldest of four boys plus some sisters must have been born minimum 10 BC. Would Aananus II willingly risk losing his High priesthood in 62 AD, in order to kill a 72 year old, peaceful leader of the Nazarenes who had been a friend of his father [Hanan] Annas? At more than 72 years old, *I find it surprising* that having been thrown from the Temple pinnacle, with both legs broken, he would still need to be stoned and hit with a fullers club to die. *This suggests that Jesus was born in 6 or 7 AD, which I favour rather than the more usual 4 or 6 BC; and if he was Jesus' younger full brother, he would only have been in his early 50s, but then Mary could not have remained, as the Roman Catholics say, a Virgin perpetually.*

Dr. Schonfield says Joseph had 5 sons and 2 nameless daughters: - Joshua called Jesus. - Jacob called James - Joseph - Simeon - and Judah who had two grandsons James and Sokker who were crucified in the reign of Trajan 98-117 AD, together with Simeon son of Cleophas. The words 'Thomas' and 'Didymus' are not names they both mean 'twin' so some say Jude was Jesus' twin, *but I say he could have been the twin of another brother.*

D I S C I P L E S,

(The Followers of Jesus)

The Apostles were:-

Andrew,

Bartholomew,

James the son of Alphaeus,

James and John, the sons of Zeberdee, a boatowner, who knows the
   High Priest socially.

Judas Iscariot, - Matthias replaced Judas

Matthew, Capernaum's customs officer; for Antipas' Galilee
   & Phillip's Gualantis.

Phillip,

Simon called Peter, which means rock. Rocky is the nickname for a
   tough. He illegally carried and used a sword and cowardly denied

Christ three times. Robt. Eisenman on page 694 thinks Peter killed 3 gaolers escaping from Prison, and was junior to James the brother of Christ.

Simon the Zealot,

Thaddaeus or Judas the son of James,

Thomas,

Jesus has 72 other unnamed disciples fully employed because they have to leave their homes.

John the Beloved Disciple is not on the above (Apostle / Disciple) list from the Bible. John the son of Zeberdee has to follow a man with a water pot to find the secretive and favourite disciples house where the last supper took place according to Schonfield. *So he can not be John the Beloved*

Two of St. John the Baptist's disciples follow Jesus. Simon the Zealot [a nationalist fighter, the Romans called them 'robbers'] bore also the name Iscariot as would appear in some MSS in John iv 71; xiii 26 then he was the father of the traitor Judas. If he were as some traditions say a son of Clopas, or Alphaeus it might appear that all the apostles were related to each other and to our Lord. Six would be 1st cousins and Judas his 2nd cousin. But this supposition depends on dubious conjecture. Most authorities agree that some of the apostles are cousins of Jesus, usually because for snobbish reasons they claim to be related to his distinguished kinsman the High Priest, but different authorities champion different disciples. However many of the Apostles were brothers, two of Zeberdee, two of Jonas, three or four of Alphaeus and two of Tolmai beside a father and son. To favour ones family was normal at this time.

The two disciples (note they are not on the list of twelve) who thought Jesus was a stranger when they met him after his death; were Cleophas, Jesus' uncle and Simeon [Jesus' 1st cousin]. Simeon became leader of the Nazarenes after Jesus' brother James the Just was killed by Ananus II. Farrar being Church of England believes that Peter never went to Rome, and therefore never founded a church there.

Many of the disciples were fisher folk. Did Jesus demand that their families starved to death, or did he pay them? At one time he recommends them to sell a garment to buy a sword. A second hand Saville Row suit would not buy a sword today. *To have 12 well dressed servants that are not slaves makes Jesus very rich, or reveals that he must be funded by someone very rich.*

THE GOSPELS

The Gospels [Good News] were written by the following with the approx. dates:-

Matthew 80 AD

Mark 71-72 AD

Luke some years after 80 AD

John (between 75-115 AD) says he is known to the High priest, but High Priests ceased after the fall of Jerusalem in 70 AD.

There were probably thirty Gospels, many of them written by Gnostics. Thomas, Peter, Mary and Judas were all found in the 20th century. The Archbishop of Canterbury in 2006 poured scorn on the leather bound papyrus written around 300 AD believed to be "The Gospel of Judas", found in Egypt 1978, and translated in 2002 AD. Because it claims that it was Christ himself who asked Judas to betray him. Christ says "You [Judas] will exceed all of them (*the other disciples); f*or you will sacrifice the man that clothes me." This suggests Jesus has a financier backing him, or that he is employed by a greater richer man than himself. *Caiaphas may want to know who this is and therefore hires Judas.* Jesus is well known, he was welcomed with palms before his feet he can not need identifying.

The Roman Catholics decided what was and what was not to be included in the Bible and probably destroyed all the original Gospels plus many other reports c325 AD. They made the man a saint; who burnt down the library at Alexandria which contained 700,000 scrolls, many unique copies. Because some reports about Jesus were not very flattering they judged it as heretical, information, and destroyed it. They were particularly frightened of the Gnostics who believed in individual research and judged them as heretics whom they could kill. All their literature was destroyed, but the Nag Hamadi scrolls were found buried in the 20th century.

A 2nd century Bishop wrote about secret Gospels in which Jesus takes men into the Garden of Gethsemene for secret initiation rites. I cannot explain and nobody else seems to be able to do so, who the naked young man was, who ran away in the dark. [Mark 14.51] The playwright Christopher Marlowe thought the apostles base fellows, and Christ a homosexual bastard, he was murdered in 1593 during his blasphemy trial aged 29.

JOHN, JOHN, & JOHN

Historians are in a muddle. There were most probably two or three Johns in Ephesus. They are variously called John the Beloved Disciple; John the Evangelist, the Gospel writer, who says he was known to the High Priest and wore a Mitre at Ephesus. John the Epistle writer; (John the Divine of Patmos), who wrote Revelations. Any one of them could have been the John who was the Bishop of Ephesus, when he was a very, very old man.

Nearly everyone disagrees as to who John the Beloved Disciple is; he was not one of the twelve disciples. Hugh Schonfield says, 14 people were at the last supper, Jesus plus the 12 apostles, and his host the Beloved Disciple John. It is in his house, that the last supper takes place; it is situated on the outskirts of Jerusalem in a large garden on the road to Lazarus' house at Bethany. Da Vinci makes him look feminine; *this could be the reason why Jesus sits next to him as he is the host. John must have been rich to have an upper room in which 14 men could lie on divans to eat, 20 foot by 30 foot is the smallest I can plan it, only two million pound homes to day have rooms that size.* Da Vinci has got it all wrong to have them sitting at a table. Two of his disciples, one of whom is John the son of Zeberdee are told to follow a man with a water jug. I believe this means that John the Beloved disciple does not want it to be known that he is an important plotter or disciple. Everybody knows Jesus, he does not need to be identified, *I think Judas Iscariot is hired to identify John the beloved* and since Jesus knows about it *he goes to a public area to be arrested.*

Non-Christian detectives make 'John the Beloved Disciple' their central character in proving that Jesus was a political adventurer. Some writers say he was a close friend of St. John the Baptist. He is held by some scholars to be a kinsman of Annas, reading gnorimos instead of gnostos. He is thought to be the John who after Jesus' arrest was described in John's Gospel 18 26 "another disciple that was known to the High Priest went into the High Priest and went into the palace of the High priest. Peter stood at the door outside. Later the other disciple who was known to the High Priest came out, and invited Peter in".   St. Peter *who I name 'Petulant' is jealous of him.* After the crucifixion, John the Beloved fled from Jerusalem with Mary the mother of God [and some say Mary Magdalene was in the party] to Ephesus were he founded the most viable Christian church. St. Paul must have known him.

He is a very secretive person and he is the only one that understands the workings of the Sanhedrin court. The John Gospel is based on his view. The language and style of the John that wrote Revelations is very different and his apocalyptic ending of time has a Zoroastrian feel.

John in his first Epistle in the New Testament Chapter 3 describes all us ordinary people as "sons of God .... and we shall be like Him." Presumably this means that calling Jesus the Son of God means nothing special.

E P H E S U S

Ephesus was the capital of the Roman province of Asia from 129 BC. Built 550 BC, the Temple of Artemis, was one of the Seven Wonders of the ancient world, the ruins are still impressive. Pliny describes it as the ornament of Asia. The great wealth of this town did not arise from a rich hinterland or through trade; its port was silted up. Its wealth came through selling religion. St.Paul was arrested by the Ephesians silversmiths for reducing their sale of statuettes of Cybele and Diana. Artemis' priests were eunuchs assisted by virgins. Young men who did not wish to risk the 66% chance of dying from castration and the certain loss of sexual *enjoyment might have chosen employment* in a dull brick Christian church which would hold hundreds, rather than serve in a magnificent marble temple holding thousands.

After Jesus' crucifixion, John the 'beloved disciple' went to Ephesus with Mary the Mother of God and Mary Magdalene *[Christians used to say she was a prostitute, to travel with the Virgin in this way I would have described her as a thwarted fiancé or wife].* The Virgin's cottage was discovered about four hundred years later in

214

the middle of a circle of stones set out as the birthplace of the Virgin Artemis.   From this cottage the Assumption of the Virgin Mary to heaven took place.   Protestant guides suppress this information to tourists, but two Popes in the 20th century have visited it.   The early Christian church is genuine and Timothy was the first bishop of Ephesus and he died in 97 AD.

Artemis was descended from the Minoan Goddess, and her nymphs did wild and lascivious dances but after Homer she became a virgin and was simultaneously Goddess of childbirth!   Diana is sometimes said to be her Roman equivalent.   An Ephesian said "If Christ does not rise tomorrow we shall have no corn this year".   St. Paul lived at Ephesus for three years.   He addresses his letter to the 'saints that live at Ephesus' and tells servants to be obedient to their masters with fear and trembling.

Bertrand Russell says in his history of Western Philosophy "The religions of Egypt and Babylon, like other ancient religions, were originally fertility cults.   The earth was female the sun male.   The bull was usually regarded as an embodiment of male fertility and bull gods were common.   In Babylon, Ishtar, the earth goddess was supreme among female divinities, throughout Western Asia; the Great Mother was worshipped under various names.   When Greek colonists in Asia Minor found temples to her, they named her Artemis and took over the existing cult.   This is the origin of "Diana of the Ephesians".   Christianity transformed her into the Virgin Mary and it was a council at Ephesus that legitimised the title "Mother of God as applied to our Lady".   Acts XX 34 "Great is Diana of the Ephesians."   If the idea surprises you that the Virgin Mary is a reincarnation of an ancient fertility goddess, the Encyclopaedia Britannica II 912 says, "The Baltic goddess Zemes mate [earth mother] whose functions were later assumed by the Virgin Mary".

The inhabitants of Ephesus were massacred at the end of the 11th cent. And again by the Mohammedans in 1283, and yet again by Tamberlane in 1401 who plundered it for a month and in 1405 the Turks conquered it.

THE MAGI, MITHRAS AND MOLOCH

The Talmud 500 AD (*the Jewish bible*) says Jesus learnt magic in Egypt. The word Magi [three wise men] comes from the same root as magic, they would have been Zoroastrian Holy men, and they would have believed that one can manipulate fate by participation, they would be members of the same international priestly guild as the Sadducees, regardless of a mere difference of religion. "We three kings from Orient are," is synonymous with 'Magi' because the role of priest and king were usually combined. In memory of this custom, Roman Emperors were Pontifex Maximus, and our Queen is head of the church. Science was yet to be invented, but they would be learned men, or astrologers [the star of Bethlehem]. The sort of astrology, which was believed in at that time, was the worship of celestial deities who controlled ones fate in a non-conspicuous way. Prophecy was generally believed in, it was not like today, a sceptical age. Mystery religions with initiation ceremonies such as baptism and circumcision produced group loyalty. The Mithraic communion says, "He who shall not eat of my body nor drink of my blood, so that he may be one with me and I with him, shall not be saved." [Resurrected in the future.] Roman Catholic communion wine is only drunk by the priest but some Protestant congregations all share it, at blood heat.

Christianity *does not forget to incorporate the nasty* Moloch or Melak [the first born baby eating God], Jesus is God's first born and God sacrifices him. The Virgin Mary knew that human life had a value, as all Jews did at that time. The custom of burning your first born children alive as a gift offering to YHWH the jealous God was less popular at the time of the birth of Christ but if Jesus was his first born, Joseph would have had to pay 50 shekels tax to the temple to avoid him being burnt alive. It was cheaper to have daughters you only had to pay 30 shekels. This was the full cash value God had put on babies lives, despite the fact that the civilised Romans had made the burning of anyone illegal. *There is no record of Jesus disapproving of this custom but if my fiction about Jesus is correct it would explain why he would not have wanted to reduce temple dues.*

M I R A C L E S

"Supernatural" means "unnatural". Farrar says Jesus' first miracle is the conversion of water into wine at a relations wedding *where he speaks in my opinion disrespectfully to his mother like a nervous man before performing on stage.* He has travelled 60 miles to the wedding so he cannot have seen her for sometime. *It is the ideal location to practice in front of a friendly audience, if he is found out, he could turn it into a joke, the guests are already happy. His first trick is successful. But is increasing the consumption of alcohol, a Gods first job?*

Jesus is constantly asking the cured to keep their cure a secret, Matt xii 16, Mark i 25 &45. iii 12, viii 30, Luke iv 35, v 14, vii 56, *is this to hide the trickery?* Although he knows it will eventually receive publicity.

On another occasion Jesus appears with *[two actors]* Elijah and Moses to three of his previously sleeping disciples. The three men are illuminated in the pre-dawn desert by a bright light. A loud voice says "This is my beloved Son; hear him", the light goes out, Jesus comes down to the disciples who were too frightened to rise *and investigate and* says "arise and be not afraid", and so the day dawned. *It is obvious how with a caste of extras a miracle like that can be performed. The desert is not a sandy one, but full of changes of level, rocks and plants to hide behind.*

Gladstone, the retired prime minister and Thomas Huxley publicly debated whether Jesus would be hung under British law because he destroyed the Gadarine swine as a result of transferring devils from an insane man into the swine. *Did he compensate the owner?*

Farrar says that Lazarus, who was a respectable citizen, was a close friend of Jesus, others say his sisters Martha and Mary were even closer. Lazarus was buried in a stone tomb with a stone door, so breathing was no difficulty, *as a child I used to worry how he could breathe in a coffin with earth on top.* He only stayed there four days. But Jesus gathered a big crowd to watch, it was only four miles from Jerusalem, and Lazarus lived for another 30 years. The story is only told in John some 60 years after Jesus died, to protect Lazarus's family. Caiaphas the high priest thought he should be executed, playing games with tombs was against Roman law; the Pharaohs didn't like thieves. However, Acts 26 23 says Jesus was the first person to rise from the dead, *so presumably they assume Lazarus' rising was a trick?* Elisha restored the son of the Shunammite woman to life in II Kings 4.8-37, so Jesus was not the only one who could give life.

Jesus walked on the non-salty waters of Lake Galilee. I have seen a photo of someone lying on his back in the salty waters of the Dead Sea reading a newspaper without getting it wet. *Water with such unusual buoyancy characteristics would naturally give rise to stories, which could get exaggerated and displaced. I think it was Paul Daniels a magician on TV who said he could walk on fresh water.*

One of the only miracles in all four gospels is the feeding of the five thousand men plus women and children. Farrar says it is on the evening of the day Jesus walks on the water. He speaks of 70 followers going ahead of Jesus *obviously some of these could arrange props for a magician. He was able to obtain a good crowd as most of them were Passover Pilgrims on their way to Jerusalem. They would have watched Jesus' boat being delayed all day by adverse winds so they could see that he personally could not prepare any tricks. The food must have cost 200 denarii and the disposal of the rope and wicker baskets must have been the biggest problem.* Remember Mary the sister of Lazarus spent 300 denarii on the spikenard she used on Jesus' feet.

Miracles convert people to Christianity even in the 1950s, at a meeting at Haringey, given by Billy Graham, he called for those wishing to collect advertising literature to come forward, in the darkened auditorium, then there was a hymn and a fiery sermon which made the congregation forget all about the people coming to collect free advertising literature. Then he called forth the converted and before anybody could forget this call, the spotlights were shone in the faces of those coming forward to collect advertising literature which made them bow their heads, *and everyone was amazed at the numbers that had been 'converted'.* But we never seem to have any miracles in the news on TV. Yet they always seem to get dramatic photos of other things that very seldom happen, like fires, riots and accidents, the only sensible conclusion is that miracles do not happen, now that we have better methods of investigation.

In 1870 the Vatican council declared a belief in miracles, [not every miracle], was obligatory and that anyone who does not believe in them is anathema [cursed] and that the Pope in saying so, was infallible. [Subject to no possible error]. However if all the pieces of the Holy Cross approved of by the Roman Catholics were put together, the resultant shape would not be a cross and it would be made of many different types of wood including English oak.

The Holy Turin Shroud has been proved a fake by carbon dating. Goethe said, "The miracle is the dearest child of faith." Hume denies the possibility of miracles, because they are improbable. 18th century thinkers found the vastness and complexity of the order of nature more impressive than any alleged exceptions to it. Cicero believes in causes and says there are no miracles, but adds that they may be necessary for the piety of ignorant folk.

The placebo effect has been demonstrated in modern medicine and is statistically more effective with church goers than with agnostics, and with people who pay rather than those that get it free on the National Health, the effect is better if the patient has faith in the healer.

THE MESSIAH

The word Christ is Greek for Messiah; it does not mean God it means "anointed one". A Messiah was usually a Priest-King. Their contemporaries knew High Priests as 'Priest Messiah' or 'Priest Christ'. Ref. Page 342 of the Holy Blood and the Holy Grail. However, the Jews thought the later ones appointed by the Romans, were false and therefore there was a vacancy of a sort. *To me Messiah means messenger.*

The Jews did not believe that Jesus was the Son of God, they believed in a Messiah which is different. St. Paul did not think of Jesus as God, but non-Jews could misinterpret his delicate description of Messiahdom. The gentiles were familiar with lots of Gods that could die and be reborn, so they had no problem believing in him.

The Magi said he was the King of the Jews and gave him anointing oil. Mary of Bethany anointed his head with nard, a smell that would remind those that smelt him on Palm Sunday of the smell of God in the Temple. Because women were imbeciles at law it would be hard to punish her; *and she could say "I bought it for my dead brother Lazarus, and since Jesus found him alive, I was so grateful I used it on him because I had no further use for it".* On the other *hand Mary might have been a descendant of David and the Holy Scriptures might not have specified the sex of the anointer because in a patriarchal society it is so obvious it could not be a woman. Was he expecting to be anointed by a priest, say Nicodemous, in the Temple at the Passover? Did Mary anoint him, just in case he was arrested too soon?* "Are you the King of the Jews?" said Pilate, not 'why did you whip the bankers in the Temple?'

Jesus the Son of God never claimed to be the equal of Adam who is described in the Old Testament as in the likeness of God, *why should one son be immortal if the other is not?*

Alexander the Great and the Emperor Augustus of Rome had both found it necessary to be declared Gods especially in their Eastern provinces. Alexander had worked wonders, miracle cures in front of a large audience.

The Old Testament predicted a Messiah. In 715-686 BC Hezekiah [13th king after David] and his son Judas were both recognised by the Jewish people as Messiah Kings. Cyrus, a foreigner, was said to be the Messiah because he freed the Jews in Babylon and returned their temple treasure to them. Judas Maccabeus had been a Messiah in 166 BC but his Hasmonean dynasty had been a disaster. Everyone was certain the Messiah was coming and wanted to be the first to identify him. It is reported that a thousand Jews between Judas Maccabeus and Christ had claimed they were the Messiah, none of them are remembered now they are dead; but during the Babylonian captivity it would have been treason to talk of King David's heir, so they spoke elliptically of a Messiah or anointed one. *Later this patriotism got mixed up with Jesus and God.* Apollonius Tyana born in the 1st century AD was a Neo-Pythagorean wonder worker, who performed miracles and was possessed of Divine cosmic power. There was widespread conviction that a Jewish Messiah was going to rule the Roman Empire. This actually happened in 67-68 AD a wonder worker who could heal the sick and who proclaimed himself to be God, was proclaimed both God and Emperor of Rome for the first time on Jewish soil; and indeed he was worshipped as God throughout the Roman Empire. The only error was that he was an Italian by birth and his name was Vespasian.

In 115-116 AD another Messiah in Cyrene prepared to return to Zion. The Romans martyred Ben Kochba in AD 132-135, he was against the Christians, and he was a freedom fighter who held out in a fortress for two years and had his own coins struck. The war lasted 3½ years and hundreds of Jews died. Hadrian had to bring Severus his ablest general from Britain to beat him.

The Dead Sea Scrolls refer to someone who is not Jesus as the "Messiah of Righteousness" and they are full of Messianic hope. The idea that the Messiah is the eternal word of God [logos] comes from Philo not Jesus. Jesus *is devious* he does not clearly say I am GOD. In John's Gospel, Jesus says, "I am, in many forms, bread of life, light of the world, door of the sheepfold, good shepherd, resurrection and the light, the way, truth and life, true vine, I and the father are one, before Abraham was I am". Jesus says to his Apostles "whom do men say I am?" They say that Herod Antipas fears that he is John the Baptist, an Elijah, a Jeremiah, a prophet or precursor. "But whom say ye that I am?" Thou art the Christ, the Son of the living God, says Peter. Christ is *flattered* and gives Peter, who later is to *attempt a murder and fail* while resisting arrest, the key to Heaven and Hell and heavenly contractual powers.

Ezekiel 4.1 addresses the general reader as the 'Son of Man' at the time of the Babylonian captivity. This same phrase is used 80 times in the New Testament to describe Christ. Robert Eisenman says 'Son of Man' means 'Son of Adam' in both Aramaic and Hebrew. In Daniel, the Saints in the plural who are to possess the Kingdom are already likened to the Son of Man. The emphasis on King David and the phrase King of the Jews *is related to the later idea of the return of King Arthur.* The punishment for claiming to be King of the Jews is stoning, not crucifixion. When Jesus was asked "who is your father" he must have always had a problem, he could not say Joseph because that would not be true, he could not say I am a bastard because that would be rude to his mother, and might subject her to verbal abuse, or even stoning by lawless urchins, so he had to be enigmatic. He could not say he was his mother's son, because contemporary thought said women do not have children (Homunculi). His statement that he was the 'son of man' was absolutely true, the fact that it had a double entende meaning that he was the Messiah, *must have amused him, but if my fiction is correct he would be determined not to give away his natural father even if it meant death.*

In an incomprehensible way, God and Joseph were both at

the same time father to Jesus; otherwise there is no point in the male line to David. The Pharaoh likewise was a son of the Sun and the previous Pharaoh. It must be possible to have an earthly father and a heavenly one at the same time. Possibly Jesus became the Messiah when his first cousin poured water on him. He only started his ministry seriously when St. John the Baptist was dead. The Greeks thought that immortal Gods could become mortal.

NAZARETH, NAZARENE, NAZIRITE, NAZORITE.

The squire 'of Nazareth', would not have been very pleased with Joseph being called 'of Nazareth' if he was just one of his workers, *the phrase suggests that Joseph was that squire.* A Nazarene is a follower of Jesus of Nazareth. The word Nazarene can mean a Christian or a Jew from Syria; it is not a very precise word. But Nazarene could mean Nazirite a 'Concentrated' or 'Separated One', like Samson who could not touch dead people, let a razor touch his hair or have any contact with grapes, ie alcohol or raisins. *I disagree with the many who say Jesus was, a Nazirite, (a long haired hippy) because he believed that nothing that entered the mouth of a man defiled him,* [Matt 6 25 "Take no thought for what you shall eat or drink".] and it is likely that he tasted his miraculous wine at Cana, surely even doing miracles with the stuff should be forbidden, but the dead he touched came to life which possibly avoided his defilement. Did Christ wear a turban like the Sikhs? Some Nazarenes did not believe in St. Paul or the virgin birth and were very Jewish. When James the brother of Jesus, refused to deny that Christ is the Son of God; Ananas son of Annas judicially murdered him. James' cousin Simeon is said to have become the leader of the Nazarenes. An Arabic copy of a manuscript originally written in AD 66, says Paul has turned the religion of the Nazarenes into the religion of the Romans.

The Old Nazarenes or Mandaens like the Samaritans were opposed to Judean traditions, they were vegetarian, rejected animal sacrifices, practised circumcision and observed the Sabbath and festivals and believed in St. John the Baptist. *Did Jesus and St. John see eye to eye?*

THE ARREST

Jesus says in Luke 36 & 38 «and he that hath no sword, let him sell his garment, and buy one». .... And they [the disciples] said, «Look! Here are two swords, Lord». «That is enough». He replied. .. The British Government bought ordinary swords for soldiers at £1.600 each in the 1960s *so the apostles must have been very well dressed for fisherfolk, which suggests Jesus was very generous to his staff.* When the disciples saw what was going to happen, they asked, «Shall we use our swords, Lord?» And one of them smote the servant of the High Priest, and cut off his right ear. And Jesus answered, Suffer ye thus far. And he touched his ear, and healed him.» Matthew and Mark record the smiting off of the ear but not the healing. St. John «Then Simon Peter having a sword drew it, and smote the High Priest's servant, and cut off his right ear. The servant's name was Malchus.»

Rupert Furneaux in an all too credible book says on page 51, that the carrying of arms by civilians was illegal in Palestine under Roman law and I see no reason to doubt this statement. He paints Jesus as a patriotic self-seeking terrorist as do many other modern writers. *However I am too sentimental to like his Christ, I can not bring myself to believe that the world's greatest religion which stresses love can really have arisen out of the exploits of an ineffective Zealot.* Readers of the Bible see nothing wrong with the carrying of swords because in uncivilised England up until the nineteenth century it was legal. But today when they are an offence we should be horrified. It is criminal to resist arrest with weapons.

Certainly Peter goes on to use his sword. *It is not easy to cut off someone's ear when they hold their head upright, if they move it to one side to avoid a blow this presents the head at just the correct angle. Swords in those days were made of iron and did not have a cutting edge as sharp as modern swords. Malchus must have been very bruised.* The attempted murder of an arresting officer going about his official business is an offence the majority of Christians today would think deserved the death penalty and a modern jury would judge Jesus to be an accessory to attempted murder, because he approved of the carrying of swords knowing he was going to be legally arrested. Yet Jesus rewards Peter with the keys to the gates of

Heaven and Hell and is the rock upon which the church is built! It is true that in Luke's gospel, the last one to be written. Jesus is cleared because he heals Malchus. It does not clear Peter and *looks like an after thought* to show Jesus in a more peaceful light.

The Good News Edition of the Bible says Malchus was a slave, *I have no idea where they have got this information from but I guess the word they are translating means "very devoted, loyal and obedient servant" for it is hardly likely that a named leader of a cohort which has five hundred men in it is likely to be a slave.* But even if not all versions use the word cohort they are all agreed that he is accompanied by a very large crowd that carries swords and staves. The King James' version of the Bible describes Malchus as "The Servant" *which equals "Chief Servant"* of the High Priest. Some think this is Caiaphas who was the High Priest. But John 18.12 – 18 24 says he was taken to Annas and the High Priest questioned him and the sent him bound to Caiaphas' *another* High Priest. The Bible frequently inaccurately calls Annas the High Priest. (Luke 3.2) In John 18.26 Malchus is said to be a kinsman of the High Priest and he is resident in the *High Priest* Annas' house. Jesus Christ is a kinsman of Annas to whose house Jesus is taken for this preliminary interview. This makes Malchus a kinsman of Jesus Christ.

Malchus did not just offer his cheek he offered his ear. *Malchus behaved like a God, not Jesus. He forgave Peter,* despite a cohort under his control, he did not arrest any of the disciples, and he meekly obeyed his instruction to arrest Jesus. He stayed up all night and recognized Peter as the man that nearly killed him, and yet he never arrested him, only reported that he had lied three times before the cocks crowed.

Is Jesus a spin-doctor who says "Love your enemy" while acting as an *evil* patriotic terrorist? Or a God that practices *unjustified* physical violence? Or is there a third alternative? In my probable fiction I am proud of my solution to this conundrum.

C R U C I F I X I O N S

Crucifixion was a punishment, which spread from Persia, to Palestine and via the Carthaginians, to Rome. Spartacus's slave revolt was put down with 6,000 crucifixions along The Appian way.

Varus, the Roman Governor of Syria, crucified 2,000 ringleaders of a Jewish revolt in 4 BC. The "wicked priest" in the Dead Sea Scrolls crucified in 152 BC, 800 Pharisees while feasting with prostitutes.

Not all crucified people died, quite a lot were alive when they were taken down, after several days. *Jesus a healthy man was probably on the cross for less than one twelfth of the average time (72 hours) it took to die. He was taken to a tomb which probably had six shelves for dead bodies, with a heavy sliding stone door which would have been impossible to open from the inside. Similar to the one that Lazarus had spent a few days in. It is clear that Jesus was resuscitated not resurrected it is possible that the original language did not have both words.* Herbs, myrrh & aloes which are for healing not embalming were amongst the 100 lb taken in to *resuscitate* him.

George Moore in 'The Brook Kerith', D.H.Lawrence in 'The Man who Died' and Hugh Schonfield in 'The Passover Plot' suggest Jesus did not die. The Sales Koran i 64 124 says, "They slew him not, neither crucified Him, but He was represented by one in His likeness," *[This is yet another way of denying the miracle].* It also says he was on the cross from soon after noon until nearly sunset, and the inscription on the cross was "King of the Jews" Not son of God. Jesus cried "My God, my God, why hast thou forsaken me". *If he himself was God, that is rather an odd sentiment. Or did he say father?*

Jesus said he was thirsty, *with so much pain to think about, so minor a discomfort so soon is surprising,* but a vinegar soaked rag on a pole was handed up to his mouth, *it would be possible for him to have bitten off a pain killing drug which would make him faint, such as opium or Bella Donna.* Jesus being presumed dead did not have his legs broken like the two robbers alongside him, instead he had a lance thrust into his side and this did not wake him up but it bled blood and water. Since water is an odd substance for a God to be made of. I think it meant *the blood flowed,* which proves the heart was still pumping, dead bodies hardly bleed.

Prisoners were nailed or tied to the cross piece first, which was then raised together with the prisoner. It normally took two days to a week to die. But death can occur reasonably quickly, through asphyxiation, if the arms take the weight of the body. The other robbers clearly had something to stand on, even if it was only a nail that is why some one kindly broke their legs. It is therefore probable that Jesus had something to stand on. Renaissance painters frequently show a block of wood under his feet, this makes it easier to nail them. This means he had to wait till shock, thirst, starvation or exposure killed him. If the nails went through the hand as Justin the Martyr said they did, [the stigmata] open hands would not have carried the full weight of the body, the flesh of the hand would have ripped, thus releasing it, so the body must have had some support. If the nails had large square heads, by closing ones fist one can get the weight taken on the two centre finger nails, which quickly get trapped so one can not open ones fingers, it's painful but the hand might not pull loose, the exquisite pain is in the shoulders which take the weight. But it is likely that his forearms were also tied unless the nails went through the wrists, between the radius and the ulna. If the victim was, as was sometimes the case, tied to the cross, or given a seat peg, it took longer to die, which was crueller. Some times there was one nail per foot, sometimes one nail for both feet. Historical tradition shows that the crucified were quite naked, and the Jews believe that Christians always paint him wearing a nappy; because they do not want the uneducated to see that he is a circumcised Jew, and this might stop Christians happily murdering Jews as the crucifiers of God. For example there was no real protest by Christians about Hitler's holocaust.

In a survey; of the Church of England clergy only half believe that faith in Christ is the only route to salvation, and a third of the 2,000 out of 10,000 doubted or disbelieved in the Physical Resurrection, the most important Christian belief. *Was the 'Resurrection' a translation error for 'resuscitation'?* Aloes were taken into the tomb these are not for the dead.

JOSEPH OF ARIMATHEA AND NICODEMUS

Joseph of Arimathea was a member of the Sanhedrin. [Arimathea was formerly in Samaria, but boundary changes now called it Judea]. John describes him as a secret disciple.

The Druids according to Caesar 54 BC believed that the immortality of the soul was the principal incentive and reason for leading a virtuous life, this could have influenced Christianity because William of Malmesbury who had access to the books in Glastonbury library before it was burnt down said Joseph of Arimathea was a minister of mines to the Roman government, Decurio Nobilis. Joseph owned tin mines in Cornwall, and had land given him rent-free by the King of England and is buried at Glastonbury. Victor Dunstan says he was uncle to both Joseph and Mary. Roman law says that only close relatives may claim the bodies of the crucified, which is why some say weakly that he might have been Jesus' natural father.

Crucified persons must have a dishonourable burial; only very important people could have got Pilate to overlook this at short notice. Jesus was crucified in Joseph of Arimathea's private garden, where he had a new rock hewn tomb, *the type with shelves for the corpses and a sliding door,* the sort that only one man in ten thousand could afford to be buried in, the sort that Lazarus had. The weight of balm they took into the tomb with them was twice the maximum personal luggage weight permitted on an aeroplane today, which must have represented in value hundreds of people's annual wages.

Joseph of Arimthea arrived late at the crucifixion and he rushed off to Pilate to ask for the body [soma]. Pilate gave permission for the corpse [ptoma]. Joseph returned with clean linen and spices and Nicodemus.

Jesus calls Nicodemus the "Master of Israel"; he was the third most important member of the Sanhedrin, [chakran] 'a ruler of the Jews'. He came to Jesus by night, which suggests he did not want to be seen. He became a disciple of Jesus after the Crucifixion and was baptised by Peter and John. The Jewish authorities then stripped him of his office, beat him and drove him out of Jerusalem. He sheltered in Gamaliel's, country house who was his kinsman.

CONSTANTINE, EUSEBIUS & CHRISTIANITY

The Emperor Diocletian ordered a particularly severe persecution of Christians in 303AD. Eusebius, and his friends were arrested and he alone escaped by denying Christ. With virtually no literate Christians left he was made Bishop of Caesarea in Palestine, a more important city than Jerusalem. Constantine was born in the Eastern Empire where there were many Christians, both his mother and mother-in-law were very interested in Christianity. In 306 AD Constantine was declared Emperor in York England by his troops. Through conquest he became sole Emperor in 324 AD.

Constantine was totally ruthless to his political enemies, decreed that all non-monotheistic religions were illegal; this caused a problem for most Christians who like Bishop Arius of Alexandria believed Jesus was a secondary separate God to the Father. Eusebius Bishop of Caesarea did not want to be personally crucified, or for his Christian friends to be killed. So he got Constantine to call the council at Nicaea 325 AD. There were several calendars in use at that time, and by varying which one was being sent to each Bishop he arranged for the majority of those against his ideas to arrive too late to affect the vote, however he had to murder a few late comers who protested. He declared that 3 = 1 an arithmetical nonsense by declaring that God was one substance and that the Trinity was one. This meant that the post of Messiah was vacant *and he permitted the Emperor Constantine to think that he was the Messiah,* and could work miracles. This started the Christian belief that all subsequent kings were divine and could cure ills. St George of England is not a Roman Catholic saint because he did not believe in the Trinity.

Eusibus said that Constantine was the Saviour of the world, and was the Logos incarnate. Constantine himself believed he was the Son of Sol Invictus, the invincible Sun and was prepared to tolerate the idea that God the Father was the Sun. It helped to transfer worship of the virgin born Mithras the Iranian God of light who was born several thousands years earlier on the 25th of December from a rock watched by shepherds to Christ. By 200 AD the God Mithras had more adherents than Christianity. *The Roman Catholics adopted his bread and wine ceremony.*

Astarte "the Virgin Goddess" brought forth a child, an actual baby every year to represent the rebirth of the Sun on 25th of December. In 321 AD Christians changed from the Sabbath [Saturday] to Sunday [the day of the Sun God]. Constantine had portraits of himself issued showing himself as the Messiah with the Sun's aureole behind his head, this later became the Christian halo, *and may account for why portraits of Jesus do not make him look Jewish.* Constantine was not very well educated and he fell for Eusebius' flattery, and gave considerable support to Christians and helped them change a religion of love into a religion of conformist law by punishing intellectuals, whom we now know as heretics. Constantine continued to crucify non-monotheists but abolished the crucifixion of Christians and branding them as criminals. He commissioned Eusebius to make new copies or translations of the Gospels.   No pre-Eusebius Gospels survive *because he altered them, and eliminated and altered Josephus' text concerning Jesus.* Constantine made Christianity a legal religion, his heir made it mandatory. In 337 BC Constantine was baptised on his deathbed by half a dozen different religions including Christians. The world thinks of Constantine as very Christian because Eusebius wrote an unreliable history saying he was so. In 747 AD a council at Nicaea condemned Eusebius as unstable. In 750-800 a forgery called the Donation of Constantine, made Constantine look Christian by giving to the Bishop of Rome the Papal States [represented by one rung of his triple crown] as well as making him Pope with supreme power over all Christian Bishops.

CHAPTER VIII
A FICTIONAL GODLESS LIFE OF JESUS CHRIST

Professor Richard Dawkins says "Faith is for the non-thinking" "God is fiction." *So my fiction is no more right or wrong than the word of God.*

PREFACE

How did a religion of love and kindness, the greatest the world has ever known, *arise out of trickery and magic?* The good historian must above all be a questioner. He must question the assumptions of the past and of previous histories and he must force the past to yield up its secrets, by studying the experiences of the people who lived in that period. He should also look with hindsight at what they should have done, see if any tried to do it, and if they tried, why they failed. Some also believe that like Arthur Evans at Knossos they should flesh out the skeletons.

The following is a hypothesis or scenario, which accommodates the known facts better than the well known Christian beliefs.

It is the actors and actresses that one remembers, on television and sometimes the writers, but almost never the producers, directors and financiers. Likewise, in history, Jesus and St. John the Baptist get recorded and remembered but who were the producers, directors and financiers?

To those that are frightened by blasphemy I would like to quote David Hume' "It is contrary to common sense to entertain apprehensions or terrors upon account of any opinion whatsoever or to imagine that we run any risk in the hereafter by the freest use of our reason. Such a sentiment implies both an absurdity and an inconsistency. It is an absurdity to believe that the Deity has human passions, and one of the lowest of human passions, a restless appetite for applause. It is an inconsistency to believe that since the Deity has this human passion, he has not others also, and in particular, a disregard to the opinions of creatures so much inferior."

Santa Claus [St. Anthony]; St Catherine of Alexandria, and

her cartwheel; and St. George and the Dragon have all had their saintliness denied by the Pope in 1969. *The Pope should not be offended if I take away Jesus' godliness* likewise, because of historical research. All four were actual people. Hypatia [St Catherine] the most learned woman in antiquity was a mathematician and polytheist, murdered by Christians under the direction of a bishop. George of Cappodocia, the patron Saint of England believed in two separate gods, the Father and Jesus.

Many writers suggest that Joseph was Jesus' father and that Jesus was a Zealot who planned rebellion against Rome. They quote Peter's petulant act of near murder when he chopped Malchus' ear off, and Jesus' approval of his disciple's illegal possession of 2 swords (Sicarii). Modern scholarship suggests Jesus is a criminal, like an I.R.A. terrorist.

Because I am sentimental I can not bear to think of Jesus as bad and because I am rational I can see a probable explanation that makes him a good real man, much better than the God Jesus we all know, who was rather a failure as a God. His wonders were in relation to the size of the world, domestic or parochial. He published nothing as good or clear as the code of Hammurabi, nearly 2,000 years earlier.

If one human produced a world religion, that human would have to be a man of exceptional ability. He would require a knowledge of religious history and geography; he would require a large organisation with power and authority; together with great wealth and a team of dedicated intelligent workers, backroom boys, producers, directors and may be a couple of presenters or actors to train disciples and apostles to put the ideas over.

Let us look for such an exceptional man. There is only one man who lived at that time and in the right place that is exceptional enough, and with a large enough organisation. Let us look at his life and see if he would have wanted to create a new religion. Strangely he is not mentioned in the Encyclopaedia Britannica despite being important in history and in the Bible.

THE JESUS FICTION

John Hyrcanus a Pharisee priest, a descendant of Zadok followed in the footsteps of his father Judas Maccabeus, the Jewish Messiah, and became king and high priest in 135 BC. He extended his kingdom and conquered Idumea but he did not murder all the people *as Moses would have advised or enslave all the people as the Assyrians would have done.* However, he did order them all, upon pain of death to believe in Moses' law and have their foreskins chopped off. The majority agreed and became 'chosen people of God' *as a reward for their cowardice.* The Jews do not nowadays proselytise, but John Hyrcanus did. However, we can imagine that educated, landed, Idumeans may have only superficially agreed to be Jews, but really kept an open sceptical Hellenised mind and retained some of their Zoroastrian traditions. Remember the Midianites murdered by Moses lived in Idumea. *Such a man, I imagine was Jesus' great-grandfather and as a priest willing to change his religion and co-operate with the conquerors, he gained preferment and wealth. He told his grandson, born c.40 BC this is the secret of my success, work with your conquerors, though he used the phrase "Love your enemies, praise those that persecute you." He was thinking of the persecution by the Jewish Maccabeans.*

"Do you believe in YHWH" Hanan said one day to his grandfather, when he was a teenager.

"If you promise to keep it a secret," said his father who was also present.

"Of course" replied Hanan and his father knew, he never impulsively blurted things out.

"Remember if you repeat this conversation, I will lose my job, the house we live in, and may be my life, so don't tell anyone, but the world is subject to natural laws, there are no miracles, but we priests have to pretend that there is a God, to make the stupid peasants bring us their tithes. Wouldn't it be a bore, if we had to work in the fields? That is the reason we have to encourage the people to sacrifice."

"Do you believe we should lie to the congregation," said Hanan.

"No, one can look very silly if one's caught out, and it is

*harder to remember a lie told years ago than it is to remember a real
happening. It is sensible to speak with the forked tongue of a snake,
which is our family badge, like the oracle of Delos in riddles that
can be taken both ways, or parables whose meaning can be altered
if one gets into trouble with the authorities. It is sensible to present
facts in such a way that your hearer will exaggerate and distort them
to your advantage."*

"Can you see the future dad?"

*"Certainly not, but by careful observation and logical
deduction and listening for news I can have a very good guess.
But it is our duty to help the people see the future and obtain justice
for them."*

*"Do you think the tricks the Magicians do are really
necessary? I think I know how they are all done now."*

*"Yes I know you are very clever at them" said his father,
"but the illiterates are so stupid, they would never do what you told
them to do for their own benefit, even if you explained why, they
lack common sense and they will not respect your advice unless they
believe it comes from God. Notice how Moses never says 'do this
because I Moses tell you', he says 'I am the spokesman of God' and
then orders the people to do what he wants, pretending that they were
Gods instructions, God can not contradict him because God does
not exist. Magical tricks have always been part of religion even in
the heathen temples they have jugglers and magicians on stage in
between the sexy acts".*

*"Do you believe in an after life, in heaven and hell?" said
Hanan.*

*"That is the most important part of religion," said his
grandfather who had been brought up a Zoroastrian. "The hope
and fear of reward and punishment is the raison d'etre of religion,
that is why God was invented, that is how you make ignorant people
do your bidding. Long term selfishness is a beautiful driving force,
and providing the peasants can be persuaded that there is an
after life and a bossy God, it is in there long term benefit to obey
Him."*

*Hanan was a good boy and he listened attentively to his
grandfather. The family spoke Greek all the time except when they
were in the kitchen where they spoke Idumean which was a silly*

language which one could not write. He could read and write all the languages the Old testament was written in, with facility, including Aramaic because if he was going to be a successful priest, he would have to know them, though of course many properly born Jewish priests couldn't even read the books of what we now call the Old Testament. As a rich and educated man, he was friendly with the Herods another rich and educated family who likewise were not descended from one of the Jewish tribes, *and became good friends with Herod Antipas,* who was his contemporary. He travelled to Alexandria where he became acquainted with Philo, and to Babylon. Some say he went to India *where he could have seen many miracles being performed, like the man that was buried alive for five hours.* There he would have observed blind beggars on the entrance steps to temples, as there are today, who are not blind; the priests get a cut in the takings and sighted men make better beggars than real blind ones, for they can judge the sentimentality and wealth of the giver better.

He dreamed as a child of becoming God and ruling the world *as Alexander had done, or ruling Palestine like the Messiah Maccabeus.* It was not just the power he wanted, his logical mind liked inventing social and religious systems that would benefit mankind. Unlike most dreamers, he set about achieving it quickly and efficiently. First he needed a lot more money and power. *He noticed conquests with the sword, like Alexander's are impermanent. The Hasmonean dynasty through the use of the sword had failed. However, Hillel who preached "What is unpleasing to you, do not do to your neighbour, that is the whole law." had been made Nasi [Head of the Sanhedrin] in Jerusalem with the help of Herod.* Hanan genuinely believed this philosophy and had rephrased the sentence *"Love thy neighbour as yourself"* which he kept secret for future use. *Herod demolished the Temple and set about building a much greater one. He was able to do this because he was fabulously rich as a result of the treasure trove found on his estate.*

Hillel helped Hanan to get his first post as a priest in the temple at Jerusalem. Hanan made a good marriage and had lots of children, including five sons. He cultivated his Jewish relations because with their regional accents about the house, it helped to make him appear a proper Jew. His international Hellenised accent did not reveal his Idumean background.

Anne Jesus' grandmother was desperate to have a child; *I believe she was approaching her menopause.*

So she prayed to God, *which I think means she went to a priest she was related to (Hanan) in the Temple who had given his wife lots of children.* She became pregnant and was ecstatically grateful to God. She and promised to give the child called Mary to the Temple, *in case her husband wanted it adopted. Is the giving of girls to Temples a memory of temple prostitution? Or was it because one of the priests was the real father and her husband's sperm was defective. Was the father Hanan?*

Mary was born and according to the 1st cent. Gospel of James and the 3rd cent. Nativity of Mary she was given to the Temple aged 3 by her mother Anne. Pope Sixtus V in 1585 said it was on Nov. 21st. As a cousin and a temple priest Hanan *was probably Mary's chief guardian,* and must have known her for many years which makes Hanan's approval of Jesus' death sentence surprising since Jesus was Mary's son.

THE HIGH PRIEST HANAN

Everyone is agreed that 'Hanan', 'Annas', and 'Ananus', are the same person. *I believe he was Jesus' most capable contemporary in Palestine and that he had secretly funded and organised* the popular uprising that had deposed Joazar as High Priest. In order to quieten the mob he was appointed High Priest by the Roman procurator on the advice of Herod Antipas, and general enthusiasm from the Sadducees. He never claimed he was the Messiah *because* he was not descended from King David. To retain his position as High Priest, he depended on Roman support, *and the Romans had made a bargain concerning Moses written law, which supported slavery, they did not want him deviating from the book,* by inventing oral law as the Pharisees would have him do or inventing new theories of love like Hillel. *Hanan was an idealist, and like me, he knew there was no God [He knew that, even as High Priest, God never bothered to speak to him] but unlike me he was prepared to practice magic, not just for the sake of power, even if that was nice, but because he was an idealist who wished to make a better world. To become High*

Priest he had, had to stamp, on all his own non-orthodox ideas. This did not stop him secretly, from his position of power, plotting the take over of an old religion, by a new one based, on tolerance love and kindness. He also loved the magnificent marble temple, and the Jewish idea of one God; he was not prepared to suffer a religion with lots of gods and therefore lots of friction between their respective priests.

Hanan realised that the Roman polytheist state religion had failed to grip the hearts of her subject peoples and the minds of rational Romans. The Emperors becoming new gods did nothing to help its credibility. *It was such a mess, it did not raise his antagonism, and he felt it would die through lack of interest.* It was, in any case, not really indigenous to Italy; they were internationalised Greek Gods. Etruscan matrilineal religions had been forgotten. Many new mystery cults were to make their bid for importance. *Hanan genuinely believed his mix of one God of Love, would be preferable, and had a good chance of superseding the Roman religions worldwide.* History was to prove him resoundingly right, *but I dare say it took longer than he imagined. But in the meanwhile Hanan with his Idumean co-patriots, the Herods, worked real present day miracles.* The Jews were the only people in the Roman Empire who were allowed to collect tax for their own State religion and not be punished for not worshipping the Emperor as God. *This was because the religion of Moses made subject peoples feel that their subjection was just punishment for the sins of their forefathers, and this made the Roman job of ruling them easier.*

Judas Maccabeus supported by the Pharisees had already overthrown civilised Greek rule a century earlier. The Romans were naturally scared of the gangs of freedom fighters in the hills, and the Messianic madness that accompanied it. They were wary of the five hundred or so descendants of King David. So they choose Idumeans who were not descended from David. They blocked the popular appointment of Pharisees and Sicarii [assassins] because they were anti Rome. *Hanan was for Rome, though he kept his sentiments a secret that is why nobody knows them, and I have had to guess, that because he was a good man, he sympathised and supported the minority faction within the Pharisee camp of Hillel and Gamaliel, whose good ideas developed into the modern Jewish religion.* Like

Burgess and Maclean it is possible to work for one organisation while secretly plotting for moral reasons to overthrow it.

I have said that it is unlikely that Moses wrote, "Love your neighbour," it is so out of character. Moses believed in the ethics of enmity, of Jihad, a Holy war of destruction of all non-tribal members, *he had not an ounce of love within his nature.* Hillel who said "Do not do to others that which you would not have them do to you," believed the message of love *but was not devious enough to stage manage the insertion of phrases in the Old Testament praising 'love' in a complex forgery. However, if Hanan has the character I have given him, he could have been the mystery man who slipped them in. No one would suspect him, he would not have lost all credibility even if he was discovered, which he was not. He could have called in all Old Testament copies so that the bits of disintegrated parchment that occurred in all copies at the same verse could be replaced with his revolutionary ideas.*

Coming from a despised non-Jewish background, Hanan must have been a genius to have become High Priest of the Jews and get his five sons also made High Priests. *I believe he could have foreseen* Professor Dawkins' remarkable computer studies that shows that the optimum behaviour pattern, to obtain maximum profit for all, is by rigidly playing "tit for tat" [an eye for an eye, a tooth for a tooth] but with the important addition of an optimistic first move. So if a man slaps your cheek, you don't smack his the first time, you offer him your other cheek, but if he then smacks your second cheek you must smack his, but not twice you always should be prepared to lose the first round. *This is why cheeks are chosen in the parable, one only has two, and when they are used up, you should return to the self evident Hammurabi code of the scales of justice or "Tit for tat".* It is very hard to realise unless you read Professor Dawkins of "The Selfish Gene" fame, how clever such a policy is. It is more selfishly beneficial than winning every time in the long run, and much, much better for society at large. It is true you usually loose all battles but in the long run you tend to win the war. *I believe Hanan may have grasped this complicated mathematical concept, and as most people still cannot comprehend it; know that ordinary people would never believe it without miracles to prove it and miracles are cheaper and easier than a university training for every one. He was right because half the world knows Jesus' dictum about "the other cheek". While only one in a hundred thousand has heard of Professor Dawkins' greater work.*

I believe hiding under his priestly regalia, Hanan was a highly motivated moral man, trying to get his ethical message across to the people, but because of his personal political situation, unable to do it himself. This is why he desperately needed an actor spokesman - a Messiah.

Likewise Annie Beasant the theosophist 1847-1933 AD, an English woman who was President of the Indian National Congress, decided to invent a God, to get her unusual religious ideas accepted. She trained from childhood Jiddu Krishnanamurti b.1895 and Oscar Kollastrom as a young substitute should he fail; to become the reincarnation of the Buddha and Head of the World Order of the Star. Krishnanamurti successfully became this world religious leader, and had several hundred thousand believers, many more than Christ during his lifetime, but he repudiated his position and confessed in 1928 when he was 33 years old, before his programme required him to take the U.S.A. by storm. This made it impossible for Oscar Kollastrom , whom I knew, to take over .

The idea of loving one's neighbour, or even of loving one's enemy had been around for hundreds of years, but Hanan felt it needed a strong plug. Buddha had said it, the Moists in China believed it, the Greek stoics were saying it with little force, Hillel the Nasi of the Sanhedrin and friend of Herod had said it, and Philo the Jew in Alexandria was publishing it.

ST. JOHN THE BAPTIST

St. John's birth date is not certain, *but I think it was approximately 6AD when Hanan had just become High Priest.* One of Hanan's relations Zacharias, was *a boring* priest married to Elizabeth, *having no property in Jerusalem, they liked to stay in his many-roomed house when they came to Jerusalem. He was generous with them, because* being a foreigner *he wanted it to be seen that he had Jewish relations. One day while staying, Elizabeth was in tears, because it seemed to her that her menopause was starting* and she still didn't have a child. *She had come to stay with her pretty 15 year old cousin Mary, she adored children, and they were sharing a bed.*

Elizabeth admired Hanan; he was so much cleverer than her husband and looked magnificent in his Priestly regalia. Hanan's house had a room *on an upper floor which could not be looked into from outside with a close fitting door. He invited Elizabeth into this room to pray with him, in front of a small altar dedicated to the God of Moses,* the sort of altar that in a peasant's house would have had a small statuette of Astoreth and be dedicated to the Hebrew fertility Goddess. *He said to Elizabeth, "It may be your fault and that you are poisoning your husband's seed, it may be a punishment from God for some misdeed. Would you like me as a doctor, to inspect you?"*

"Oh, yes" she said, because he was so kind and gentle. In the private room, the incense on the altar acted as an aphrodisiac. She lifted her skirt and covered her face with modesty. In the preface, I have explained that she was not wearing under pants. He kissed her c*** to wet it, and spat into it, then gently he put his hand up and found that her womb had folded down so nothing could get up it. This turned her on and she squealed with delight but he continued to intone prayers in a singsong voice, in case anyone was listening at the door, and indeed Mary was, she had come to look for Elizabeth. Later he told Mary that he had corrected Elizabeth's relapsed womb and that her husband had then given her a child.

However, Luke 1.59 reports a body of opinion, which would not believe it. In the innermost courtyard were only the high priest could go, *Hanan told her husband* Zacharias, the angel Gabriel had ordered him to act dumb. "They came to circumcise the child; and they called him Zacharias, after the name of his father. And his mother answered and said not so; but he shall be called John. And they said unto her, 'There is none of thy kindred that is called by this name'. And they made signs unto his father as to how he would have him called. And he asked for a writing table, and wrote his name is John. And they all marvelled." Once John was accepted into the congregation Zacharias' *embarrassment left him, and he* was able to chat again.

Which suggests Hanan found nothing wrong with Elizabeth,

and guessed that Zacharias couldn't ejaculate properly and so sportingly offered her some of his seed.   No one could defend her better than this great priest with his private room, she trusted him, and now that he had turned on her passion, loved him. Her hand could not resist seeking out his penis, and finding it stiff, it was not long before their pelvises were thrusting together rhythmically as he intoned his prayers.

She had often thought of going with another man, but there was nowhere private in her house. And if she got caught, Hebrew law said she should be stoned to death, and the lover knowing her guilty secret would be able to return again and again by threatening to impeach her, until it happened so regularly, that they would be *accidentally* found out

Mary had fond memories of donkey riding on Hanan's knee, as a four year old. Now aged 15 she could not help noticing Elizabeth's eyes and the suppressed excitement in her radiant face. Something very marvellous must have happened to dull old aunty Elizabeth in that upper room. She was determined to discover more about this fertility cult that not only made Elizabeth happy but which worked.

Hanan was delighted with his new son John and started to plan his future. What he wanted was more contact with ordinary Jews that is why he had been friendly to Elizabeth and her husband in the first place, now he had a hold on Elizabeth and was definitely accepted. He spent a lot of time planning the future of his natural children, *now he gave some thought to John's career. What he wanted was a rabble-rouser, like the Prophets of old, a leader of 'rent a mob' who could give to the Sadducee cause the voice of the people, may be the very poorest people so that the Pharisees would be isolated in the middle.* It would enable the Sadducees always too Hellenised, rational, reasonable, and frightened of the Romans, to institute radical change, because they could say it was just to avoid mob bloodshed. After all it was by being an expert at rent a mob he had made himself High Priest. The Sadducean weakness was their lack of popular support. *It would be difficult for John to persuade the people that he was in contact with supernatural powers unless; he could do magical tricks like the Magi, [Zoroastrian wise men.] Then he thought, as one often does, of a brilliant idea but too late, if only there could have been magical happenings at John's birth, then he could be a Messiah, he was after all of the Davidic line.*

THE VIRGIN MARY

Mary persuaded Hanan to show her his private room, with the fertility altar as she called it. Hanan had grown rich from his bribes connected with the building of the temple, and it showed in the quality of his dark red Persian rugs on his dining couches, because he lay down to eat like a Roman; with opulent soft embroidered cushions in his private apartments.

Mary *was 15 and felt suddenly shy being alone with the* recently appointed High Priest of the Sanhedrin. *He quietly and continuously intoned prayers in the language of Moses, which she didn't understand because she spoke Aramaic and Greek. They were to her as meaningless as abracadabra* or the Latin texts the Roman Catholic priests used until a hundred years ago, when preaching in English country churches; *but she knew they contained big magic. He lay on the couch, resting on one arm, just as he did when receiving important guests. She squatted on the carpet beside the couch and he firmly but gently held her hand, he had the bedside manner of a doctor, as he explained to her what she kept between her legs, and how one day she would marry and that it would become her husband's most prized possession. He explained that her husband would open the bag, which would cause it to bleed, and put his seed into her, which would then grow into a baby. And how the baby would come out head first with some pain but she must not forget with the excitement of the baby, to expel the bag, which was there to protect the baby from her feminine dirtiness. On no account must she try to open the bag with her finger, she could never give herself a baby, only men could make babies. The most important thing was to preserve her hymen for her husband; nobody else must open her bag.*

"Oh dear" said Mary "Three nights ago it started bleeding but I didn't finger it at all," she said in distress.

Hanan looked serious, "Are you sure" he said "that you

have never played with boys, I have heard you were caught romping behind the woodshed with two youths and you were screaming "No, no" what was all that about?"

"Oh they were naughty boys, one of them had his robe up and I saw his backside, and they told me not to tell and anointed my ear hole with a sticky fluid and laughed and said it would give me a baby, will I have one like Elizabeth? Mummy told me never to kiss boys."

Hanan smiled "No darling Mary, no." Mary thought doesn't he look handsome when he smiles but at that moment her look of admiration had triggered in Hanan a passion she did not know about. His eyes narrowed and his toes curled. "I better have a look," he said. She was really thankful because she had been quite worried by the bleeding. "Come and sit on my chest and kneel with one knee each side and raise your skirt" he said, she clambered onto the horse hair couch revealing everything, because religious law prohibited the dirty modern habit of wearing underpants, a wise health rule, before soap was invented, to prevent disease breeding in clothing contaminated with shit and menstrual flow. "This is a very private ceremony" he said, "You must keep it absolutely secret." It won't hurt but I am going to use a bit of spit to wet you." His warm hands ran up her soft naked thighs. He brushed aside the pubic hairs with his fingers and gently stroked the labia of her vagina; she tingled as the blood filled these lips. Then leaning his head forward he dragged his rough wet tongue upwards over her cunt, this was delicious, the labia soon opened to reveal a particularly well developed hymen which had obviously never been tampered with, only a small hole, as is usual at puberty, to let out menstrual blood.

Hanan loved the taste and went on doing it. It was a marvellous sensation, and she told him so. She somehow knew that this was more than a medical inspection. In order to raise her cunt to a more convenient height for the inspection she arched herself backwards and in order not to overbalance she put her hand down behind her, she felt something like a snake under his robe, and she grasped it firmly. Hanan was a strong man but his resolves became weak, she looked into his face and she saw an expression that told her that he had seen God.

She realised that she must be playing with his manhood "What does it look like," she said for she knew and knew rightly that Hanan would never hurt her.

He pulled up his robe there was no awkward delay wriggling out of underpants, and there it was proudly standing. She moved back so that her soft thighs were resting on his muscular ones. Marvelling she took it in her hands and started stroking it. He gazed upwards at her angelic face with a halo of tousled hair catching the rays of the sun, he felt a throb and then another one and a jet of sperm spurted into the air, in surprise Mary raised her body on her knees and the second squirt bathed her cunt about 4" inches from his penis. She wiped it away with the inside of her skirt and both of them went down on their knees to God and intoned prayers holding hands. Both knew they loved each other but they did not speak of it, she knew he was married and he knew that as long as she was not deflowered all was well. Mary returned to live under the male guardianship of the Temple, *her bedroom was probably in his office suite; but all was not well and she returned in a couple of months to report the symptoms of pregnancy. Hanan was a great man, it would ruin his career, upset his wife and her family. It had to be kept secret but if blood could flow down once in a million times sperm cold swim up. However, no body else knew this scientific fact.*

Hanan was amazed, he had always been brought up to believe it was quite safe as long as one did not break a girls hymen, nothing could happen, sperm in a girls mouth or up her arsehole, he had been told was harmless.

However, secret non-penetrative child sex abuse is common in England today; particularly by guardians.

JOSEPH THE CARPENTER

Joseph had delivered the correct timber on time and he had come from Nazareth *with his customary gift to Hanan.*

"My cousin Mary" Hanan *said introducing Joseph to Mary.*

After she had gone out, Joseph said "Gosh she's a 'smasher', now my wife's dead; I wish I could get a girl like that to look after my children".

"Ah" said the wily Hanan, "She is a virgin, but the angel Gabriel has whispered in her ear, that she will bring fourth a Messiah, would you want to be the father of a Messiah? Well said Joseph not taking it very seriously, I am descended from Abraham and David, but I would love her even if it were another man's child.

The next day Hanan spoke to Mary, "You are going to have God's child and I will witness to it. The alternative is to be stoned to death if you wish to tell anyone about what we did, and I shall deny it, because it would damage my career. But Joseph fancies you and will treat you well even if he guesses our secret. I am afraid I can not get you quickly, a younger un-jealous husband." Mary loved and respected Hanan, she knew his ideas always worked, so she quietly and firmly acquiesced, death by lapidation did not appeal to her. "I have arranged for you to be inspected by five senior members of the Sanhedrin. If they ask you why you think you are pregnant, say you saw the angel Gabriel and he poured something in your ear, act like a silly girl and don't elaborate the story and keep our guilty secret and I will make your son a king among men."

The Magicians trade union conference regardless of religion took place in Damascus, Ephesus, *and this year it was taking place in Jerusalem. Annas was by far the most skilled in foreign languages, and being on the host team, he learnt all sorts of tricks, because he had had to act as interpreter when foreign priests wished to exchange information. He learnt little ways of distracting people's attention when raising the dead, and* how to restore a man's sight by flicking the hard skin of a cataract away with his fingernail.

He pointed Mary out, to three fellow guild members of his grandfather's Zoroastrian church, *and sent them after her with scouts, to arrange a repeat* of the well known happenings with a star and shepherds that had occurred at the birth of the greatest Middle Eastern God, Mazda, and as qualified doctors, in case there were birth complications.

Joseph loved Mary and although she was pregnant after a few months, he took her with him when he had to attend a census for taxation, of his *large* estates, beyond Bethlehem, but she was in pain on the road and that slowed them, so that they did not reach

Bethlehem until nightfall. *Being rich* he asked at the five star hotel, i.e. the best and only hotel, despite the fact that hundreds of ordinarily rich people were sleeping on the streets in booths of mat and wicker work woven with leaves, as a result of the census. He was so impressive that he managed to get a room in the annexe. *The Roman Procurator's horse that was the great grandfather of Caligula's horse, which was to be made a Senator, had to spend a night in the open.*

He would not have arranged the journey so late to Bethlehem had he realised the baby was so far advanced. It was very odd, Mary giving birth so soon they were not even married yet, but he did not want to bully her at such a time. He was puzzled, what did her cover up story about Gabriel mean, she was certainly a virgin, it had been certified, he didn't really care, he had four heirs already and it would always give him power over her, because of the threat of having her stoned.

He dozed off, thinking he would lecture her in the morning, but he was woken by a lot of inarticulate shepherds burbling something about God, and a comet that could foretell the future, [Since Halley: planets can not foretell the actions of man; men can foretell the actions of comets.] Then three magnificent Magi and they were no dream for they left gold, frankincense and myrrh, presents far exceeding a bride price, *clearly only Herod or some great scion of a Sadducean family could afford such largess, or God himself which is what they all said. Mary was so loving and so modest and there had been no one else since they were engaged, it was a puzzle.*

The lighthouse at Pharos, Alexandria was 440 foot high and was built in 280 BC. The star/light of Bethlehem *could have been an oil lamp on a pole in the stable yard, to guide taxpayers and give protective lighting to the Romans. It would move in the correct direction behind trees and hills as one zigzagged towards it. A guiding light might have been an unusual idea to the locals who nicknamed it a star.*

Alternatively they found their way by "following the star" a phrase which simply meant they were educated men who could read the map of heaven and in a land with no signposts find their way either by land or sea.

The Magi arrived a trifle late as the long journey had advanced the delivery by a couple of days, *but in sufficient time, to give the most famous birthday presents in the history of the world. The Magi returning to rule their priestly kingdoms, called on Herod, either Herod the Great whose itchy balls were troubling him* or in my opinion, because *Herod the Great had been dead for a decade at the time of the census; his son Herod Antipas who now he was a ruler; could be called 'Herod the Great'. He was conducting a lawsuit to prove his rights, to his deposed brother's kingdom, which included Bethlehem. This lawsuit was eventually won much later by another Herod, Herod Agrippa. For this reason he could have wanted to massacre the infants in Bethlehem even if he had no jurisdiction there.* Hanan had arranged to be with Herod, to supervise any upsets, when the wise men came to report the miracle and collect their substantial reward from him. Herod laughed at the story of a baby inheriting his father's kingdoms, but sweated with alarm when turning to his cautious sensible friend Hanan, for confirmation that it was a joke. , "It is very likely and is foretold" said Hanan with a dead straight face. It was now Hanan's turn to be afraid. Herod, who was a bit tipsy and in a jealous rage, said, "I'll have to murder all the new born", so Hanan sent *a messenger to Joseph with money and introductory letters from senior members of the Sanhedrin to flee to Egypt.* Herod *Antipas had no jurisdiction in Bethlehem despite his brother's removal. So I doubt if* the murders took place in Bethlehem. *Joseph thought it would help to hide the birth date, so off he went to Egypt*

Aged 12 Jesus' *irresponsible* parents didn't notice his absence for a day on the sixty-mile caravan from Jerusalem to Nazareth. They then responsibly returned and it took them three days to find Him in the Temple, knowledgeably arguing with the elders. The Temple was not a single room like a church, it covered approx 25 acres and was divided into courts and was a forest of columns such that one would have had to have walked miles to have seen every part, because of the close spacing of the columns and had Jesus accidentally moved a mere five feet his parents could have missed him. This makes the first recorded words of our Lord *all the more cheeky* if we accept the Christian interpretation that 'Father' means 'God'. I quote from the 'Good News' New

Testament published in 1966. Luke 2:48 - "his mother said to him, "My son, why have you done this to us? Your father and I have been terribly worried trying to find you". "Why did you have to look for me?" He asked. "Didn't you know that I had to be in my <u>Father's house</u>?" But they did not understand his answer." *Joseph and the writers of the gospels might not know who his father was and Mary might not want to tell.* Homeless people were not allowed to sleep or eat in the Temple any more than they can do so in a cathedral today. *I suggest Jesus had left messages with Malchus, the butler and the cook for his mother, at his <u>father's [Hanan's] house,</u> where he had learnt his debating wisdom. Joseph and Mary might have been frightened of confessing to Hanan that they had mislaid, his son. Was the gold frankincense and myrrh payment for looking after him?* Luke refers to Jesus as "the son of the Most High" *Priest is the word that normally follows 'Most High', the word could not have been 'God' because that implies there are several gods, it is much more likely the word priest was crossed out by Luke who did not want us to know.* Hanan's nine-year term as Most High Priest occurred at about this time.

MIRACLES

Elijah had dressed in bulky shapeless clothing, so that he could conceal weapons and magical props. Saint John the Baptist dressed like him so that he appeared not to care about the things of this world. Hanan took his son in law the High Priest Caiaphas to see John's news worthy baptisms in the River Jordan which *he knew would include Jesus.* A voice cried out to Jesus "You are my son". *Was this God or Hanan? Jesus was about twenty (two thirds of scholars think thirty) and was a bit reluctant to become Messiah, it would be difficult to back out of, once he had started, but having seen how easy John made preaching look; he decided to give it a try.*

St John was only six months older than Jesus but he had been preaching for a few years and was already famous and much respected. John's honesty gave him stature and authority; he did not stoop to miracles or tricks. *Hanan realised he could not be the Messiah, so he used him to announce Jesus as he baptised him. Hanan had by now built up a good team of backroom boys and supporters who were skilled at crowd suggestion.* Soon John's criticism of Herod's new wife left him headless.

Jesus had to face his public, he must do miracles, and this really scared him. He finally agreed to do one that would not matter if it went wrong and that he could shrug off as a joke if it failed. Farrar says it was his first miracle. He arrived late from a distant place several days walk away and added at least five uninvited new apostles to the guests at a wedding at Cana. This caused the wine to run out which was shameful for the bride. His mother the Virgin Mary says, "They have no wine". Jesus who has not seen his mummy for along time says, "Woman what have you to do with me." John 2.4, at first sight a really rude remark, *until one realises that Jesus has butterflies in his stomach and does not want his mum to mess the trick up.* She said to the servants "whatever he says do it at once" as if she was the hostess. He asked for the water jars to be filled with water. *The water jars were probably the ones that collected rainwater off the roof which were outside and therefore easily accessible at night when every one was asleep, with necks that were too narrow for a full wine skin to be inserted and too narrow for an observer to notice anything inside. Hanan's man would have put in the previous night an empty wine skin through the narrow neck which he would have filled with high quality wine and then sewn up so that it could not be taken out, the jar would still be two thirds full of clean water should any one want some in a cup.* Jerusalem was a Roman province at this time, and the Romans always diluted their wine with three parts water to wine, and this mixture was called wine. 2 Maccabees 15 39 "For just as it is disagreeable to drink wine alone or water alone, whereas the mixing of the two gives a pleasant and delightful taste." *All some one had to do at the last moment was to pierce the bags so that the jars contained mixed wine and water. If the bags were found, that would simply prove the miracle. These jars could not be tampered with because they would be in the middle of the party. There would be a considerable number of gallons and the expense would be on its own, impressive to poor people. The trick worked perfectly, Jesus loved the adulation; from now on he was hooked on being a magician. But would a real God's first miracle upset the temperance movement, and Islam's prohibition of alcohol? However, alcohol was a method of eliminating germs in water in those days.*

The Master of the Ceremonies thanks the bridegroom for the wine, that Jesus produced *was he the bridegroom? His mother seems very bossy for an ordinary guest.* After the wedding he is referred to as a teacher and Rabbi, in those days no unmarried men could be teachers or Rabbis.

Jesus did not want the secret of his power, the great Hanan, to become common knowledge to his apostles and disciples, if they genuinely believed in Him, their wonderment would communicate it self to the people. Hanan certainly did not want anyone to know. Honest Jesus, with Delphic cunning said John 11.37 "If I do not the work of my father *[Hanan]* believe me not". *Jesus set up his ministry on the shores of Gallilee one of his disciples Simon-Peter was a tough who owed money on his boat to Jesus' father's carpentry/boat building firm. Soon Peter's debt would be so bad that he would have to sell himself as a slave for non-payment of debt, but Jesus said nothing about money, he said just come and follow me and act as my bouncer.* Gallilee was a very good location if you had a fast boat, and several of his disciples had them. Round its shores was the Decapolis a league of ten self-governing Greek cities. Being fiercely independent each had its own policing arrangements, which made the area an ideal place to escape arrest.

He chooses twelve apostles because he was *racially prejudiced* in favour of the Israelites, one for each tribe. Many were his relations but none save Judas Iscariot was his social or financial equal. One rich man genuinely wanted to join and help finance the outfit, to the apostles surprise Jesus sent him off with a flea in his ear, "go sell all you have and give it to the poor." *Jesus didn't lack money he wanted privacy. I don't believe socialists who say Jesus disapproved of the rich. I think he just did not know how to get rid of the man.*

"It is easier for a camel to go through the eye of a needle than for a rich man to enter the kingdom of heaven". Simply means that a rich man arriving at the town gate cannot enter with his trade bales on his camels, he has to manhandle them through the narrow pedestrian eye. It is called a needle because a slender tower is erected over it so that travellers can see from far away where the entrance is in the mile long town wall. If the town is in a dry area the road is sandy as is the surrounding area, it is not a different colour like mud is from grass in England. (Cleopatra's needle which sits beside the Thames is the right size.) His goods have got to be weighed and checked to pay trade tax like your virtues and sins are weighed on entering heaven. *Because he associates with rich men, his imagery of hassle is related to them.* Going through the eye of a needle was like being searched before boarding an aeroplane and customs on arrival. Jesus was a Jew not a Christian and like a Jew he believed in unbridled usurious profiteering. In the parable of the talents a man gives his servants gold or silver, its not specified which, weighing 113 lbs 13ozs per talent, he gives them no commission, but is pleased when they double it, and horrified by the man who simply returns it without interest. In the capitalist world to day, deducting inflation, the average man is lucky if he can double his money in his lifetime. "From him that hath not shall be taken away."

He told his apostles to go out and advertise his presence "Be ye wise as serpents *[the house sign of the diplomatic High Priest Hanan whose sons were described as* "a brood of vipers" in the Talmud] and as "harmless as doves". Any town that does not welcome you; move on quickly - "God will make it worse than Sodom and Gomorrah for them at the day of judgement." Later he sent out 70 disciples because there were 70 nations on earth. He promised his followers everlasting life if they suffered for his cause. Muhammad years later was to copy the idea with heaven for all those who died with wounds to the front.

According to Farrar, Jesus' first revelation that he is the Messiah is to a Samaritan woman privately at a well side. *He could hardly be arrested outside Judea and a woman's word against a man's would be worthless at law. The Pharisees are more concerned about him talking to a strange woman than the Messiah information.*

Jesus cures the son of one of Herod's courtiers. Hanan was possibly appointed by Herod, so it is not surprising that he had friends at court. But the status of the man carries weight. Jesus cures him at five hours walking distance without even seeing the sick man.

Herod's courtier could easily disclaim any part in any jiggery pokery in the event of trouble.

John 'the beloved disciple', is this a secret homosexual friend? I think not he was a rich Sadducee; we might call him a Yuppie. He had strong moral views and believed passionately that the only way to run society was through reward and punishment, and though he did not believe in God, after all he was educated, he did believe it was the duty of the priestly class to rule the inadequate silly people through faith. He was a very great showman and loved abstract poetical ideas. To him, Hell fire was the secret and he could grow lyrical about it, but that was later, for the present he was Hanan's inspired administrator of his secret service.

John 'the beloved disciple', heard from a local priest, the sad tale of a craftsman who as a slave was being forced to do the most menial tasks by a nasty legalistic employer. This slave had decided to commit suicide. So John spoke to the slave secretly. "Would you be prepared to do anything to obtain your freedom?"

"Yes" said the man "I don't mind what risk I take because I am going to commit suicide anyway, I have not got a woman, as my boss won't let me marry".

"Well" said John "can you walk and move like a leper?" The man did a convincing mimic of how the local lepers walked in their colony. John gave him some make up "Cover your skin with that, add a little each day". The man's eyes sparkled with hope. "Go to your local priest, he knows nothing of this and convince him you are a leper, if you fail bad luck, but I expect he will not want to touch you. Once he has certified you, it will be against the law for your boss to touch you; if he does I will see that he gets sent to the colony for decontamination. He will be under a legal obligation to feed you and he will be unable to make you work. If he fails to feed you, tell the priest, and he will feed you. Your masters only way of avoiding the expense of feeding you is to give you your freedom, if he does, I will send a wonder worker to do a miracle cure, but if you are found out you will have to become his slave again, and he may punish you and he saw liquid fear in the man's eyes." "When the wonder worker comes, do everything he tells you to do. Take a damp cloth in your hood and be prepared to clean yourself up quickly, go to him

when he is on his own, you do not know my name I am not a local; you will never see me again. When you are cured tell everyone how wonderful he is and that you believe in him". A year later when he had been freed and fed by the local priest from the large donation John had left behind. A man came and said "Jesus my master is coming to cure believers."

"Oh I believe in him said the leper". *The leper was watching Jesus and the crowd stayed away from the leper but Jesus left the crowd behind him and so all could see him he broke the law by touching the leper. The leper cried out loud and* clear I believe you are the son of man *and grovelled at his feet.*

Jesus said quietly "wash your face"; the leper used the wet cloth in his hood hiding the action. "Tell nobody about this." The leper jumped up ran back to his hovel and completed the clean up. After a long close inspection by the local Priest, guarding his secret, he left a free man, free of leprosy.

Jesus made it a regular feature, to tell cured persons not to tell anyone, *he knew the news would get out, but it made it much easier for him or his assistants to cover up or hide any apparatus that had been used in the miracles. Never were his miracles subject to scientific evaluation as they took place. Farrar believes he did this out of modesty, but he knew the news would get out and why not cure all the lepers?*

I cannot tell how all the miracles were done, but some, might be done by Delphic phrases that could be interpreted more than one way. After all if one man says it will rain and another says it will not, one man is bound to be a very great prophet. To cure a supposedly mental man would make no real impact with the crowd when he goes quiet and lucid, but to drive the devils out into swine is a brilliant bit of theatre, even if modern animal protection societies do not think a God need harm anything.

John 'the beloved disciple,' was staying at the house of a Roman Centurion who had donated the best synagogue in town, according to Farrar. *John realised there was no chance of additional funds, without a miracle. So John persuaded the slave, who had converted the Centurion in the first place, to pretend to be ill. The slave only had to appear to have a paralytic seizure and then recover at a particular time and John could drug him, diagnose his illness and vouch for his recovery, so it was not very dangerous for the slave. Messengers arranged the trick, Jesus, never* actually saw the slave, he only spoke to a collection of synagogue elders who asked him to do the cure. *So both Jesus and the slave could not be arrested for fraud.*

Jesus' inability to rescue John the Baptist, a man universally agreed to be a great and good prophet and one on whose good word Jesus so much depended, shows a shocking lack of loyalty, on the part of a God who could cure a man five hours walk away *but is easily understood in my scenario. Hanan could not have a spy in Herod's women's quarters and he could not sew a head back on.*

The removal of a cataract, a cloudy lens, with the flick of a fingernail is not something a doctor would do today because it leaves the seeing eyes naked to infection but it can be done. The blind man outside the temple would *of course not be blind but seeking official retirement and would have had to apply to the establishment, which suggests Jesus had establishment contacts. I will not bore you with an explanation of every miracle, for one can easily see that with Hanan his father in the background it is no more difficult for Jesus to do miracles* than for Alexander the Great or one of the Roman Emperors. And nobody today, believes theirs, and they had less time to practise.

L A Z A R U S

Lazarus was a Pharisee who like Jesus does not appear to need to work; he had built himself a rock cut tomb the sort that only one man in a thousand could afford. It probably measured 6' x 6' x 6' with three shelves on each side, and a very heavy stone door requiring three or four men to open. Lazarus was brave to agree to be buried alive, not because of the discomfort or shortage of air, but because playing with graves was against the law, and later the High Priest Caiaphas specifically wanted him executed for the offence. He must have been able to move about in the tomb, because he came out of his own accord in his grave clothes after four days. *He was no doubt looking forward to promotion by Hanan in the short term and to becoming a favourite courtier at the court of King Jesus.*

JESUS' LIFESTYLE.

Jesus' sex life is a bit of a mystery. Hanan must have wanted him to make a diplomatic marriage; say a patrician relation of one of the Caesars or at the very least a daughter of a Herod; but in order to do this he would have had to wait, until he became King of Judea. Half the middle-aged bachelors today are 'gay' but there is no indication other than the phrase 'the beloved disciple' [John] and Judas' kiss to suggest it. It is a very remote possibility that he could have been bi-sexual, and liked group sex; bi-sexual people are usually the best at keeping it secret and who was the naked man who ran away at his arrest?

Jesus' life style has been misunderstood, he was a rich man, the only evidence to show that he was poor is that he was born in a stable, which was clearly an accident, and that his father was a carpenter, "Tecton" which was a trade much respected amongst the Jews but despised by the Victorian English. His robe was so valuable when he was crucified that the soldiers played dice for it. There are very few facts that reveal his social position, but the way two women anoint his feet and then dry them with their hair is suggestive of great wealth. Spikenard is incredibly expensive and it was kept in an alabaster box. *I believe neither of the women who do it is poor.* Mary is the sister of Rabbi Lazarus who has a large villa and a stone burial vault. Incidentally Mary called Magdalene is unlikely to have been a loose woman, Luke 8.2-3, because she is listed ahead of Joanna the wife of Chusa, Herod's steward, and Susanna and many other unnamed women followers who spent weeks with him, so I take her to be a woman of substance.

According to Farrar he frequently stays at Lazarus' house and uses it as a base just outside Jerusalem. "Jesus loved Martha, and her sister, and Lazarus" [John 12].

Few Christians will admit that Mary, Martha's sister wipes his feet with her hair and rubs on spikenard, [an ointment], to this clearly stated passage in the Bible because Mary's brother Lazarus is a respectable Pharisee and friend; John 11 2; *so in their deceitful way, when faced with a story they do not like, they pretend that the gospel writer has confused the two Marys.* .The paintings on the walls of respectable dining rooms in Pompeii reveal that at that time sexual unions in unusual positions and in public were not frowned on. When discovered they invented the word pornography and pornography laws were created to hide the newly found paintings and sculpture. *Sex for fun was so strongly disapproved of. Jesus would not be human if he did not obtain secret enjoyment from the possibility that under cover of deep shadow Mary's hand could easily slip up under her hair and the hem of his robe and massage his private parts, which were unprotected by underpants. I think Christians admit this and that is why they call Mary Magdalene who also wipes Jesus' feet with her hair a prostitute, especially as Jesus is disrespectful to her, but then Jesus does not have much respect for women, he is rude to his mother, he dare not laugh at the Mass Murderer Moses' laws making it compulsory to stone women, true he doesn't actively encourage it, but he is not as horrified at the suggestion* as we would be today and then as now it would be illegal under Roman civil law, *and the woman in adultery could have been pretty. I think Jesus is very macho to have women kissing his feet and wiping them with their hair and not even speaking or thanking them while they do it, but rudely ignoring them and talking to other people. Also it would appear that unless the dining rooms are twice the size I have suggested women are considered too inferior to be allowed to eat with our Lord.*

He speaks up for the Samaritans because Nazareth a Jewish village is very close to Samaritan country, which has to be crossed on the way to Jerusalem. They really are His neighbours even if they were not the average Jew's neighbours.

The PUBLICITY CAMPAIGN

The chronologies of the different gospels differ because chronology had not become a standard method of recording history. I therefore take my events in the chronological order that Farrar a Christian has them in, I think this is fair.

Jesus does various miracles to publicise his importance followed by the raising of Lazarus from the dead.

Having had 12 disciples for two or three years; Jesus employs another 70 to take his message further a field while in Galilee. The local people start walking to Jerusalem for the Passover. In full view of this crowd he walks on water. *Fishermen organised by Jesus, with rods sit by the side collecting extra fish for the 5,000. The crowd watch in wonderment seeing him walk on water the fishermen are able to tell the crowd all about his miracles and teaching.*

He does his tricks on the water until dusk, so it is obvious that he can not be helping with the preparation of the food for the 5,000 that evening. *But with 82 followers many of whom could have family servants and slaves to help can as a result of pre-organisation easily arrange to amass baskets full of food without his help together with financial aid from his daddy.* He then feeds 5,000 men plus their unimportant women and children *who he can not be bothered to count.*

He then goes to his friend Lazarus and gets his daughters to put on smelly ointment, a Royal oil that everybody's unconscious memory reminds them of Kings. This costs one and a half times as much as the feeding of the five thousand and then rides into town. He does not travel in a coach with 82 soldiers in uniforms with swords. He enters on an ass because this is written in the Old Testament. *The 82 helpers throw their cloaks before him, and have had palm branches cut ready for his passing to lay on the muddy track and they get the crowds to cheer him and follow him to add to his authority to do, what he must do in the temple.*

THE BUILDING OF THE TEMPLE

Herod destroyed and rebuilt The Temple. It took decades to build; but not as long as a medieval cathedral. It was built in the Greek style, on the edge of a naturally occurring cliff face overlooking the Kidron or Kedron valley. The North South Route ran close up to the vertical cliff wall of the Temple site. *Could this route be called the Kedron road?* The Temple was rectangular; its side was straight like the side of the Parthenon, though many times larger. In front of this cliff, on the other side of the *Kedron road, but the same side of the Kedron valley was a pinacle of naturally occurring stone shaped like a penis called the Twin Cedars of Olivet. The architect might have wanted to demolish it. But I believe it was sacred to the memory of the leader of the Jews who first led them to Israel.* I think this pinnacle was where *the bully* Abraham *stole the hereditary feminine power of his wife Sarah,* by threatening to kill their only son whom she loved.

The building contractor would certainly not wish to destroy the bridge across the Kedron road to the stone pinnacle , because it was the ideal place to hoist up blocks of stone, timber and other materials delivered in bullock carts, or by other means if too heavy for carts. By taking out a few planks in the bridge to make a hole and by erecting tree trunks along the lines of a pyramid and fixing a pulley at its apex, it made an ideal crane in the best place. So that building materials did not need to pass through the twisting narrow shop lined streets of Jerusalem. If this was the builder's access point, he would have required the top of the pinnacle as a yard for the storage of building materials delivered early, and the bridge would have been fenced off from use by the general public.

While the temple was being built over thirty years; large areas of the 25 acres must have been waste land, which could easily be used without comment by the builder for storage of stones and timber and as a workshop. So no one would object to the presence of thousands of sheep and other animals awaiting slaughter on the altar and doves and money changer's tables.

This particular Passover was to celebrate the formal opening of the completed temple. The builder was persuaded to relinquish his use of the bridge as a crane. At long last it was possible to obey the ancient regulations prohibiting temple trading. But the Temple traders who had been on unbuilt land did not want to go. I think popular opinion has been misled. I think Jesus' aim was to give the temple the right to do the trading not ordinary people.

THE MONOPOLY OF "THE LEGALLY PURE "

When the temple was originally planned the old rule that there was to be no trading in the temple was part of the plan. The ugly Twin Cedars of Olivet was scheduled as the place where shopping could take place without spoiling the architecture. There was enough room for four shops where 'legally pure things', birds *and possibly animals* could be sold. They were approached by a bridge across the Kidron from the Temple, and so were not on the main circulation route. If four different families, as was intended, had owned the shops, prices through competition would have been reasonable.

Farrar in his Life of Christ refers to these shops on pages 142, 642, 654 and 655.

How Hanan ended up owning all four of the plots we do not know, but at this time maybe no one else realised that he did. The average expectation of life in Rome at this time was 22 years. *Therefore ownership of the four shop plots, on the top of this natural rock, could have changed hands through inheritance. Many owners might not have appreciated their value. The builder may have frequently damaged them, or the bridge, and the owners may have been called on to repair them or pay rent for useless land, or because they owned them have great moral pressure put on them to contribute to the building of the temple. Everyone had to wait until the Temple was finished and the other owners may have become impatient.*

Hanan must have feared that the Sanhedrin would repeal the ancient laws of Zech if he violently threw out respectable bankers, for his private profit. To call in the Roman Soldiers would be tantamount to admitting that the Sanhedrin could not manage their own affairs. He must have prayed for a revolt by the worshippers.

Hanan was no longer High Priest. Why did not Caiaphas the High Priest (Hanan's son in law) put a stop to temple trading with his 100 gatekeepers? To get rid of the traders must have been very difficult since I guess some of the 100 gatekeepers would be susceptible to bribes. According to the ancient laws of Zech; no one could sell anything in the temple. For Hanan's family monopoly to work, it was essential that no one was allowed to trade except on his land, because building work had left large areas of the site where unblessed trading had been allowed to take place on potential temple land for thirty years.

Jesus put a stop to all Hanan's competitors trading in the temple. Presumably the Jews which Jesus whipped were selling things in the Temple as 'legally pure', who would want a non-legally pure dove?

If so they were spoiling Hanan's trade because no one would want to cross the bridge when they could buy cheaper, in a central arcade.

R. Simeon son of Gamaliel objected to paying a gold coin

for one dove. Long after Hanan was dead it was reported that his family (the Ananus family) charged 250 times the normal price for their wares. Every woman who became pregnant had to buy a pigeon [dove] *and these could have been homing ones that returned to them for resale.*

This monopoly of the right to sell all things legally pure; was one of the most profitable recorded in history. Hanan's family could not have charged 250 times the correct price for a dove if the stated "Monopoly" did not exist.

Finally 3 years before the Temple was destroyed the Jews with hysterical jealousy stormed these four shops called the Chanujoth and destroyed them because they hated Hanan's sons most of whom had been high priests.

Christians think they were doing the same thing as Jesus had done decades earlier; *but this must be nonsense*, his traders were in competition and doing it inside the temple area on trestle tables not in permanent built shops approached by a bridge. However the Christians have failed to see why Caiaphas had his kinsman Jesus killed for enabling him to make his wife's family one of the greatest fortunes in the Roman Empire? To discover you must continue to read my Jesus Fiction. Was he as High Priest taking bribes?

THE CLEANSING OF THE TEMPLE

This is the most important thing that Jesus ever did. This was *an especially important* Passover *because it was the ceremonial opening of the Temple.*

The numbers of temple traders must have increased dramatically and those already trading must have required even more space. The traders were not priests but townsmen. If Hanan sent in toughs he would be madly unpopular, Zech's ancient prohibition on temple trading *would be cancelled. Hanan knew that a morally indignant, non-priestly people's riot was the only method of driving them out. So what he wanted was a brilliant orchestration of crowd psychology. Success could only be guaranteed if nobody could connect Hanan with the fracas.* Unfortunately St. John the Baptist was dead. *His only remaining bastard; Jesus must do the job, all the years of expensive arrangement of miracles was going to pay off.* The wonder worker comes, huge crowds surround him, many of them are from the group - the feeding of the five thousand men - he journeyed in with,, [there is no free lunch] and the seventy, extra disciples, who even if they were not being paid must have been receiving expenses because they had to leave their homes, showing that his organisation was not short of money, and led by twelve men not in uniform but who are efficiently trained. *However they are unarmed and* the temple staff could have easily arrested Jesus, standing there with a whip, *like Allah.Jesus preaches to them and establishes the fact that he stands on high moral ground and his cheerleaders get the mob to utter great cries of approval, whose emotions can be understood even if their Galilean regional accents cannot. He points to the notices saying* no trading in the Temple ordered by Zadok High priest at the time of King David and with a cheering crowd he overturns the moneychangers tables, *to the delight of the crowd who help themselves. He knows the money changers themselves have all been invited to a pre-Passover dinner in Hanan's priestly palace, leaving their normally reliable slaves as shopkeepers* who know they must not touch an aristocratic descendant of King David, even in self-defence.

Jesus overthrows the moneychangers' temporary trestle tables, coins run in all directions, *the defence are uncoordinated; they are all on their hands and knees rescuing or stealing the coins. Finally he clears out all the temporary hawkers with their sheep, cows and caged doves, which have dirtied the white marble with their excrement. Now the temple has space for the great crowds who were waiting outside.*

Some of the temple courts could accommodate 6,000 people. During the early building-years large areas of the temple must have been non-consecrated, and the bridge to the Twin cedars of Olivet, was out of use, it would only be on completion that the traders would have had to move.

The slaves in charge of the money don't know what to do and flee. For incompetence they will be made to work in the fields and no new slaves are willing to take over in case the people rise up again. Farrar says he cleanses the Temple twice.

To hide the connection Hanan votes for Jesus to be arrested. *This is why nobody else to my knowledge has guessed that he is*

Jesus' father. The people discover Hanan's 4 shops just across the bridge and realise that this is much neater.

Having lost his cool in the temple were he had to whip some people, Jesus feels like a snack and finds a fig tree which because it is out of season, has no figs, so he causes it to shrivel up and there is no mention of compensation to the owners. *I don't suppose the Greens or the Friends of Trees are very impressed by this un-God like behaviour, even if it was a dramatic illustration of a parable.*

Judas Iscariot's father owned a large house, *costing over two million pounds in modern day money. He had at least one room capable of accommodating a minimum of 14 divans round a table for the 12 apostles. I doubt if Judas would be disloyal for £300 in today's money* though this seems a lot, to reveal the whereabouts of such a well-known public figure as Jesus who could have been arrested by the 100 doormen in the temple.

Caiaphas, on the other hand, might think it worth more than that to discover who the secret 'Godfather' really was. I think the bribe was to identify publicly John 'the beloved disciple', kinsman to Hanan, (Ref Schonfield's Passover Plot) by catching them all in his house. It was here the last supper took place, in "a large upper room furnished and prepared" [14 men minimum {Jesus, *his host,* and 12 apostles} *had had space to lie down and eat; in an age of poverty this room is very large and grand. I think it more likely that Judas was Jesus' spy in Caiaphas' camp, but this view is peripheral to my thesis.* "This took place to fulfil the prophecy" is a recurring theme throughout the gospels. Modern authors think this is not chance but deliberate policy on the part of Jesus. Jesus and Judas deliberately collude because it is foretold that the Messiah will be betrayed for 30 shekels of silver.

This is confirmed in the Gospel of Judas written 300 AD which claims that it was Christ himself who asked Jesus to betray him.

MAP OF JERUSALEM

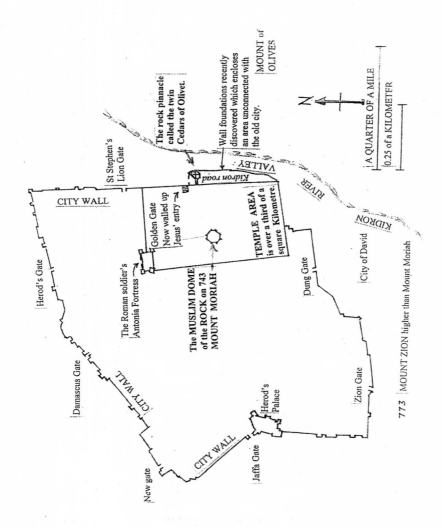

The rock pinnacle called the twin Cedars of Olivet.

Wall foundations recently discovered which encloses an area unconnected with the old city.

MOUNT of OLIVES

N

A QUARTER OF A MILE

0.25 of a KILOMETER

St Stephen's Lion Gate

KIDRON VALLEY

Kidron road

CITY WALL

Golden Gate Now walled up Jesus' entry

TEMPLE AREA is over a third of a square Kilometre.

RIVER

KIDRON

The Roman soldier's Antonia Fortress

The MUSLIM DOME of the ROCK on 743 MOUNT MORIAH

Dung Gate

City of David

Herod's Gate

Damascus Gate

CITY WALL

Zion Gate

773 MOUNT ZION higher than Mount Moriah

New gate

Herod's Palace

CITY WALL

Jaffa Gate

The FOUR CHANUJOTH SHOPS

were sited on a rock pinnacle *called the Twin Cedars* of Olivet. They were approached by a bridge from the Temple, across the Kedron *Road. The Annas family* many of whom were High Priests had a monopoly of all the four shops and charged 250 times the properprice for doves which had to be bought on the birth of a child. Jesus by cleansing the Temple of common traders; created this profitable monopoly.

Gamaliel a friend of St. Paul and a grandson of the Pharisee High Priest Hillel destroyed the Chanujoth *pinnacle 3* years before the Romans destroyed the Temple. The fire melted the gold stored in the shops so that it *ran into cracks in the rock and as Jews love gold they pulled the natural rocks to pieces and left no trace of the foundations.*

From the Kidron Valley, the pinnacle would break the skyline and so before accurate sea level height measurements had been invented, Abraham *could well have thought this was the highest rock* to sacrifice Issac on.

There is still a conspiracy, even in the gospels written fifty years later, to conceal the important role of John 'the beloved disciple', Jesus knew he was going to be arrested, so he crossed the brook called Cedron, (*Kidron or Kedron?*) *so no suspicion should fall on John the beloved disciple. He arranged to be* arrested in a garden, by Malchus and his men, *so that the Sanhedrin could not officially identify John and his house, as part of the plot. I believe the records concerning Jesus are so incredibly full, that they must have been kept by literate members of the Sanhedrin, who even fifty years later would want to keep this information restricted, despite the sacking of Jerusalem.*

The arrest provided another opportunity to perform a miracle, the apparent replacement of an ear. *Steel with a really sharp cutting edge had not been invented, so it was not possible to cut off an ear without risking or intending murder. If the attack were from the front Malchus would move his head to one side, which would expose his ear at just the right angle to be cut off by a blow aimed at the crown of his head. If the attack was from behind and the sword missed, his jugular would be cut. Was, Simon nicknamed Rocky, a skilled swordsman?* (Simon called Peter. Saint Peter [Petra] the Rock on which the Roman Catholic Church is founded.)

Peter took a swipe at Malchus, who screamed with pain *and squashing a sausage skin of cow's blood screamed*, you have cut my ear off. *Jesus picked something off the ground and held it to the side of his head and said "there, do you feel better now?" It was a pitch-black night, not the sort of trick for the daylight in public. Who on earth could suspect the High Priest's servant who was also a kinsman of the High Priest of being in the plot, but if there is no God, he must have been, and it is not likely he would play so small a part being an important named man, unless his master was also in the plot. Malchus took Jesus to Hanan's house. [John 18.13 & 24].*

According to St. Jerome an early translator of the Bible into Latin; Jesus gave his grave clothes to Malchus.

Jesus' cleansing of traders from the Temple must have delighted Hanan and he must have wished to reward him, but it was essential that their connection remained a secret. At first sight it seems Hanan [Annas of the Bible] sends his servant Malchus to arrest him and have him killed. It's possible, but I cannot believe that the founders of the greatest religion on earth lacked common loyalty. Though dead men cannot speak, Jesus would have had time on the cross to speak out about the shop monopoly. The irregularity of Jesus having a trial at night in Hanan's palace is a mystery to historians.

Malchus and his guards, brought in Jesus, *into the richly furnished reception room of Hanan's* [Annas] private palace, for he was not High Priest at the time, *though he might have been second in importance to his son-in-law, Caiaphas on the Sanhedrin.* The Bible implies that a trial took place but electric light was not invented and the Sanhedrin never met in the evenings.

Malchus explained about his ear, Annas gave orders for no further arrests to take place. Otherwise how was the unnamed disciple, thought by some authorities to be John the 'beloved' Disciple, actually inside the High Priest's palace? And how did he have the authority to ask *petulant* Peter into the palace compound and protect himself and Peter from being arrested when Peter was recognised by two maids and Malchus? The stated fact that Malchus spoke to Peter in the courtyard shows that he was not in bed at the time that the cock crew, *this suggests that he did not go to the doctor, and that his missing ear was not troubling him. No one except Malchus would know about Peter denying Jesus thrice, so it is probable that Malchus reports this story, to the Gospel writer, which is told to prove that Jesus can see into the future. Peter would have been too ashamed to publicise it and nobody else would know. If my interpretation is correct Malchus would think it was a big joke, and must have been a Christian to have loved his enemy Peter so much that he did not want to arrest him, for having attempted to murder him!*

Three gospels say Malchus' ear was cut off, only one says Jesus put it back on. *This sounds like someone who is embarrassed by the God Jesus' unloving behaviour, inventing the idea that he stuck it back on. However it could be that Malchus willingly took part in the miracle as part of a team hoping for promotion, but two days later when Jesus was crucified, being a bit frightened of being found out especially w*hen he heard Caiaphas the high priest wished to execute Lazarus for doing the miracle of rising from the dead. He *therefore did not wish to confirm the miracle publicly.*

Hanan dismissed his servants so that he could be alone with

Jesus, but one loyal servant who was not in the plot advised him to remember his age, [he was past modern retirement age] "It may be dangerous for you to be alone with a violent man whose associate only half an hour ago tried to murder Malchus while resisting arrest".

Hanan said "I have the strength of God on my side I am not afraid". As soon as they were alone Hanan whispered, "Thank you very much, you did a terrific job of clearing out the temple traders. [The fact that he made so much money proves they never came back]. *We will need all the money we can get out of those shops to finance the big take over next year* when amongst other things Herod Antipas is attacked by his disgruntled Arabic father in law whose daughter he has exchanged for Herodias, especially as currently he has disinherited his sons for plotting against him. *It must be seen, that I had nothing to do with the clearing of the temple, the Sanhedrin has not dared to accuse me of cleansing the Temple, especially after Bar Ben Buta brought in 3,000 sheep for sale!*

Our scheme for your political takeover is coming on very nicely, this is a marvellous opportunity for you, everyone is calling you Messiah, God, King of the Jews and goodness knows what else, I am going to arrange for you to be charged with this. We won't charge you with raising Lazarus from the dead. He and his sisters did a first class job, but this will give you even more publicity, and save them from any legal action.

I have spoken to Herod he is very embarrassed by the execution of your cousin John the Baptist. *He says he is not frightened, that you will cause unrest and approves of your message of love; he says he would rather leave the judgement to me. Pilate liked your defence of Roman forced labour, when you said,* 'Whoever shall force you to go a mile, go with him two'. *[This referred to angaria or military requisitioning of labour]. And he liked your phrase* "render unto Caesar, that which is Caesar's" and your defence of usury in the parable of the man who failed to invest his master's money so that it did not double, as it should have done.

Whatever happens don't let them force you into saying you are God, the Messiah or the Son of God, and definitely not King of the Jews or you will be stoned. Leave them to put the words in your mouth, I have arranged for you to be accused in this way. Keep turning the tables on your accusers by saying it is not I that am claiming it but you who for some reason believe it. They will find your refusal to deny the accusation irritating but it is not against the law if you stick to the meaningless phrase "Son of Man". They won't know what to make of it, because there are some obscure references to it meaning "Messiah"."

"Are you sure it is alright for us to have this meeting, it is most unusual to talk privately with the judge before the trial." said Jesus

"Do not worry," said Hanan, "they will never guess in a couple of thousand years, I am far too respectable".

FAIL SAFE ARRANGEMENTS

"Pilate has to release a criminal because it is the ancient custom at Passover".

Hanan continued in a low voice. "Pilate is very pleased with me for tipping him off about Barrabas and the timing and location of his proposed damage to Jerusalem's clean water supply. It is just as well to get rid of these murderous toughs. I am sure Pilate will not release Barrabas; he is so very keen on his clean water aqueduct. It is his only personal achievement. Barrabas dead will be marvellous for our cause; alive he would be a liability".

"I am certain that nothing will go wrong, but if it does I have arranged with the soldiers, for a small bribe that ropes rather than nails will be used to fix you to the cross, and we will get you some pain killing drugs, and then after half an hour we will arrange a distraction and a fight in the crowd a hundred yards down the hill from the cross. The guards will leave you surrounded by seated women who will then stand up on the brow of the hill to obscure any backward glances, but the magic tricks and fighting should engross everybody for ten minutes giving time for four strong men to cut your bonds and hide you in *Joseph of Arimathea's new rock cut tomb* which we have had specially cut just behind the execution site and away from my arranged drama. When they notice you are gone there will be several men pointing to the sky saying they have seen a vision, their voices only returning when its all clear. I doubt if the soldiers will tamper with a tomb my men will pretend to help open the door but actually bolt it with pebbles in the secret slot and it takes three men in any case.

If they do go in you will appear to be a corpse with something over your face, and we are arranging for a musty smell, if they drag you out we will anger the crowd and rescue you. Even if your arms are giving you pain you should be able to run on your legs and if you can't you will be carried. You should say you are thirsty if you want drugs". They then discussed other secret distress and information signals. *"However I am sure all this will be unnecessary, as you are bound to be the prisoner which it is the tradition to release for Passover".*

"When you are released we will send messages to all the priests throughout the country saying that you are the Messiah and are the official king that has taken over Archelaus Herod's kingdom. *They will never suspect the Sanhedrin of giving you support if we recommend your execution now. Are you alright"?*

"Yes" whispered Jesus "thanks, I am quite looking forward to the challenge". They both knew the principle that if you wish to become the prime minister of an ex-British colony you have to have served some time in a British jail. *The idea was to get Jesus a place in the prime minister's university. Hanan and Jesus desired to co-operate with Roman civilised authority, but it was essential for him to prove to the people he was not a spineless quisling.*

"You must be able to obtain the respect of the freedom fighters and sicarii, and the only way of stopping them creating a blood bath is to become their leader without using their methods" said Hanan. "They are already very suspicious of you preaching, "Love your enemies". *'Enemies' is surely a synonym for Romans, and* "render unto Caesar what is Caesar's". *They are saying you are a Roman stooge, especially* as one of the apostles is a tax collector. *But being arrested will put a stop to that suspicion and* the charge of being King of the Jews will advertise the idea that you really are the Messiah and King.

Your release can be made to look almost miraculous, and it would be difficult to recharge you ever again for the same offence. "I love you Jesus, take my blessing, my own dear son", and his voice broke as he clasped his forearm.

"Don't worry daddy, I'll back you with the last drop of my blood, we must get a religion of love accepted by all men and from my miracles I've done so far, I can see people are taking my

teaching seriously already. We both believe in Hillel's teachings, and I promise not to go so far with my teachings concerning liberty, equality and love as to give the slaves any hope of a revolt. After all our family owns hundreds of slaves and when I become king I will not just have 2 or 3 but thousands. Like you I am sure, these are early beginnings, we are going to succeed, I will become Priest and King of the Jews. I notice you have already got the rumour out that the next Roman Emperor will be declared in Judea; *your forward thinking is fantastic."*

"Good luck" whispered Hanan, "Once you can fake sincerity you will be able to achieve anything." He started intoning prayers in a monotonous voice, as he tingled a little brass bell, "Bind him firmly," he said in a hard voice. "Take him to Caiaphas, across the public courtyard, don't use the back alley." Hanan had complete confidence in Caiaphas he had always been his 'yes man'. What could go wrong?

Caiaphas was Hanan's son in law *and he had got the job of High Priest through recommendation from Hanan. I imagine him as a self seeking clever man who was always obedient to Hanan's spoken and unspoken will and an extremely efficient administrator, but totally lacking real commitment to the cause of reforming the government of the world through love. He had got the job in advance of many of Hanan's natural sons because his eldest children were girls and he was 10 years older than his wife.*

Hanan had retired due to some physical weakness that prevented him standing and shouting long speeches for many hours and cutting the throats of hundreds of cattle in an afternoon. Over the years Hanan had come to rely on him, he had never challenged him, but he forgot that now he had been High Priest for many years he was no longer dependent on his patronage.

Caiaphas and Hanan's natural sons were seething with rage because of Hanan's plans for Jesus. To make his favourite Jesus; the King of the Jews, a God, and possibly High Priest. Hanan did not know that Caiaphas was jealous of Jesus, and that he wanted Lazarus dead. *But Ananus, Hanan's natural son on the night of the trial flushed out some rumours that Jesus was Hanan's bastard, and their half brother, on confirmation, of this suspicion, Caiaphas turned against Hanan.*

Hanan knew that custom decreed that a man always had to be released on this particular feast day. It worked; Pilate released Jesus into the safe hands of reliable young Caiaphas. So Hanan retired for his siesta and took his usual sleeping draught for his physical ailment that had caused him to resign his post of High Priest to a younger man and fell contentedly asleep. Hanan had arranged for all Jesus friends and his own trusted servants and friends to deliver letters to all the important priests in the provinces; Caiaphas or his assistant where to issue them as soon as Jesus was released. Jesus was released and sent back to Caiaphas.

However Caiaphas sent them all out with blank parchments or ones containing banalities in sealed rolls. The messengers thought they were a call to the long awaited rebellion. They rushed off forgetting about fail-safe plans for Jesus, believing that he did not need them any more. Caiaphas sent Jesus back to Pilate. Pilate had Jesus mildly whipped, but again refused to convict him. *Only when Caiaphas assured him that Hanan had wanted* Jesus Barrabas released not Joshua nicknamed Jesus Christ did he change his mind, *especially when Ciaphas promised him that the Sanhedrin would give him the money* for his pet project of the water supply, only then did he wash his hands of these priestly squabbles and convict Jesus. Reluctantly he released Barrabas because someone had to be released by custom. *Caiaphas if he was to fight his powerful father in law, realised he would need the protection of the zealots.*

The authors of "The Holy blood and the Holy Grail" say, "Of all the discrepancies and improbabilities in the Gospels, the choice of Barrabas [to release] is the most inexplicable. Something would clearly lie behind so clumsy and confusing a fabrication."

Hanan slept, nobody told him, everyone knew a crucifixion was going on, so the noise did not disturb nice people who did not like the sight, John the Beloved Disciple had been dispatched to the country by Caiaphas, Malchus who had been up all night knew his master never wanted him during the siesta period so he fell asleep. Jesus was alone. Joseph of Arimathea was a great friend of Hanan's and had consented to the use of his tomb for Jesus, as part of a fail safe plan, he was partially party to, as was his close friend Nicodemus, but both had voted for Jesus as they had been asked to do by Hanan, but had been out voted.

When they heard Jesus was crucified, they rushed round and realised something was wrong. They told Hanan, a message was sent to Pilate who released the body *but by now the plot was in disarray, Pilate was guessing that this Jesus was more important than appeared on the surface to Hanan.* Meanwhile, Christ called out "My father *[Daddy Hanan]* you have forsaken me." *These are odd words, for a God that had created the world. Jesus spotted the servant with a drug who was part of an elaborate fail-safe plan, which had not been activated. He cried I am thirsty, considering the level of pain he must have been suffering this seems an extraordinary suffering to complain about. Someone raised a wet rag to Jesus calling it vinegar. Is it normal to carry vinegar around with you plus a long stick and a rag?*

Shortly afterwards Jesus slumped which is unusual, in a mere three hours. Frequently, normal people live on the cross for several days till thirst, hunger, pain and exposure kill them, if they do not die of the first shock. The other two robbers had their legs broken and the soldier no doubt gave them a sharp tug in an attempt to dislocate their shoulders, which is a sort of kindness because it helps to kill a man by stopping breast expansion and reducing oxygen intake and also through shock. A lance was stuck into Jesus' side, out came blood and water. *Are Gods made of water? Water or any clear liquid defies medical explanation, so it must mean free flowing blood.* Blood only flows freely when the heart is pumping. *Jesus was alive but unconscious.*

Joseph of Arimathea and Nicodemus did the best that they could with drugs weighing as much as two person's maximum luggage allowance on a modern airliner. Aloes, which were included, are for the living, not the dead. It was resuscitation not resurrection.

As a result of the bungle, Jesus gave up teaching and retired to obscurity. Hanan quarrelled with the High Priest Caiaphas, but could not quickly get rid of him. However with his vast savings richly endowed the Christian cause, and died soon after. Joseph of Arimathea and Nicodemus joined with the apostles and James the brother of Jesus in Nazareth, under Herod, were they were comparatively safe from that "viper brood of Hanan's". *[ie his sons]. The house with the wisdom of snakes.*

Whether or not Jesus died on the cross I know not, but he

certainly retired from public life, which is strange, for his job as teacher was but part done. He left, if he was God far too many conundrums for god-fearing men, let alone questioners like myself. But if my tale is correct it all fits.

On the cross he suffered traumatic learning, if he survived he must have been very shaken, the nails would have been sterilised in the making by a red hot fire, so he may have avoided gangrene. His optimism must have taken a severe jolt, when he heard his father apologising for being asleep while he suffered, and he must have realised how serious it would be if Hanan should die during any future miracle or election stunt. Also, he now realised, Ananus II and Caiaphas were very serious rivals whereas he had thought of them as friends.

Furthermore, the bungle had blown Nicodemus and Joseph of Arimathea's cover, together with John the beloved disciple's. He himself found it painful to write because of the damage to his hand, which is why he never wrote his own Gospels. Judas Iscariot, a genuine lover of the poor, was disillusioned, when he realised that he had been cynically used by every one and had lost all chance of promotion in the church with so many plots and counter plots. He committed suicide.

May be, it was at this time that the flight into Egypt took place, and Jesus stayed incognito with Philo. John the beloved disciple with the 'virgin' Mary, and Mary Magdalene fled to Ephesus in Turkey. There John built up an enormous reputation, which years later was to rival the importance of Artemis whose temple was one of the seven wonders of the world, a very large plain brick church still exists.

Even if we disregard Jesus and all he stands for, we should remember that historically the century before the destruction of Jerusalem was Palestine's finest, in terms of culture learning and wealth, and at that time it was the jewel in the Roman Empire.

The apostles, had been recruited as crowd controllers, and were not very educated, so the Christians appointed seven deacons, in imitation of a Synagogue. They were distressed that Hellenised widows as opposed to Jewish widows were receiving no charity. St. Stephen was one of these deacons, and not only did he do miracles like Jesus but he preached, and at his trial by the Sanhedrin he said Jesus was going to make a second coming. *Caiaphas who was no longer*

High Priest was furious and arranged for him to be illegally stoned to death. By this time, we can assume that Hanan was dead.

Saul, later called St. Paul, was an educated Roman citizen, who was one of the Jews of the Diaspora. He came from Tarsus in Turkey, to seek his fortune in the city of Jerusalem, which was the centre of, and recipient of taxes for the whole Diaspora area. He studied under Gamaliel with Stephen, but decided to work for Caiaphas. He watched approvingly while Stephen was stoned to death, and set off to Damascus to kill all the Christians, not bothering with the apostles who remained in Jerusalem for they were too unimportant, and nearly illiterate. The six other deacons fled, *Caiaphas believed Jesus was biding his time in Damascus, having announced his intending return through St. Stephen. [His Second coming] Saul went to murder him.*

On the journey he realised that if he were successful, he would be a wanted murderer under Roman Syrian law, he would have to be dependent on Caiaphas rescuing him and giving him the high office that he promised he would. Syria was a totally separate province, where the Sanhedrin could give him no protection. *He learnt that Caiaphas did not always keep his promises. He had broken his promise to his father-in-law to save Jesus' life. He learnt the secret that Caiaphas, did not disapprove of Jesus, or his teachings, but was just vindictively jealous of his half brother. Caiaphas was very old; he could easily die before the present incumbent of the office he had promised to Saul died.*

On the other hand, he received a message from Jesus that while he slept; Christians had been in his room that could easily have killed him, just as King David had twice left messages for King Saul while he slept. Saul [St. Paul] began to think following conventional methods of promotion was very dangerous. If he was successful the Christians would have good reason to kill him, likewise the Romans under the law, and Caiaphas being untrustworthy might do so simply because he knew too much.

The Christians believed in love not war, so they offered him a post, and Saul realised his chances with them were much better. He liked the Gamaliel/ Jesus love thy neighbour idea. *Many rich Sadducees belonged to this secret society, and when Jesus ruled there would be lots of posts for his helpers.*

If Jesus, who was ill, died or retired, there would be a vacancy for the sect leader. Until then, there were lots of good posts going in Diaspora towns.

He saw the light; he changed his name to Paul. *Caiaphas in pique* wanted him killed, but being a Roman Citizen, he could not be executed, he got the Romans to transport him out of Jerusalem, and finally to Rome for Trial, he like Jesus before him knew if one was to become prime minister one must graduate from your colonial ruler's Jail, and have been whipped by the Romans.

The way Christianity spread is almost a miracle but it took hundreds of years. Everywhere throughout the Roman Empire, there were sizable populations of Jews living in towns. If only 10% of the total population lived in towns and 10% of the population of the Mediterranean was Jewish that could mean half the townsfolk were Jewish, because there is no record of them doing agricultural work abroad. They certainly handled the trade and were artificers and doctors.

The Christians found it convenient to leave Jerusalem, long before the Romans burnt it down. The burning of Jerusalem cleared the Jews out of the city, and put a stop to sacrifices. Buddhists had preached for hundreds of years, that it is a waste to give sacrificial animals to priests. The Christians prospered because being gentle honest and peaceful, they offended nobody. They needed no churches, "where ever two or three are gathered together there am I", *if they were attacked or persecuted they simply moved to another town, and they kept in touch with other communities through people like Paul.*

Jesus had played the part of the Messiah better than all the other hopefuls. St. Paul soon realised that it did not matter whether Jesus was alive or dead, if he physically never came back because of ill health or domestic bliss, or lack of a peaceful opportunity it was unimportant. From Paul's point of view it made it better, he could behave like Moses and make God say what he wanted him to say.

Lazarus was not named in any written work, until after Caiaphas was dead, for Caiaphas it is reported wished to kill him, after all there is one thing you do learn when you are High Priest, there is no God and therefore miracles can't happen. Later Jesus' brother James was killed, possibly this was because he became a greater threat when Jesus died in exile of natural causes.

A SUMMARY OF CIRCUMSTANTIAL EVIDENCE

The conventional version of the Bible *must be false, because it is as ridiculous to believe in a God as to believe in fairies.* Therefore there has to be a new interpretation. Mine may be wrong, but if it fits the facts, it is better than the Christian one. Because Christians will dismiss my research as sacrilegious rubbish, I must, at the risk of being repetitious, like an Agatha Christie's detective, set out the clues that led me to *the man that popularised goodness as an ingredient in religion and who was the creator of Christ in more ways than one.*

If natural law says 'Jesus had an earthly father'; who was he? No one clue proves any thing, but the build up of circumstantial evidence is impressive.

My version does not need to explain away or re-write parts of the Gospels. Whereas, I am able to list 5 examples, and there are many more, where Christians suppress, or try to explain away parts of the Gospels that embarrass them.

1) How Jesus the God of Love can be an accessory to attempted murder, or at very least, condoning the carrying of illegal offensive weapons, and why he did not disown Peter his own disciple for the attempted murder of Malchus?

2) Why Jesus had a foot fetish. They say that 'Mary', the sister of Lazarus, is a copyists muddle for the 'Mary' called Magdalene, who they then with no evidence go on to describe as a prostitute. Likewise they never translate 300 denarii spent on the spikenard used for His feet as anything more than £3 despite inflation, which at 1% pa would equal £5 million. [£3,000 to £5,000 min.]

3) Why on the two occasions Jesus speaks to his mother, he is rude to her.

4) His destruction of a fig tree, and the Gadarine swine. This is destruction of private property without compensation, and should offend the Green party.

5) His failure to preach a sermon upon his return from the dead, his general lack of clarity including not writing a book, or making a clear statement as to who he is, and his inability to do really useful miracles to improve the lot of mankind, by teaching them about electricity instead of providing wine for a party. Also he forgot to free the slaves, and reinstate the importance of women by saying

that homunculi (fully formed babies in men's sperm) do not exist.

I maintain that Hanan's motive was an altruistic belief in a philosophy, that Hanan wanted the world to accept, just as I want the world to accept my ideas. His secondary motive was power for his family. The idea of a God King would be natural to him; *he associated with the Magi,* who were usually a composite of High Priest and King.

Terms like 'son of man' suggest no more than a prophet. He knew that Alexander the Great claimed that he was born of a virgin, and had worked miraculous cures in order to claim the people's acceptance of his claim that he was God. To Hanan the idea of a Messiah was banal, so many had tried it and failed. He knew, an Arab of good family like Herod the Great, who had become rich as a result of finding a treasure trove on his property, could achieve Kingship and there had been rumours that Herod had, had an outside chance of being chosen as Emperor of Rome, because he was such a successful administrator.

Hanan *knew the value of 'rent a mob';* he had become High Priest because of a popular uprising against Joasar. When Herod's son who had inherited half the kingdom, including Idumea was deposed for bad rule, Hanan must have been an obvious candidate. He was already in charge of receiving taxes and it was more normal for the High Priest to be King as well.

Who put about the rumour that finally materialised for Vespasian, that the Pontifex Maximus and Emperor of Rome would be proclaimed on Jewish soil? No one else would have found such rumours useful. His own incredible recorded success makes his enormous vision seem reasonable. Being Idumean makes it probable that he would combine Zoroastrian magic with the rationalism of the Greek language, which he used in daily life. As High Priest, his congregation had ten times as many people as Herod Antipas ruled over; this gives him the power and facilities.

The Roman and Jewish religious straitjacket provides a motive for him, to wish to get the 'love' message over by an unusual ruse.

No one would expect Joseph's child to be born in a humble stable, so this suggests the birth was hurried and unplanned. Only Mary could know how soon the baby was coming, *Joseph must have thought it had another couple of months to run.* If the Magi were doctors, they arrived too late to supervise the birth. Who had the power to send Priest Kings [Magi] as mere messengers with gifts? If God is not Jesus' father, his father must be someone very near to God; nobody is nearer to God than a High Priest.

Judea was much more powerful than the little countries on her southern border, and the Magi *could have been attending the High Priest's inauguration.* The High Priest would have easy access to the enormous quantities of frankincense and myrrh stored in the temple for burning, and he could easily distort the records of how much was actually burnt; besides he was rich in gold.

The concept of planning a coup 25 years ahead, suggests a brilliant organiser and operator, there are none other than Hanan who have that reputation. Bethlehem is on the road to Idumea, Hanan's birthplace. The shepherds, the star, the virgin were all important pointers, there is too much for mere chance, all commentators suggest that Jesus' ministry followed a plan. A father that gave such valuable gifts at birth would be likely to continue giving secret gifts there after, to support the Great man role he had sketched with such theatricality.

The Bible says Annas [Hanan] and Caiaphas were High Priests when Annas was <u>not historically,</u> which suggests that Hanan was very important. Annas had been High Priest and Caiaphas his son in law was now High Priest, *and I suggest got the job because he did what Hanan told him to do.* Why did they walk 40 miles to the Jordan River to witness St John baptise Jesus? Annas might have liked to think he was High Priest, because in the distant past some High Priests had retained their posts until death.

But why would the Christians want to promote him when they say he killed Jesus? When the New Testament was written, Annas [Hanan] and his family had all, long since, been killed by the Jews whose rabbis [Pharisees] described them as a 'viper brood', because they were hated for the great wealth they had obtained from their monopoly of the Chanujoth, the four shops across the bridge from the temple.

Why did Hanan not defend Jesus? He was likely to know who Jesus' father was, because he was the Virgin's kinsman and as head of the Temple, he was her legal guardian.

Hanan was fertile. Secret, gentle, non-penetrative child sexual abuse is common today. Nearly all the participants were related to the 'High Priest'. Why do the Gospels tell us this, when it appears to be irrelevant snobbish information? Could it be a sort of code to tell us who were genuine members of the conspiracy by the remnants of the Annas faction? Some authorities say all the apostles were related to Hanan [Annas the High Priest], others say three of them came from another family, but either way it is sufficiently peculiar to raise questions as to which side he was on. Mary Cleophas married Joseph of Nazareth's brother and her sons the apostles Andrew and Peter were partners in a fishing fleet with James and John (Zeberdee) who were sons of Mary Salome a 2nd cousin of the Virgin Mary.

Zacharias was assassinated between the temple and the altar for proclaiming the Miraculous Conception of Jesus. When his wife Elizabeth was told of her cousin Mary's pregnancy, "the babe (John the Baptist) leapt in her womb."

The Virgin Mary, Jesus, Elizabeth, John the Baptist and Malchus are all related to Hanan. Lazarus is an employee and friend. Malchus is chief servant. Thus, the majority of the named recipients of miracles are all connected to Hanan in the Gospels. It really is incredible if this is just chance. It must have been fairly important to someone, for it to be mentioned.

Yet the Christians assume Hanan was responsible for Christ's death! The raising of the daughter of the ruler of the synagogue shows Jesus had priestly connections. Nicodemus, and Joseph of Arimathea serve with Hanan on the Sanhedrin. Nicodemus a ruler of the Jews came to Jesus by night, suggesting secrecy. Joseph of Arimathea must have been a relation because Roman law only allows relatives to collect the bodies of the crucified. Jesus' brother James is kinsman and friend!

If gnostos is a mistranslation for gnorimos as some scholars think, even John the mysterious 'beloved disciple' in whose house the last supper took place is a relation. John the beloved disciple's movements are worked out in 'the Passover Plot' by Hugh J Schonfield where he is shown to have entered Annas' (Hanan's) palace, after Jesus' arrest and to have sufficient authority to invite Peter in. He shows how the whereabouts of John's house is kept secret, and feels that the chroniclers for some reason are always trying to hide his identity. This is the John who after the crucifixion "took her (The

Virgin Mary) unto his own." John 19:27.

The feeding of the five thousand and the four thousand shows that someone beside Jesus and his apostles was behind the birth of Christianity. Jesus never in general attacks the Sadducees but always the Pharisees; he is a liberal Greek in thought, supporting Rome, like Hanan.

The greatest clue is the cleansing of the Temple of traders; Jesus' final act; which must have given Hanan the earning power of ten thousand ordinary people, and benefited Hanan and Hanan alone. Why, oh why, would Hanan want to kill Jesus so shortly afterwards?

Information about his monopoly of the four shops comes from Jewish non-biblical sources, which Christians are often ignorant about; this could explain why this clue is not more commented upon.

Caiaphas who might have been taking bribes secretly for trading space in the temple must have been severely shocked by Jesus acting with arrogance in his temple. Viewers of soap operas will not find it strange to find sons in law, supported by natural sons ganging up on a secret take over bid by a bastard rival, who wishes to take their jobs. But before the days of Burgess and Maclean the double life may not have readily occurred to Hanan's contemporaries, and his children would not want to expose him since their own careers were tied to his august respectability.

Annas plus Caiaphas visit St. John the Baptist to witness Jesus' baptism, and together release St. Peter. Caiaphas on his own will not accept Jesus' release, desires to kill Lazarus, and employs Saul [St. Paul] to chase Christians

Malchus was incredibly kind and Christian not to arrest Peter for attempted murder if the sword stroke had been real. After all he was accompanied by a 'great multitude' at the time of Peter's attack and later Peter was recognized by maids at Hanan's palace.

The Malchus incident proves that Malchus is a stunt man willing to risk his job, or if his job is not at risk, it is surely likely that his master Hanan connived at it. If the High priest were able to speak to God, he would know the ear was not cut off? Or, if like me he knew that there are no Gods or miracles, he would know that the miracle healing of Malchus' ear was a trick. If Hanan is in the plot, he is no minor figure.

Victor Dunnstan in 1985 says, "And Ciaphas, the High Priest of Judaism, flew in the face of the might of Rome. Later in the trial, when the defence of Jesus seemed to be winning the day Caiaphas engaged in a travesty of Justice which perhaps had not been witnessed in the legal history of the Jews and which has perhaps not been witnessed since. He took the prosecution case out of the hands of the prosecution council, and under took the prosecution himself. He cross-examined Jesus himself and did not allow the defence the right to reply. The fear, malevolence and haste hide something far more than the detestation of a local preacher who proclaimed himself to be a God. The Sanhedrin voted 40 to 31 for the dismissal of the case against Jesus"

"PILATE PRONOUNCED JESUS INNOCENT ON NO LESS THAN FOUR OCCASIONS". Pilate wrote "Jesus of Nazareth the King of the Jews." He refused to add the words "he said he was."

The guards on the tomb were not Roman soldiers as is commonly supposed but Sanhedrin guards (Matthew 27:65) while they collected some food or drink in the middle of the night; *Hanan could easily have got an officer to substitute for them, for a few vital minutes*

The Greek idea that His body is 'a temple' is vital to the promotion of Jesus from being a mere Messiah [herald] into being God. John 13.42 "Nevertheless among the chief rulers [a phrase used elsewhere to describe members of the Sanhedrin which was headed by the High Priest] also many believed on him [Jesus]; but because of the Pharisees did not confess him, lest they should be put out of the synagogue." This may explain Farrar's puzzlement *as to why the Priests knew more about his body being the 'temple', than his disciples, who did not bother to come to his crucifixion.*

The jealous hatred that caused Caiaphas' to have Jesus crucified was carried forward by Hanan's legitimate son, Ananus, who lost his job as High priest to murder Jesus' brother James, when he was an old man. *I think Ananus and his brothers could be trying to regain inheritance money that had been left by their father to the Christian cause.*

The main popular errors, which have thrown people off the scent; are :-

A) The belief in Jesus' poverty. Based on his father being a working class carpenter, the stable birth and the way in which he ate gleanings in the fields. Jewish law on gleanings is extraordinary in the West, but is still practised today throughout the Middle East. It is not a sign of poverty only a sign that he is travelling.

B) The belief today that the Pharisees were the establishment in Jesus' time, because Rabbis are their ideological descendants. The Sadducees could not correct this error because they were wiped out with the destruction of the temple.

C) The assumption that a father and son in law, because they both are called High Priest would see eye to eye on everything.

D) The surprise that any normal person would hint that they were God because they did not know it was a fashionable at that time, to say one was the Messiah and hundreds did so.

E) And finally: The total disbelief that any body, especially a High Priest, could dissemble all their life like Burgess or Maclean (Russian spies).

For Jesus to have, done the job of actor presenter, as brilliantly as he did, he must have had first rate back up and production. When you remember famous films, one always remembers the actors, rather than the directors and producers who may have lost fortunes to present it. So it is not surprising that his backers and financiers are forgotten.

Hanan was the only person who was the right age and had the wealth, power, and intelligence, to be a successful bidder for religious leadership and kingship; it may have failed but years later it did sweep the world. Jesus Christ is undoubtedly the greatest man in History, and I think he was right to choose not to physically have a second coming; it would not have been peaceful.

It is up to us to bring peace on earth and I am very hopeful we are very near to being able to do it. I would feel very guilty, exposing an historical system, which has helped peace. If I did not believe that I have the method of achieving it in my 2nd volume currently called Cupid's City"

"Treason never prospers, what's the reason,
For if it prospers, none dare call it treason,"

"Men are we, and must grieve when even the shade
Of that which once was great has passed away."
Wordsworth wrote it of Venice;
I think it applies to Christianity

EPILOGUE
RAPHAEL'S CODE,

OR HOW I DISCOVERED THE FATHER OF JESUS, AGED 8.

I received a card from friends in Scotland with a picture of a dinosaur in a lake. It said underneath "This is a genuine photograph of the Loch Ness Monster". Nobody would tell me if it was true, in the end I guessed it was a photo of a model of a dinosaur superimposed on a photo of Loch Ness and then photographed so that it was a genuine photo. But why; had no one been honest with me?

As Christmas approached my mother asked me what I wanted Father Christmas to leave in my stocking. I said I didn't know, but that I didn't want all those oranges he had left last year. Besides our bedroom did not have a chimney. Previous bedrooms had always had a chimney even if they had been blocked up by a gas fire.

Half my Christmas cards had Father Christmas on them; only a tenth had a picture of the baby Jesus whose birthday it was.

Who was Father Christmas? He was not my father, he had not married my mother, was he Jesus' father? God is referred to as 'The Father'. Is Father Christmas God? With another name he is a Christian Saint?

I awoke in the middle of the night my mother was in the room and in the dark had dropped some oranges on the floor. My mother had lied to me and like a thief I had caught her in my room. I had always trusted my mother, why did Christians have to tell lies. Was it just a way of making children obey grown ups, by frightening them with stories of Hell Fire?

The only explanation I got from my mother was that with the war on it was difficult to buy presents and the little wrapped gifts did not fill the Christmas stocking which was why she put the oranges in as fillers.

Our house had been bombed and my mother was divorced so we were staying with my grandmother. My Grandmother said at Sunday Lunch. "Had I ever been in India?" "Yes" I said. My mother said "No, of course I hadn't". I felt snubbed. So I said "Yes I have in my mummy's tummy!" My grandmother got up from the dining table and walked out of the room, before desert had been served, saying to my mother, "The things you tell your children".

When we had eaten the Christmas pudding my mother told me to apologise to Granny. She was worried, as we had nowhere else to live. So I knocked on the drawing room door and said "I am sorry", but I did not know what I was sorry for or how to lengthen the sentence. Grudgingly sitting in her fireside chair she said "That is alright" and then sat silent not explaining why calling a stomach a 'tummy' was so shocking that she had thought it was so important that she had missed pudding. I stood in front of her not knowing what to do, or say, it seemed a bit abrupt to walk out of the room. I felt her disapproval had something puzzling to do with Christianity.

I noticed above her head an oil painting which is on the cover of this book. I said slightly puzzled "Is that the Holy Family?" She replied "Of course it is". I said "Who is the extra child." "John the Baptist" she said. I was shocked. Only two hours earlier I had been at a Quaker Sunday School, and the woman lay teacher had told us about how St. John had baptised Jesus in the Jordan River watched by the High Priest Annas and his son in law Caiaphas. One of my fellow pupils had asked "How did John recognise Jesus, had they met before, were they friends?" The teacher replied "No they had never met before, but John had recognized him by the light that radiated from his face and body." I thought my granny was talking nonsense about the picture on the wall, but I did not dare say so.

So I pressed on enquiring who everyone was. She explained that one woman was Elizabeth the mother of John, and the other woman was the Virgin Mary, I was not surprised by her emphasis on Virgin, I knew she was very important. After all she had said it was the Holy Family, and although I didn't have a father because my mother was divorced, I knew it was usual. So I said "Who is the man in the background? Is he their father? Firmly and angrily she said wagging her finger, I told you it was the VIRGIN Mary. "Yes" I said "I know that but who is the man?" With a shrug she said he is the High Priest Annas and then with more emphasis she said it is a secret and you must never discuss it with anyone. You must promise never to speak about it again. So I said "I promise". "You can go back to your mother now" she said.

So I asked my mother if the Sunday school teacher was correct and that John the Baptist had never met Jesus. She was busy but said "I know your teacher and I am sure she must be right. So I burst out laughing, "Granny must be an idiot then". My mother was alarmed. "Why". I explained the picture in the drawing room showed the naked Baptist playing with Jesus naked. Oh said my mother "Granny is very very knowledgeable about those sorts of things and I must believe every thing she says". I dare not discuss my promise to Granny that I would never discuss that Annas was the father of Jesus and John the Baptist, because she had agreed the picture was of the Holy Family. I had no idea that Virgin was a sex word, I didn't even know what sex meant; I thought Virgin was a Christian name.

You may say that the word of a woman ten times my age is no proof that Jesus' father was the High Priest, but this is the beginning of the chapter and you must read on to discover the truth, but this misunderstanding led to a lifetimes interest.

A few days later I returned to my boarding school. There I learnt that Joseph was only engaged to the Virgin Mary when Jesus was born, and therefore could not possibly be Jesus' proper father, but this was all a bit of a mystery and hush hush. Well I knew the answer; the father was the High Priest, but I kept my mouth shut.

Written on the cross was "this is the King of the Jews". Jesus kept saying I am the Son of Man, he didn't keep saying I am the son of God. On the cross he says "My God, my God why did you forsake me? Well if he was not a separate person from God that is a very odd thing to say *but if the word should be 'father' not 'God' as some translators think, he could have been referring to his real father who was taking a siesta thinking him released by Pontius Pilate.*

Then a speaker at a Sunday service told me nearly all the disciples were Jesus' cousins; and Jesus was kinsman to Malchus, (Jesus' arresting officer) who was kinsman to the High Priest. Later I asked a teacher "What does 'Kinsman' mean". "Oh related" said the teacher and the bell rang. This surely meant that Annas was related to Jesus.

Later still I heard how Joseph and Mary journeyed in a large group from Jerusalem to Nazareth for a day and then noticed Jesus was missing so they had to waste 3 days, to find what I took to be a naughty 12 year old. They found him in the Temple having a serious discussion with the elders. Instead of apologising Jesus said "Where would you expect to find me, except in my **father's** house". Another boy asked "Did he sleep in the Temple? Is it not like a church with no bed or kitchen?" "Well he most probably spent the night in the High Priest's house which I think was on the Temple Mount" said the master. Well that was it; the school master knew my Granny's secret.

Then I learnt that Annas and the other High Priests had had Jesus crucified. I began to think it was unlikely that Annas would want to murder his own son.

But there was something awfully odd about the repeated references in the Bible to one man being released at the Passover, and Barrabas a robber was favoured despite Pontius Pilate wanting Jesus' release. The civics master told me that it had greatly helped both Ghandi and Nehru in their careers; to have short sentences in British prisons. Another boy asked "Is that why Jesus wanted to be arrested" and the master said "Quite probably. The Romans were the colonial masters, just like the British, and prison would give Jesus good publicity and establish his patriotic credentials as a descendant of King David".

My mother had told me That Dr. Marie Stopes had achieved fame by being put in prison for one day for recommending contraceptives in her book Married Love and as a result the book had become a bestseller.

Pontius Pilate the Roman ruler had released Jesus but something must have gone very wrong. The Jews had welcomed Jesus' entry into Jerusalem with palms before his feet. *I think the Jews that wanted him dead were not the general population but Caiaphas' supporters.* Because the Bible says Annas and Caiaphas were both high priests simultaneously which is clearly nonsense children assume that Annas was high priest when he was not and that there could be no disagreement between Annas and Caiaphas (Annas' son in law) and therefore they both wanted Jesus' crucified. However it would be natural for his legal sons and son in law to be offended by Annas concealing his plans to make Jesus a king; and to be very jealous if they thought that Jesus was his bastard son. They could all have dreamed of becoming King as well? The Roman

Emperor was a God and a King, and it was usual for the King to be the High Priest in other countries.

Because only 3 professors understood his book about mathematics; my mother thought Bertrand Russell the most intelligent man in the world. Russell said he could not prove that there was no teapot circling the sun, because telescopes were not powerful enough; but just because he could not prove there was no God that did not prove there was both a teapot and a God.

'Can God make a stone so heavy he can not lift it?' This schoolboy conundrum proves that God is not infinitely powerful. Science does not need God to explain history.

If Jesus was such a good man that when he died he became God, his life seems reasonable. But if he was already a God when he sucked the Virgin's breast he appears to me, to be a bit disorganised in his priorities.

He never bothered to teach anyone how to cure blindness, or tell women they produced half the babies DNA and that it was not as generally supposed throughout the Roman civilised world that males only produced homunculi (tiny babies) in their sperm. Surely he should have corrected this scientific error; that caused women to be third class citizens because they had no part in the making of babies. If He knew; why didn't He tell the world? If He was a God he must have known about electricity, television, and petrol engines. But He never bothered to tell any one. Or even publish a proper book explaining good and bad behaviour. He behaved like an excellent man but hardly like a God. If his miracles are magician tricks then he believed in deceit and told lies.

Thinking about this as a ten year old, I awoke in the middle of the night, when all the other boys were asleep in my dormitory, to hear the random banging of a casement window in the wind and with pure innocence I prayed to God. "Give me a sign" I said, "to show that you exist, bang three times in equal rhythm, I don't want to believe silly people who say you don't exist. So I prayed to God silently. He failed the test I was rather shocked by the thought that God might not exist, was he like Father Christmas? "Suffer little children to come unto me", indeed. When I said to a schoolmaster, God would not speak to me; he said I would have to be a very good boy before I could expect God to be bothered with me. *This encouragement to goodness is why many good men continue to say there is a God when they are uncertain.* So I said the only person I can remember God talking to was the murderer called Moses, surely he was hardly a good man. "Oh" he said "He had confessed his sins so that was alright; read your Bible".

So I read my Bible to see what sort of men God liked talking to. The wicked and evil mass murderer Moses seemed to be his first choice. And I was shocked by reading about a man who in order to steal land murdered the troops of his wife's family who had surrendered; besides innocent women who hadn't even fought to defend their inherited land. He was at least as evil as Hitler. Hitler didn't kill British troops who had surrendered. I did not know, at this time, about his Christian minions murdering the Jews. He said "My God and the German People". I think Hitler learnt from Moses how to govern his 90% Christian country. His troops' belt buckles had "God is on our side" written on them and he was patriotic like Moses for Gods chosen people only God's chosen were Germans not Jews.

Long after the war I learnt that Pope Pius 12th saw from a Vatican window dozens of Jews being forced to stand on a lorry to be taken to a concentration camp which they thought meant slave work, but which he knew meant the gas chamber and he made no protest. Can the Pope when he is infallible talk to God? Some Roman Catholics want to make Pius 12th a saint! Even today the majority of the American armed forces are "poorly educated, patriotic evangelical Christians".

There are no properly scientifically recorded miracles; the original pieces of the Holy cross were of many types of wood, including English oak. An eye specialist told me that with his little finger nail he could flick off a cataract to restore sight to a blind man. He guessed that Alexander the Great had done this in public when he worked miracles and Jesus could have done the same. However he wouldn't do it because the patient could easily get an infection and be dead in three weeks. About this time I became an atheist.

Thomas Aquinas' dictum which was based on Aristotle, said that the soul did not enter the embryo for 40 days for a boy and 90 days for a girl. The Pope in 1869 said the soul entered the embryo on day one. Rich people, pay priests to say Holy Communion to avoid

Hell when they are dying. But young married women very frequently eject embryos into the latrine. Why don't R.C. priests insist on going to the W.C. with them? Is the last sacrament a useless incantation? Surely every soul is equal.

My mother told me that her mother my Granny had told her that babies were delivered by storks or found under gooseberry bushes. Mummy knew when she got married neither was true but was shocked when my father produced his urinary device. I then realised that Christians (like my middle class grandmother) by refusing to speak about sex had confused me. I think in her deceitful ignorance, she may have chosen the man to be a High Priest because she imagined that all priests were celibate like Roman Catholic ones. But by now she was dead; so I could not ask her. But because I had believed Annas was the father of Jesus, for several years, the idea was naturally in my unconscious. All though I am an Atheist I still in a moment of danger say to a companion "For God's sake don't".

When I was young, to say one was an atheist was very daring, and most people regarded you with as much affection as if one had said one was a thief.

However the average aristocratic family has to pay death duties every 30 years so that family fortunes don't last long. But they say Jesus never dies, so the church avoids death duties.

God has failed to get his *slaves* (humans) to translate The Word of God (the Bible and or the Koran) into most languages, and certainly took along time doing it for most people. There are approximately 6.800 languages today and one dies out every fortnight. Mandarin Chinese has one billion speakers, English has half a billion. More people are travelling to remote parts of the world, and human racism like Hitler's Nazis and Christian inquisitions are no longer popular. So there is a chance I will not be murdered by Al Queda.

My Uncle died and I inherited a leather bound book called The Life of Christ by Farrar which had been a best seller in Victorian days. I read it. Farrar believed everything in the Bible was true, so he had great difficulty in explaining stories that were reported differently in different Gospels. His usual way out of this difficulty was to say those things that did not fit together where separate items; not the same item reported wrongly. As a result he says Jesus had six trials. And he had fed thousands of Passover Pilgrims twice and cleansed the temple twice, with a three year gap. In a note he introduced me to the monopoly of the 4 shops on the Chanujoth which were vandalised by Jewish looters, 3 years before the Temple was levelled by the Romans. Taanith 4: 8 *However the Aramaic for 8 is very like 5 and I think he means 5.* It is sometimes spelt Ta'anith.

I think bird sellers would have shops full of wicker birdcages which would burn well. They also had "money changers" *(bankers?) and therefore I think metallic money would be stored on the top of this rocky pinnacle. In fact I can not think of a safer place to store it. Local shops in the centre of Jerusalem would only have mud walls. A thief would have to climb a near vertical surface 100 feet or escape across a bridge into a Temple with 100 paid gate keepers.*

I think the Temple was completed about the time of Jesus' crucifixion about 50 years after it was started. It is true builders were employed for another 30 years. *These I believe were finishers,* people who smoothed and polished marble, and of course goldsmiths who applied the thick gold plates to the walls of the Holy of Holies, which with some other buildings had roofs. But 'Temple' is a Roman word describing a grand roofless space so most of the space was open to the sky surrounded with *5 foot diameter Greek Corinthian columns.* Here there was space for preachers like Jesus and St Paul, a sort of Hyde Park Speakers Corner.

Other colonnaded areas were for the hundreds of cattle and sheep which were to be executed and the people to watch and collect the bulk of their dead animal. I am afraid Jesus did not cleanse the temple of animal droppings only of cheap goods and money.

The Romans destroyed the temple in 70 AD and then again in 135 AD to make sure there was no place for the Jews to make their *evil* patriotic assemblies.

When the Romans first destroyed the Temple, they burnt it down so everyone around could see that something dramatic had happened. The result was that the gold became liquid and because they had not used mortar it ran into the joints between the stones and collected in the foundations above the natural rocks that had no cracks.

So the Jews left no stone on the Temple Hill unturned in their search for spaces between the un-mortared joints into which the liquid gold might have run. Mortar was not used between stones in Egypt. The stones in First class buildings were fixed with copper clamps; as a result long ago the best buildings in Egypt, have been demolished for the copper. But the ignorant tourists think the second class buildings are stupendous. *But the Jews love Gold (money is the current phrase,) patriotism and possibly God.*

In case you think I am prejudiced against the Jews for saying they are money grubbing. I now give the Jews some praise. For two thousand years throughout Europe the cleverest children especially the really clever ones that could read and write became priests and Rabbis. However the Roman Catholic priests, monks and nuns, about 10% of the population of Italy, by refusing to have children have deliberately destroyed their cleverness genes. In contrast the Rabbis got married and had lots of children. *As a result the Christian population by a small fraction is not as clever as the Jews.*

Farrar thought hatred of money changers was normal and that Jesus must have hated them despite the fact that Jesus thinks that one's servant should double your money for no profit while one is away on a trip. Matthew 25 14-24. I wish my stockbroker could double my money annually. But in Luke 19 11-27 he thinks a servant should turn one gold coin into ten!

However for the Annas family to charge 200 times the proper price must mean a monopoly of all trading in or near the Temple. Therefore this monopoly has been created by Jesus Christ putting a stop to all Temple trading. Jesus is clearly revealed without possibility of doubt as Annas' rent-a-mob captain.

The Jews who decades later wreck the Chanujoth are undoing Jesus' bullying of the *slave* money changers with a whip.

Why? Why did Jesus make Annas one of the richest men in the Roman Empire? Why did he risk being nailed to a cross to achieve it? Annas had to keep it secret otherwise if the public knew Jesus was Annas' man the whole moral pressure on the traders would have been lost.

Where did Jesus get the money to feed thousands and have his servants' dressed in cloaks that second hand were worth a sword? The easy answer is; *his mother's guardian gave his bastard the money and hoped to make him King of Archelaus' kingdom* which Herod Antipas had lawsuits to obtain. Who but a High Priest would have the foresight and sufficient wealth to have given him Gold

Frankincense and Myrrh and arrange for birth events to correspond with those foretold?

Long after Jesus was crucified, the four shops on the Chanujoth were used as the premises for the Sanhedrin (the priestly legal council); when it condemned men to death. This might be because the Annas' family dictated its policy; or maybe for safety's sake. But three years before the Romans had to expel the Jews from Jerusalem; the rabble fired and destroyed the Chanujoth.

Abraham copying the religion of the surrounding country in which he was a wanderer decided to follow Moloch or Melak's custom of murdering the first born on the highest mountain. Mount Zion in Jerusalem is higher than Mount Moriah but the Moslems believe the Dome of the Rock 692 AD is built on the site of Abraham's altar and the point were Muhammad's body miraculously journeying from Mecca changed direction and went vertically to heaven. This rock which measures 58 foot by 45 foot in area is only 3 or 4 feet higher than the surrounding tableland. Because this is reported *I guess it is one of the largest rocks. The separate pinnacle on which the 4 shops stood must have been the same height as the temple plateau for a bridge to have linked it. Col. Everest's equipment had not been invented. If one looked from the Kidron valley up at the cliff face a pinnacle of the same height standing in front of it would break the skyline and thus be said to be the highest rock by Abraham's illiterate goat herders.*

Due to splits millions of years old it must have been made of many rocks. I suggest the winching up of heavy stones on to the bridge may have given it an occasional jerk when things went wrong. If the natural rock had hairline cracks or fissures in it, I guess the gold ran into it, and so at every opportunity people were keen to dismantle it. Is this why the Jews are said to love gold?

Why did the High Priest Caiaphas, on his own initiative return the freed Jesus to Pilate for execution? An obvious reason for his hatred would be jealousy. He would not want Jesus the bastard getting the throne and authority over him. When he had hoped he might achieve that position himself. Is this why he wished to kill Lazarus; and send Saul (St Paul) *to kill Jesus* in Damascus?

I have asked 12 non-Christians to judge if Annas is Jesus' father and they all agreed that if they were jurors at a trial they would say he was. The Christians I have asked all dithered, but after all it would mean throwing a side a life time's belief.

SOME ATHEIST IDEAS.

Bin Laden says Allah has declared a Jihad on America and kills 3,000 in the World Trade Centre, thousands of Pakistanis, many illiterate. shout approval in the streets. President Bush's word 'crusade' to describe his anti terrorist policy suggests that Jesus does not object to the killing of a few Afghan and Iraqi civilians. Why can Jesus and Allah not have a debate on television to say if they are the same God or rivals? What sort of God would be content to let his loving adherents kill each other over genuine misunderstandings about his word, and not set about clearing up anomalies? *He is an appallingly bad communicator.*

A Bishop of Durham has had doubts about the Virgin birth and Christ's miracles. Nowadays miracles are not reported in the daily papers or on television. God has never once appeared on television. A DUMB GOD is unfit to be a ruler or communicator of rules, *and so must be sacked, because he is incompetent, uninterested or non-existent. Why if he was all knowing was he so lazy* that he never told us about electricity? *Why could he not have worked a miracle and restored the lives of the World Trade Centre victims?* If this God or Gods do not care for Human life why should we care for them, *because they terrorise us*? If God is so much cleverer than us, why does he want our praise?

Saint Augustine believes that women should be punished more for a stolen apple than men for Abel's murder of his brother. He said that men are born in the image of God, when defective children are born does this mean that God is defective? Or does God not believe in equal opportunities for all. Ref John 9 3. Or, *has he not only failed to have written a moral code, but does not believe in morality.*

The Bible is muddled; Jehovah's witnesses say it is the word of God. *Is God muddled*? Differing religious groups go to war about detailed interpretations of God's word. This proves that God is a poor communicator, and does not care for mankind, or that he does not exist.

"Thou shalt not kill" is one of the clearest instructions that

God gives. Yet history shows it is the favourite occupation of the followers of Moses who wrote it and Christian crusaders.

For example Luther the founder of Protestantism said, "How much more ought we to break on the wheel and kill.... hunt down, curse and behead all usurers." *Is this what we should do when the Chancellor of the Exchequer raises interest rates?*

Assuming that there are no atheists and counting religionists by their countries, two thirds of the world does not believe in any form of Christianity, though half the world believes in Moses. No Christian church has more than half the Christians believing in it, they are hopelessly divided. The Muslims knowing all about Christ reject his divinity. Not a single word of the Bible has been translated into 60% of spoken languages; only one out of 16 languages has a full translation. For 1,500 years God never bothered to speak to backwoods tribesmen, *which suggests that he is racist.*

In England less than 10% of the population goes to church, if that became general only 3% of the world would vote for a Christian party in a world election, and it could never obtain a majority. Since 1969, 1,600 Church of England churches; and 6,000 out of 14,000 Methodist chapels have been declared redundant. In 2002 regular Sunday worshippers had fallen by a third over the previous two decades to 3.500,000. In the U.S.A. in the 1950s church going was higher, this was because the workers were becoming middle class, and wanted to behave as they thought the middle class behaved. *There was a great movement of people from one town to another and the vast variety of churches put them in touch with their ethnic group and like-minded people. By becoming socializing agencies, they sold real religion.* In Italy the number attending church services is less in proportion to the population than the number wearing the 'habit' at any time from the renaissance to the 18th cent.

The majority of the peoples of the world believe in some sort of spiritual force, and have done so throughout recorded history, so there must be a very good reason why they all think; He, or this force exists. Less obviously if He doesn't exist, the need that created the myth must be fantastically important. I hope this volume shows the origins and development of the idea of God, and explains simply why man wanted to create him, despite an absence of evidence for the paranormal.

294

I personally have never felt the pangs of conscience, may be I have been too good (laugh). I have only felt embarrassed exactly the same feeling I have if I have made an arithmetic error. I would be interested to meet someone who has, so they could explain to me what it feels like. It is possible that it is only felt by intuitive and emotional people but never by logical minds as defined by Jung. Bertrand Russell says "And conscience is a most fallacious guide, since it consists of vague reminiscences of precepts heard in early youth, so that it is never wiser than its possessors nurse or mother."

The law allows me to, and I wish to attack, subvert, and deny the Christian religion. A publication is blasphemous if it contains any contemptuous, reviling, scurrilous or ludicrous matter relating to God, Jesus Christ or the Bible. It is not only that I do not desire to go to prison, but I genuinely greatly respect the God concept, I respect and believe that Jesus is the greatest man in history, and that the Bible is the greatest literary work and I agree with Spinoza who changed the view of the Bible from a record of the literal truth to an imperfect but fascinating historical record. I do not desire to be indecent, abusive or intemperate, and I apologise, if in my inexperience I have sailed too close to the wind, because I think it wrong to speak of a hand held terrain re-design implement when I mean a spade.

Jesus said "I am the son of man". He did not say "I am the son of woman" because his contemporaries did not believe that women could have children they were simply bags. My tourist guide in Laos told me her elephant riding grandfather believed that women contributed nothing to the birth of a child save food. Jesus did not say he was the son of God because he did not want to lie. He simply wished to hint that he was the Messiah who wanted to take over part or all of Herod the Great's kingdom and return it to the Jews. If he had said his real father's name, his father would have lost the monopoly of the Chanujoth. Joseph was only engaged to Mary when he was born.

Pope Alexander VI said, "It has served us well this myth of God". *I believe it to be morally wrong to kill the myth of God without replacing him. So I hope to publish a sequel in which I recreate God's ability to record and reward good and bad behaviour with greater accuracy than any historical God could do, in a non-supernatural way - by the use of the 'God Card'.*

INDEX

CAPITAL LETTERS means it is a heading relating to the subject. Illustration numbers and headed areas are in heavy type. Single references are left out as they can be found on the computer

APPENDIX

Primary sources: Four shops (chanuyoth or chanoth) under the Two Cedars of Olivet selling ritually pure doves (Lamentations Rabbah 2.5). The arched-causeway extending from the Temple to Mount Olivet (Mishnah, Yoma 6.4; Mishnah, Parah 3.6; Mishnah, Shekalim 4.2). Shops belonging to Sons of Hanun (B'nai Hanun— Yerushalmi, Peah 1.5, Lieden Ms.) or House of Hanan {Beth Hanan—Yerushalmi, Peah 1.5); equated with Beth Hint near Jerusalem destroyed in first Jewish War (Neusner ed. vol. 2, Peah, TOO). Shops of Beth Hini destroyed [in Jewish War] (Bavli, Baba Metzia 88a; Bavli, Hullim 52a). Shops of B'nai Hanun destroyed 67CE (Siphre Deuteronomy 14:22 [105]). The Sanhedrin said to have taken up residence in the shops (Bavli, Sanhedrin 41a; Bavli, Rosh ha-Shanah 31a; Bavli, Shabbath 15a). Ruin of the Temple attributed to avarice and the bullying of high priests (Tosefta, Menahot 13.22; Tosefta, Qodoshim 13:21), Monopoly of dove sellers (Lamentations Rabbah 2.5). Talmud complains of monopoly maintained by High Priests' bullying, including that of Beth Hanin (Bavli, Peshahim 57a; cf. Josephus, Jewish Antiquities 20.181, 205-7, 214). The extortionate prices of sacrificial doves (Mishnah, Kerithoth 1.7). The high priesthoods of Annas' five sons (Josephus, Jewish Antiquities 20.198). Annas son of Annas captures Temple courtyard and besieges zealots within Temple in 67 CE, but is killed by zealots and Idumeans in ensuing massacre (Josephus, Jewish Antiquities 20.197ff; Jewish War 2.563, 648, 651; 4.160ff., 314ff., 508; Life 38f., 44, 60.

Editions: H. Danby, The Mishnah, Oxford: Clarendon Press, 1933; I. Epstein, The Babylonian Talmud, London: Sonico Press, 1953; J. Neusner (ed.), The Talmud of the Land of Israel, Chicago: University Press, 1990; J. Neusner, The Tosefta, New York: Ktav Publishing inc., 1981; H. St. J. Thackeray et a/., The Works of Flavius Josephus in English and Greek; Jewish War, Jewish Antiquities, The Life, Loeb Classical Library; London: Heinenmann, 1926-1965.

Secondary literature: J. Derenbourg, Essai sur l'histoire et la geographie de la Palestine, Paris, 1867, 467ff; J. Jeremias, Jerusalem in the Time of Jesus: An Investigation into Economic and Social Conditions During the New Testament Period, London:SCM, 1969 pp. 19-20, 49-50; Schürer, E., G. Vermes et al, (eds.) 1973-1987. The

History of the Jewish People in the Age of Jesus Christ (175 B.C.-A.D. 135), in 3 volumes. Edinburgh: T. & T. Clark Publishers; H.L. Strack, P. Billerbeck, Kommentar zum Neuen Testament aus Talmud und Mischnah, München: Becksche Verlagsbuchhandlung 1924.

David Hyde-Harrison [The Son of Woman] is an architect, sculptor, and painter who was brought up a Christian. As a result of prudery concerning the word virgin I misinterpreted what I was told to keep secret as the name of Jesus' father, so when I came across an Aramaic report I immediately connected Jesus as the man that helped to make one of the greatest Roman fortunes. This book includes the first report of this discovery.

I am descended through Plantagenet Kings of England from Charlemagne whose mother and wife were Merovingian princesses. Which as a result of the Da Vinci Code's publicity are thought to be descended from Jesus!

I went to good Christian boarding schools. My divorced mother's home was bombed at the beginning of the war, so I spent my holidays as a social equal with the owner of Battle Abbey. She, though not a church goer, appointed the C of E Deacon, not just a vicar. She wrote a book. She invited Winston Churchill for the weekend and he accepted; true he didn't come, but his cousin wrote a poem about my mother's ankles. I therefore learnt like Moses to be upper class and that I could write a book, so here it is.

I studied at Camberwell School of Art and the Architectural Association. I married an architect and we designed and built our own house. I have also written a book called **Functional Junctions** a rational solution for transport in cities ISBN 1 84019 006 X www. Func-Junc.co.uk
or www. d.hydeharrison@blueyonder.co.uk

Printed in the United Kingdom
by Lightning Source UK Ltd.
123715UK00002B/241-261/A